LOST TALENT

WOMEN IN THE SCIENCES

In the series
LABOR AND SOCIAL CHANGE
edited by Paula Rayman
and Carmen Sirianni

LOST TALENT

WOMEN IN THE SCIENCES

Sandra L. Hanson

Temple University Press
Philadelphia

Temple University Press, Philadelphia 19122
Copyright © 1996 by Temple University
All rights reserved
Published 1996
Printed in the United States of America

♾ The paper used in this publication meets the requirements
of the American National Standard for Information Sciences—
Permanence of Paper for Printed Library Materials,
ANSI Z39.48-1984

Text design by Arlene Putterman

Library of Congress Cataloging-in-Publication Data

Hanson, Sandra L.
    Lost talent : women in the sciences / Sandra L. Hanson.
        p.   cm. — (Labor and social change)
    Includes bibliographical references and index.
    ISBN 1-56639-446-5 (cloth : alk. paper)
    1. Women in science—United States.   2. Women science students—
United States.   I. Title.   II. Series.
√ Q130.H365   1996
    500′.82—dc20   96-219

To Rebekah and Steve

CONTENTS

TABLES AND FIGURES

TABLES

FIGURES

ACKNOWLEDGMENTS

This research was funded by grant SES-9122802 from the Office of Research Evaluation and Dissemination, and the Sociology Program of the National Science Foundation. The opinions expressed here do not necessarily reflect the position of the National Science Foundation. Many thanks to Michael Ames, Paula Rayman, Larry Suter, and Steven Tuch for helpful comments, and to Marcia Annis, Lynn Dunlap, Helen Harkless, Dot Kane, Mei Chu Lin, Darcy Straus, and Fengang Yang for help with analysis, tables, and figures.

LOST TALENT

WOMEN IN THE SCIENCES

1

INTRODUCTION

Young girls do not start out with low achievement in science. (In this book, the term "science" is often used to refer to the areas of science, math, and engineering.) Early in the high school years, however, many girls experience the beginning of a departure from science typified by enrollment in fewer science courses, lowered achievement and increasingly negative attitudes. The significant loss of talented young women from science education and occupations is the focus of this book.

Even though women have been entering the formal workplace in record numbers since the middle of the twentieth century, they have not entered jobs in science at a similar rate. Women represent 46 percent of the U.S. labor force, but they hold only 22 percent of the jobs in math, science, and engineering (National Science Foundation, 1994). Somewhere along the way, between the earliest training and entry into the labor market, gender stratification occurs. Science jobs are among the highest paying, highest status jobs in the labor market. The shortage of women in this area helps maintain gender inequalities and represents a significant amount of lost talent.

Recent Reports on Gender and Science

There is considerable agreement among researchers, educators, and policy makers that the last few decades have seen progress for women in science. Young women are now as likely as young men to take certain high school math and science courses. The gender gap in average math proficiency scores has disappeared at ages 9 and 13 and has nearly disappeared at age 17. The number of women earning advanced degrees in math and science is increasing, as is the number employed in math and science occupations (National Science Foundation, 1993, 1994; National Science Board, 1993; American Association of University Women [AAUW], 1992; National Center for Education Statistics, 1994). In spite of these

1

gains, however, the gender gap in science has not disappeared. Recent reports using information on students and workers in the 1990s provide alarming evidence of the persistance of the gender gap in science:

■ In elementary school, young girls are less confident of their abilities in science and math and less interested in careers in science and engineering than are young boys. This is true in spite of similar exposure to courses and similar achievement (National Science Foundation, 1994).

■ Surveys of 17-year-olds show that young women take fewer advanced courses in math and are less likely to take chemistry and physics courses than are young men (AAUW, 1992; National Science Foundation, 1993, 1994; National Science Board, 1993; National Center for Education Statistics, 1994).

■ Surveys of 17-year-olds also show that gender differences persist in math proficiency scores at the highest levels (e.g., algebra and multistep problem solving) and in math achievement test scores. Beginning at age 9, there are gender differences favoring males in both science proficiency (what the student knows and can do) and science achievement (what the student should know and should be able to do) test scores (National Center for Education Statistics, 1994; National Science Board, 1993).

■ In their last year of high school, young men are more than three times as likely as young women to expect to pursue a career in science, math, or engineering (National Science Foundation, 1994).

■ In many areas of science at the secondary and postsecondary level, teachers are overwhelmingly male. Teachers at all levels of education and of both sexes discriminate in the classroom and have lower expectations in science and math for females than for males (AAUW, 1992; National Science Foundation, 1994).

■ Parents also discriminate against daughters. A majority of parents believe that their sons are better in mechanics and math than their daughters, and they fail to give their daughters the most elementary training in the use of tools to build or repair mechanical objects (Vetter, 1992).

■ Although women have earned the majority of bachelor's degrees in all fields combined since 1982, they earn a smaller portion of bachelor's degrees in science and engineering (44%). Women are especially underrepresented in engineering, where they earn only 15 percent of the undergraduate degrees. Although the proportion of master's degrees and doctorates earned by women in science and engineering has increased, women are still underrepresented here as well. They receive 45 percent of the master's degrees in science and engineering fields and 29 percent of the doctorates. In engineering, women account for only 14 percent of the master's degrees and 9 percent of the doctoral degrees. At all postsecondary levels, women are more likely to drop out of science and engineering programs than are men. A vast majority of women in science programs are in life sciences, psychology, and social sciences. Recent evidence suggests that the 20-year trend toward less sex segregation in fields of study has slowed down considerably (National Science Foundation, 1994; Hollenshead, Wenzel Lazarus, & Nair, in press; Fox, 1995; Jacobs, 1995).

■ Women make up 42 percent of the labor force but only 22 percent of the science and engineering labor force. Within this labor force, they hold lower status positions, receive smaller salaries, and are more likely to be unemployed or underemployed compared to their male counterparts. Many of these differences persist when qualifications are taken into account. Despite initiatives on the part of industry to recruit and retain women, women scientists are less likely than men scientists to be employed in the industrial sector of the market (Rosser, 1990; Rayman & Brett, 1993; National Science Foundation, 1994; Fox, 1995, in press; Long, Allison, & McGinnis, 1993; Zuckerman, 1991).

■ Institutional practices that begin in graduate school and continue in the workplace function to keep women out of science. In a recent survey of engineers, 56 percent of the women said that they were aware of cases where females had been overlooked with regard to career opportunities. Another survey of women scientists showed that large numbers had experienced or witnessed sex discrimination or harassment. There is considerable evidence that the culture of science in the workplace continues to be a male culture (Rosser, 1990; Vetter, 1992; Fox, 1995, in press; Alper, 1993; Zuckerman, 1991; Devine, 1992; Rayman and Brett, 1994).

The Science Pipeline and Limitations of Past Research

Many researchers and policymakers use the imagery of a science pipeline to think about the relative access of women and men to the fields of science, math, and engineering. The image is one of a training pipeline running from early training in primary and secondary school through advanced training in the university to the hiring of qualified scientists in the labor market.

Berryman (1983) was one of the first to introduce the notion of the science pipeline and the formation of a scientific talent pool from which science professionals could be drawn. Aptitude, course taking, and achievement are often used to determine whether a student is in or out of the pipeline. When visualizing the pipeline, it is perhaps more accurate to think of it as a funnel, since all elementary school students are in the pipeline but many drop out along the way. Research on women's participation in this pipeline shows a pattern of declining course taking and achievement along with increasingly negative attitudes about science. Most researchers have suggested that this decline begins in high school and worsens in the undergraduate and graduate years (Office of Technology Assessment, 1988; Oakes, 1990; National Science Board, 1993; AAUW, 1992; National Science Foundation, 1993, 1994; Rayman & Brett, 1993; Brush, 1991; Barber, 1995). Sells (1978; 1980) considers advanced high school math classes the "critical filter" that keeps many women from entering the male-dominated math and science professions.

Although the pipeline imagery is becoming pervasive in the literature, and descriptive information on the number and characteristics of men and women in math courses or with high math scores is available, the research in this area has a number of limitations. These limitations go beyond the well-known problems of unrepresentative samples and inconsistent measures that have led to conflicting findings (Oakes, 1990). There is surprisingly little research that provides insight into the complexities of the process by which so many women opt out of science.

A good example of the lack of attention to these complexities in past research is the tendency of many analysts to focus on single dimensions of the science experience or single dimensions of factors affecting science experiences. For example, Oakes (1990) has noted that much attention has been given to women's math experiences, but that very little attention has been aimed at their *science* experiences. In a similar fashion, researchers often focus on a particular dimension of experience, such as achievement, course taking, or attitudes. The implicit assumption has been that the different areas of experience are related in such a way that knowledge of the experience in one area reveals insights into the experience in other areas. There is, however, evidence that the different dimensions of experience in math and science are not so perfectly correlated (Oakes, 1990). In fact, young girls' attitudes about math and science may turn from the positive long before they stop taking the classes (Mullis & Jenkins, 1988). And even after many girls stop taking the math and science classes, those who stay in the classes do not get lower grades than their male counterparts, although their standardized scores are usually lower (DeBoer, 1984a; Linn & Hyde, 1989).

In my research, I explore four aspects of experience in both math and science: achievement (e.g., grades and standardized test scores), access (e.g., course taking), attitudes, and activities (e.g., use of calculators, microscopes, computers and the like). The first three of these have been given some attention in the literature, but we know less about young women's *activities* in math and science. Researchers and the federal agencies that monitor science achievement in the United States have suggested that these areas of science are important dimensions of students' science experience (National Science Foundation, 1993; National Science Board, 1993; National Center for Education Statistics, 1994; Oakes, 1990; Morgan, 1992; Smith, 1992; Catsambis, 1994). Importantly, I consider all four of these dimensions and their interrelationships in trying to understand women's experiences in the sciences.

In general, we know much more about women's experiences than we know about the causes of these experiences. When researchers do look at causes, they often follow the same unidimensional approach that they use to describe science experiences. Some researchers have focused on schools and teachers, some on personality characteristics and choices, and some on family characteristics. Although these studies are important, they do not provide a view of the entire process leading to success in science or of the complexities in that process. For example, when researchers focus on personality characteristics (e.g., Meece, Wigfield, & Eccles, 1990), explanations for the original source of the personality differences are often not attended to.

In my study of women in science, I consider four sets of causal factors: gender, family resources, school resources, and individual resources. I describe women's science experiences as being at the end of a complex path of causal influences. That is, the influence of gender is not necessarily just a direct influence, but rather it might also work indirectly through family experiences that affect school experiences and that ultimately affect individual characteristics and experiences.

Additionally, researchers have been slow to realize the ways in which the individual and social factors that are typically seen as causes of science experiences might interact with each other to affect those experiences. Likewise, these individual and social factors might interact with experiences in one area of science (e.g., attitudes) to in turn affect experiences in another area of science (e.g., achievement) (Oakes, 1990). This research acknowledges the fact that women's resources in one area of life might interact in a unique way with resources in other areas by carefully examining interactions between multiple causes of science experiences. A set of interactions that are particularly important for understanding the complexities of women's science experiences are those involving gender, race, and social class. Special attention is thus given to these interactions in this research.

Although some researchers have used multidimensional models to examine women's science experiences (Wise, 1985; Ethington & Wolfe, 1986; Ware & Lee, 1988; Marsh, 1989), these experiences have typically been addressed in a relatively static way (see Rayman & Brett, 1993; Wise, 1985; Lee, 1987; and Marsh, 1989; for studies that are an exception to this static approach). Some researchers use cross-sectional data to infer causal relationships (e.g., Boli, Ramirez, & Meyer, 1985). Even when longitudinal data are used, science experiences are often seen as a one-time outcome, with early science experiences included as independent variables predicting later experiences. Some researchers use longitudinal data to present "snapshots" of students' experiences in the different time periods. In effect, they are using longitudinal data in nearly a cross-sectional fashion. This is especially problematic given evidence that the science pipeline is very fluid, with many students entering and exiting (Berryman, 1983; Office of Technology Assessment, 1988). It cannot be assumed that snapshots of students at various points in time (even snapshots using longitudinal data) represent the same pool of students. In addition, longitudinal studies examining the pipeline from high school into careers are rare. A long-term approach, which does not stop with the end of education, is important given the evidence showing a considerable exiting from the sciences after college and graduate school and before young people enter occupations (Berryman, 1983; National Science Board, 1993). In this research, the fluidity and long-term nature of experiences are recognized by following young people and developing patterns of experiences over time—science trajectories. These trajectories begin with early training in high school and extend to postsecondary school and occupations. For example, some individuals will have early success and interest in science but will drop out at critical decision points (e.g., after their sophomore year in high school, after their senior year, after college) while others will drop out later or stay in the pipeline. In other words, this research describes distinct patterns or trajectories that women experience in science and the school, family, and personal/psychological experiences as well as resources that are associated with the trajectories. Few researchers have looked at multiple sets of experiences in the sciences over time as outcomes to be predicted. The research reported here follows the life course perspective in acknowledging the fact that science experiences, like other individual experiences, are not one-time events but rather are dynamic and constantly changing, with much variation between individuals in the way they are encountered (George, 1993).

Another limitation of the literature on women in science is its atheoretical nature. The typical approach to the problem is to create a long list of independent variables and test them for statistical significance. The emphasis is on statistical sophistication, not on theoretical development. Thus when statistical relationships are found, there is no broader conceptual context within which the findings can be interpreted and understood. In the research presented here, a conceptual framework involving the creation of lost talent through selection processes and unequal resources is used to look at the role gender plays. Both differential treatment on the basis of gender and differences in family, school, and individual resources are seen as critical factors in understanding why so many talented women leave the sciences.

Another critical shortcoming of much of the research on gender differences in science is the tendency to make conclusions about "boys" and "girls" without paying attention to important statuses other than gender, mainly race and class. We know that low-SES (socioeconomic status) and non-Asian minority youth have lower achievement in science than do their upper-SES white counterparts (Oakes, 1990; National Science Foundation, 1994). But some have found that African American youth hold more positive attitudes about science than any other subgroup (Hueftle et al., 1983). Thus we cannot assume that some or all of the science experiences of African American women will be more negative than those of white women. Interestingly, some have found African American girls to be more positive about math and science than their white counterparts (Dossey, Mullis, Lindquist, & Chambers, 1988). Can we conclude that the gender pattern among white youth is duplicated amongst nonwhite youth? The limited research which is available suggests that we cannot. For example, athough overall gender contrasts show boys in more advanced high school math courses than girls, among African American youth, the opposite pattern prevails (Mattews, 1984).

A final limitation of past research on women in science involves the emphasis on the individual actions and decisions of women in the science education realm as separate from larger structural processes involving education and occupation systems. That is, the link between the reproduction of power and status at the macro level and the individual expectations and attitudes of young men and women is seldom acknowledged. Work by Kerckhoff (1976), Bourdieu (1973), and others that shows how culture is reproduced and how personal education and occupational choices draw on real structures and opportunities is essential for understanding the loss of talented young women from science. Fox's (1995, in press) work on women in science occupations provides further support for the importance of structural factors over individual factors in understanding women's success in science. When different school, family, and individual experiences of young women are examined in this research, they are viewed as reflections of gender differences in power at the macro level.

Recent work showing how advances for women in science training have not been equally matched by their increased entrance into scientific occupations sheds more light on the need for a structural approach to women in the sciences (Stockard, 1985; Charles, 1992). In spite of these findings, the majority of work on women's access to science professions assumes that training is the key to occupational equality and focuses solely on the factors that would enhance that training (e.g., teachers, curriculum, nonbiased books, etc.) (Ware & Lee, 1988; Fennema & Peterson, 1985; Eccles & Jacobs, 1986; Hess & Ferree, 1987; Fox, Brody, & Tobins, 1985).

These limitations leave many unanswered questions about women's experiences in science. Do young women lose interest in science at the same rate as they lose interest in math? Is this true for all women, regardless of their social class and race? Do they experience a decline in all aspects of math and science, including achievement, course taking, attitudes, and activities? Does gender have a direct influence on science experiences, such that equally qualified girls and boys end up with different experiences, or does it indirectly affect science experiences through the unique family, school, and individual characteristics of women? What are the characteristics of women who stay in science? Are their families different? their schools? Are these characteristics causes of perseverance or just correlates? In sum, although the alarm has been rung on the shortage of women in science, we have not come very far in our understanding of the complexities of women's experiences in science nor of the complexities of the explanations for these experiences.

In this research, groups of young women are followed over time in an attempt to begin to understand these complexities. Using large, national samples of young people and a conceptual framework that suggests that deficits in resources are a key in understanding the loss of scientifically talented young women from the sciences, the research seeks to discover the complicated patterns of women's experiences in diverse areas of science. It also presents a picture of the successful woman scientist—what her family is like, what her school provided her, and what personal strengths she had that made the difference in beating the odds. Before describing these women and their experiences, it is important to consider the larger social and economic context of science in the United States.

The State of Science and the Economy in the United States
We are living in a society that is increasingly reliant on science and technology. With the Soviet launching of Sputnik in 1957, a push to produce more and better U.S. physicists, chemists, mathematicians, engineers, and medical researchers began. Since then, the United States has been an international leader in research and technology. But whether the United

States can retain that lead is far from certain. Noted scientist Carl Sagan (1989) has concluded that we "live in a society dependent on science and technology in which hardly anyone knows anything about science and technology." Changes in the economy have not resulted in larger numbers of students going into science and engineering. The percent of college students majoring in science and engineering has remained constant over the past 30-some years (Vetter, 1987; National Science Board, 1993). Others suggest that interest in these fields may actually be waning. In 1988 less than 1 percent of college freshmen said that they would major in mathematics, down from 4 percent two decades ago. Physics and chemistry majors fell from 3 percent to 1.5 percent. (Tift, 1989). The late 1980s saw a similar decline in interest in engineering, although in 1990 and 1991 enrollment in engineering programs increased slightly after a 9-year decline (National Science Board, 1993).

International comparisons of students provide additional cause for concern. The best American students are not competitive with their peers in other countries when it comes to math and science. The Second International Math Study (SIMS) and the Second International Science Study (SISS) look at students from 20 countries, including the United States. They show that students from many other countries, including Japan, Hong Kong, England and Wales, and Sweden, know much more math and science than do even the best students in the United States. One of the findings from the science study is that U.S. students were tied in science with students in Singapore and Thailand for fourteenth place in a group of 20 countries (International Association for Evaluation of Educational Achievement, 1988; McKnight et al., 1985).

Concern about U.S. competitiveness in science and technology is rampant. It is fueled not only by the state of science education in the United States but by the consequences of weakening competitiveness for America's economy, standard of living, and national security. It is in the nation's interest to have high-quality education in science and engineering. Well-educated workers are increasingly seen as the "human resources" or "human capital" that is required for a competitive advantage (Office of Technology Assessment, 1988; National Commission on Excellence in Education, 1983). The state of science education is not the only problem looming in the country's science future, however. Demographics add a further complication.

Demographers (Wetzel, 1988), labor economists (Leontief & Duchin, 1986), and concerned government and business leaders (Brock, 1986; Perot, 1988) recognize a potential problem in the nation's labor pool. Projected retirements in the science and engineering sector during the 1990s will reduce this segment of the work force by about half (Finkbeiner, 1987). According to the National Science Foundation, 60 to 70 percent of current faculty members in engineering and natural sciences will be retiring or leaving their positions in the next two decades (Teltsch, 1991). Regardless of whether the number of exiting scientists is as large as this, the documented stable or declining interest in science and engineering majors in recent decades does not suggest a labor pool rising to fill these openings.

Future work cohorts will include increasing numbers from two groups—women and racial minorities (Oakes, 1990). Most of the college freshmen of 2005 were born by 1987. Demographers tell us that because of the low birth rates of the 1960s and 1970s and the resultant "baby bust" generation, the number of 18-year-olds is declining and will not stop doing so until the mid-1990s (Office of Technology Assessment, 1988). At the same time the number of women getting college degrees and the number of minority youth are increasing. Women and non-Asian minorities have not historically held degrees or jobs in mathematics, science, or technology (Oakes, 1990).

Although women have been entering the work force at an increased rate since the end of the Second World War, they often occupy lower status, nontechnical jobs in the service sector of the economy. One of the major labor supply challenges for the United States over the next two decades is to develop a balanced work force possessing the technical skills necessary for jobs in science and engineering. To do this, women will have to be integrated into the technical and scientific sectors of the labor force to a far greater extent than at the present. Education, family, and occupation systems in the United States have consistently turned a majority of females away from science education. Many young girls who start out doing well in science end up with little scientific interest and knowledge. It is this training and education that provide the critical link between labor force needs and supply. What happens to the talented young women in this educational process? Recent work on educational systems suggests that gender is one of the major classifying characteristics in determining who will succeed and fill high-level positions. This assumption is at the core of the conceptual framework used here.

The Conceptual Framework: Selection,
Resources, and Lost Talent

Beginning with the work of Blau and Duncan (1967) and continuing in the "Wisconsin" model of status attainment (Sewell, Haller, & Ohlendorf, 1970; Sewell, Holler, & Portes, 1969), the research on educational and occupational attainment in the United States has primarily relied on a functionalist, socialization model (Horan, 1978). That is, the research assumes that differences in attainment can best be understood by differences in learned skills and motives, and thus that the attainment system offers a fair system of rewards to the most talented.

Prior to the introduction of Blau and Duncan's status attainment model, theoretical work in the United States and Europe focused more heavily on the structural factors that affected attainment, irrespective of individual merit (Kerckhoff, 1984). The inability of the status attainment model to explain equally well the achievements of blacks and whites, men and women, and upper class and lower class brought about a renewed interest in the structural impediments to achievement (Giddens, 1973; Wright & Perrone, 1977; Portes & Wilson, 1976; Alexander & Eckland, 1974; Treiman & Terrell, 1975). Theories focusing on class (Giddens, 1973), allocation (Kerckhoff, 1976), sponsored mobility (Turner, 1960), the regulation of ambition (Hopper, 1973), cultural capital (Bourdieu, 1973), and segmented labor markets (Beck, Horan, & Tolbert, 1978) all questioned the ability to understand achievement without considering social structures.

These arguments about the import of nonindividual factors in social mobility systems suggest that there will be a considerable number of youth who are talented and motivated but who do not achieve because of their placement in the stratification system. In this research we are interested in exploring this "lost talent" among young women in science.

The conceptual framework that is used here to approach the problem of talented young women exiting the sciences is one that stresses structural barriers or selection processes that directly affect science achievement through gender discrimination but that also indirectly affect science achievement through the transmission of "gendered" socialization and unequal allocation of resources in family and school environments.

Kerckhoff (1976) and others have questioned the socialization model of achievement and argued that young people's expectations are not so much developed through the socialization process as through knowledge of the real world. Although everyone may want to succeed, people in different strata have different expectations as to their chances of success. For youth in more disadvantaged social positions, these expectations may start out high but tend to be lowered over time as they observe the successes and failures of others like themselves (Han, 1969; Siegel, 1965; Kerckhoff, 1976; Oakes, 1985).

The link between position in the social structure and individual attitudes is discussed in a number of theoretical works on the achievement process. Bourdieu (1973) suggests that societies reproduce themselves and maintain a system of power by means of the transmission of culture.

The reproduction of culture through education plays an important role in the reproduction of the whole system, and culture is arbitrarily imposed by dominant groups. Bourdieu suggests that education systems control mobility by selecting out the students who will achieve. The selection process is one that assures the continuation of the status quo of the system and is based on categories such as gender, race, and class. Those who are not in favor then begin to develop more negative attitudes toward school in anticipation of the barriers that confront them.

Other work on the role of status effects in educational systems is remarkably similar in noting the selection process and the anticipation of success reflected in students' attitudes. Kerckhoff (1976) discusses an allocation process whereby individuals are not free to achieve according to their talents but rather are subject to social forces that "identify, select, process, classify, and assign individuals according to externally imposed criteria" (p. 369). Students' expectations for their future are then affected by these observed constraints.

Further insights into the notion of lost talent come from Turner (1960) and Hopper (1973). Turner made important contributions to our understanding of the role of structural factors in educational systems by distinguishing systems that allow free competition (contest mobility) from those that stratify early on (sponsorship mobility). Hopper (1973) added to this notion by stressing that societies need to be assured that high-level positions will be filled. They must, then, develop ambition in all youth. Through the process of selection by external criteria, some but not all will succeed. Hopper suggests that societies must then "cool out" the ambition of the unsuccessful in order to avoid social conflicts. Education is a major vehicle in both the selection and the "cooling out" processes.

Little empirical work has been done on the intersection between status in the stratification system and loss of talent. Although there is research that shows that the status attainment model works less well for women, blacks, and individuals from lower SES backgrounds (Portes & Wilson, 1976; Kerckhoff & Campbell, 1977; Alexander & Eckland, 1974; Treiman & Terrell, 1975; Treiman & Hartman, 1981; Rosenfeld, 1980; Sewell, Hauser, & Wolf, 1980), it often does not explicitly look at stratification status and the selection process. In my recent (1994) examination of lost talent among U.S. youths I found considerable loss of talent through mismatched aspirations and expectations and through reduced educational expectations. This loss varied with gender, race, and class.

One way to examine the selection process is to look at changes in expectations over time. Much of the evidence on women's educational expectations suggests that women are more likely than men to adjust their educational expectations downward over time, especially with the advent of marriage and children (Haggstrom, Kanouse, & Morrison, 1986; Randour et al., 1982; Marini, 1984). Research has shown that boys' educational aspirations *and* expectations exceed those of girls, and that there is a greater consistency between the aspirations (hopes) and expectations among young men than among young women (Crowley & Shapiro, 1982; Marini & Greenberger, 1978; Hanson, 1994). One of the few researchers who has not found gender differences in educational expectations and aspirations is Mickelson (1989). Her unique sample and measures may be a partial explanation for her findings.

In Gaskell's (1985) study of working class females, she found that young women believed that they were making personal educational choices but that those choices drew on real structures, and opportunities. The choices tended to reproduce class and gender structures, with the working class girls choosing nonacademic courses of study that would prepare them for clerical jobs.

In sum, research on the general educational aspirations, expectations, and achievement of young people suggests that gender is an important factor in creating lost talent. What does the research show about science education? Although it is clear that women are underrepresented in science, longitudinal examinations of the extent of lost talent and the process leading to it are rare (for exceptions see Oakes, 1990; Office of Technology Assessment, 1988; Rayman & Brett, 1993, 1995). The first goal of this research is to describe carefully women's and men's experiences in the sciences in order to assess the nature and extent of talent loss, especially among young women. But how does the lost talent process work? How are talented young women "cooled out"? Evidence from science research grounded in feminist theory and focusing on power and status in science occupations (Schiebinger, 1987; Rosser, 1987; 1990; 1992; Atkinson & Delamont, 1990; Rossi, 1964; Rossiter, 1982; Hollenshead et al., in press; Zuckerman, 1991; Fox, 1994, in press) and from the structural theories reviewed above suggests that inequalities based on gender are maintained by differential treatment based on gender alone as well as by differential access to resources that favor young men over young women. The assumption is that different ties to the power structure creates gender stratification but that differential access to resources is necessary in maintaining the stratification (Chafetz, 1984; Giele, 1988). Although economic structure at the macro level will not be measured in this research, the conceptual framework used here assumes that the differences in resources flow not from natural individual differences between the sexes but from gender differences in these ties. As the discussion below suggests, the family and school play a major role in redistributing resources that are potentially important for success in science from the larger system to individuals. How does this process work?

Literature on Resources and Science

FAMILY RESOURCES.   Family socialization and resource allocation are key ingredients in maintaining the sex stereotypes and norms that keep the gender stratification system intact (Parsons & Bales, 1955; Chodorow, 1978; Entwisle & Baker, 1983). Beginning with birth, parents give children cues about appropriate gender-linked behaviors. These cues act as resources for children's later educational activities and interests. For example, mothers' communications with sons contains more of the verbal stimulation thought to foster cognitive development (e.g., explicit speech, and teaching and questioning that contain numbers and action verbs) than does their communication with daughters (Weitzman, Binns, & Friend, 1985). Boys and girls are given toys, clothing, physical environments, and rewards for two distinct types of behavior. Boys are encouraged to be outgoing, aggressive, independent, and analytic, while girls are encouraged to be passive, dependent, and nurturent (Lake, 1975; McDonald & Parke, 1986; Fagot, Leinbach, & Kronsberg, 1985; Rheingold & Cook, 1975).

Likewise, parents encourage mathematical achievement more in boys than girls (Eccles & Jacobs, 1986) and accept lower mathematics achievement in girls than boys (Maccoby & Jacklin, 1974). Parents hold different educational and career expectations for sons and daughters (Casserly, 1980), and these expectations influence those of their children (Armstrong & Price, 1982). Even parents of mathematically gifted students have been found to view careers in mathematics as less appropriate for daughters than sons (Fox, 1980). These data are complemented by children's perspectives. Boys perceive their parents as being more positive about their mathematics achievement than girls do (Sherman & Fennema, 1978).

Research on women who succeed in science education and occupations shows that these women often had family backgrounds that allowed them to develop independence in an environment with diverse role models. They tended to have families characterized by well-educated, parents, family stability, parental encouragement of androgyny and of achievement in science, and maternal employment. These women were also more likely than others to be first born (Smith, 1992; Mullis & Jenkins, 1988; Casserly & Rock, 1985; Auster & Auster, 1981; Rayman & Brett, 1995; Association for Women in Science [AWIS], 1993; Brown, 1990). Experiences in their family of procreation have also been found to be associated with women's entry into and success in science. Women with husbands and with young children fare less well than do other women. These family experiences do not appear to work to the disadvantage of men in science (Shenhav & Haberfeld, 1988; Long, 1990; Fox, 1995, in press; Culotta, 1993).

SCHOOL RESOURCES.   Three areas of school influence have been stressed in the science achievement literature—the "hidden curriculum," course taking, and peer influence. This literature shows how teachers, courses, and peers act as resources for achievement in science. They stress gender differences in treatment and access that limit women's resources and accomplishments. Advocates of the "hidden curriculum" thesis propose that teachers hold different expectations for the two sexes, which they communicate in subtle but pervasive ways. It has been shown, for example, that teachers give more attention to boys than to girls (AAUW, 1992; Sadker & Sadker, 1986), invest more cognitive time with boys than with girls in mathematics (Brophy & Good, 1974) and science classes (Morse & Handley, 1985), and hold higher expectations of mathematics achievement for boys than for girls even before actual differences in achievement appear (Becker, 1981; Hallinan & Sorensen, 1987). Girls also receive less encouragement and information about courses and careers in math and science from high school guidance counselors (Oakes, 1990; Fox et al., 1985). And these teachers and counselors have effects on decisions that last well beyond the high school years (Ware & Lee, 1988). Teacher influence during the high school years also comes in the form of role modeling, for having women science teachers in high school increases chances that a young girl will choose a science major in college (Matyas, 1986) and do better in college science courses (Boli et al., 1985).

The gender gap in science course taking has been well documented. On average, girls and boys perform equally well in mathematics up to about grades 6 to 8; however, the number of females who continue to take mathematics courses drops precipitously during high school years (Office of Technology Assessment, 1988; Oakes, 1990; Fennema & Peterson, 1985), and this differential course taking in mathematics is found even when achievement and ability are controlled (Fox, 1980). Further declines in science course taking among women occur in college. Women choose science majors at a much lower rate than do men (Commission on Professionals in Science and Technology, 1986; Oakes, 1990). One obvious implication, then, is that as early as junior high school females choose not to undertake the advanced training in math and science that leads to careers in the science and technical fields (Ernest, 1976; Sells, 1980). An additional loss occurs through lack of exposure to scientific thinking and, perhaps, leads to a lack of appreciation for the kinds of understanding scientific knowledge can provide (Maccoby & Jacklin, 1974). Women's knowledge and course taking in math are important resources for access to high-status occupations. Their lack of knowledge and course taking in math acts as a critical filter that keeps women out of a host of occupations, including chemistry, physics, engineering, computer science, and occupations in the social sciences and business that require an understanding of statistics (Sells, 1978, 1980). Numerous studies show the importance of gender differences in attitudes and achievement in math and science during high school for determining persistence in the scientific pipeline in the college, postsecondary, and early work years. For example, interests and performance in college math and science courses are strongly linked to math course taking and achievement test scores in high school (Wise, 1985; Ware & Lee, 1988; Boli et al., 1985; Wilson & Boldizar, 1990; Ethington & Wolfe, 1988).

Finally, we can think of the school peer group as a resource for young women's science achievement. Studies have shown the importance of support from female friends for young women's continuation in science (Boswell, 1985; Fox, Tobin, & Brody, 1979). Peer group norms are at least part of the explanation for the success of single-sex girls schools in recruiting young women into math and science courses and, in general, in preparing women for nontraditional occupations (Fox et al., 1985; Schwager, 1987; Tidball, 1980; Rice & Hemmings, 1988; Lyall, 1987). Finally, a recent ethnographic study of college women showed that the peer group was a major factor in shifting young women's goals away from careers and interests in science and toward romance and heterosexual relationships (Holland & Eisenhart, 1991).

INDIVIDUAL RESOURCES.   How do individual characteristics of young men and women affect their science experiences, and to what extent are they a product of the different resources allocated to men and women in school and the family? At the center of the research addressing these questions are the notions that institutions define gender roles and that these definitions become forged into a diffuse "gender belief system" that shapes the day-to-day behaviors and attitudes of men and women, boys and girls (Hess & Ferree, 1987).

Although boys and girls are equally likely to report that they like math (Ernest, 1976), math comes to be defined as a male preserve (Weitzman, 1979; Fox et al., 1985). Girls often fear that success in this male domain will make them less popular among peers (Fox et al., 1979). The content of courses may be important in conveying messages about girls' ability in mathematics. Early research showed that girls do more poorly on word problems based on male activities (e.g., woodworking and guns) than they do on the same problems put in the context of female-typed activities (e.g., cooking and gardening) (Milton, 1958). It is also interesting that girls' math skills improve when they are examined by other women (Pederson, Shinedling, & Johnson, 1968).

There is ample evidence of the effect of cultural norms on women's perceptions of their abilities. For example, a number of studies have shown that students' achievement in math depends on its perceived usefulness to their future careers (Armstrong, 1985; Fennema & Sherman, 1977; Hilton & Berglund, 1974). Thus if girls do less well in math, it may be due to their implicit understanding that math skills will not be useful to them in their future family and work roles (Brush, 1980; Eccles et al., 1985), and, in fact, that the pursuit of professions that use these skills will conflict with their future family roles (Fox et al., 1985; Sherman, 1983). In both high school and college, women's identification with traditional sex roles and their perception of the incompatibility between science careers and family pursuits keep them from entering and persisting in the sciences. Men, on the other hand, do not see the pursuit of math and science as being in conflict with their family roles (Matyas, 1986; Ware & Lee, 1988). In fact, women's perceptions of the career/family conflicts for women in science careers are probably accurate given the pressure for early productivity in these careers (Linn & Hyde, 1989).

Others cite the motive to avoid success as an explanation for women's lack of achievement in math and other areas of intellectual ability. According to Horner's (1972) research, women want to succeed but are ambivalent about success in the context of social proscriptions concerning bright, successful women. However, replications of Horner's work have not reproduced her results (Fleming, 1982; Condry & Dyer, 1976).

There is no reason to believe, then, that men and women differ in their basic motivations for success, but the research stimulated by the fear-of-success concept has shown that individuals are sensitive to the social consequences of their achievement behavior and that these consequences are perceived as different for men and women in particular situations (Gravenkemper & Paludi, 1983).

Related to these social costs are the strong stereotypes held by young women. Many believe that math and science are more useful and important for and better understood by boys (Eccles et al., 1985; Zimmerer & Bennett, 1987). This stereotyping begins as early as the primary grades (Vockell & Lebonc, 1981).

Other personality characteristics that vary by sex and that have been shown to act as resources for achievement in science include confidence and self-esteem (Fennema & Sherman, 1977; Linn & Hyde, 1989); sex role attitudes (Farmer, 1976; Crowley & Shapiro, 1982); educational/occupational expectations (Hanson & Ginsburg, 1988; Rosen & Aneshensel, 1978); and locus of control (Hanson & Ginsburg, 1988; Astin, 1974; Fennema & Sherman, 1977). These personal resources persist in their importance after the high school years. DeBoer (1984b) found that one's perceptions of one's ability in science and one's attribution of success in science to ability were important predictors of participation and performance in science during college. Men have the advantage on both of these.

Gender and Lost Talent: The Role of Discrimination

In sum, it is argued here that young talented women are more likely to leave the sciences than are young men because of structural barriers and selection processes. To some extent, the larger power structure is reproduced in the cultural milieus of families and schools that offer different experiences and resources to young women and men. But structural theories also argue that these experiences and resources cannot fully explain the differences in women's and men's achievements—in this case, persistence in the science pipeline. Gender status in and of itself is an explanatory variable to the extent that equally qualified young women and men will not have equal opportunities in science. Discrimination based on gender alone is part of the reason for young women's lack of success in science.

Recent work by Stockard (1985), Charles (1992), Hanson et al. (in press) and others documents the fact that women's advances in education (including science education) have not been met by similar advances in occupations. When Stockard looks at variation over time in the disparities between men's and women's education and income in the United States, she finds that income variations are much larger and virtually unrelated to variations in education. Stockard concludes that the ultimate explanation for the continuing disparities in the occupational world cannot, then, be attributed to women's lesser training but instead must be assigned to cultural beliefs and practices that give preference to males. Charles's (1992) examination of data on occupational segregation in the United States between 1950 and 1970 confirms Stockard's analysis. In the same years that the economy was developing and entering a postindustrial stage in which women obtained more education, Charles finds that occupational segregation increased.

Fox (1995; in press) provides further evidence for the importance of structural rather than individual factors in determining science achievement. She finds that individual characteristics involving training and family experiences have little explanatory power in understanding the gender gap in status and earnings in science occupations. There is a long history of research on women in science that suggests that structural impediments are a major factor in marginalizing women scientists (Cole, 1987; Zuckerman, 1991; Rossiter, 1982; Cole & Zuckerman, 1984).

Thus well-trained women continue to experience barriers in the science occupations. The loose link between women's access to education and occupations suggests that although education systems have been opening up to women, gender discrimination in the work arena continues to consign them to low-status, low-paying occupations.

In sum, the research presented here utilizes a structuralist framework that suggests that gender will have both a direct and an indirect effect on science achievement. The direct effect will occur through discriminatory actions and policies of key institutions that are based solely on gender, regardless of qualifications. The indirect effect will occur vis-à-vis the unequal resources offered to young women and men. Thus both insufficient resources as well as gender discrimination are explanations for the exiting of bright, talented women from the sciences.

The Study: Data and Methods

THE MODEL. The model used to guide this study of gender and lost scientific talent is presented in Figure 1-1. It borrows from the above literature on lost talent, status and resources, and the science pipeline. In general, the model shows the different ways in which gender can affect science experiences and the relationships between key variables in the science achievement process. The time order of the key factors in the model is suggested by the left to right placement of the blocks of variables, with causation moving from left to right. All blocks of variables are assumed to have direct effects on science experiences. In addition, earlier variables can work through variables that occur between them and science experiences to affect these experiences. Gender is exogenous in the model. It is the status variable, which comes first in the process. Family and school resources and ultimately individual resources are endogenous variables, which come next. Finally, the model shows the outcome of interest—experiences in the sciences.

The model reflects several important characteristics of the science outcome. First, these experiences are multidimensional. To understand the totality of science experiences fully, four dimensions must be considered: achievement, access, attitudes, and activities. Students may be high on some of these dimensions and low on others. Hence, focusing on a single dimension denies the multiple ways in which young people can experience science. A second important characteristic of the science pipeline is its longitudinal nature. Over time information on students in different stages in the pipeline is provided to describe these experiences. In addition, this causal model operationalizes experiences in each area of the science pipeline with trajectories that represent typical paths in an area over time.

The model presented in Figure 1-1 also reflects a number of characteristics of the causal process leading to experiences in the sciences. Most important is an acknowledgment of the different ways in which gender can affect science experiences. First, gender can have direct effects on

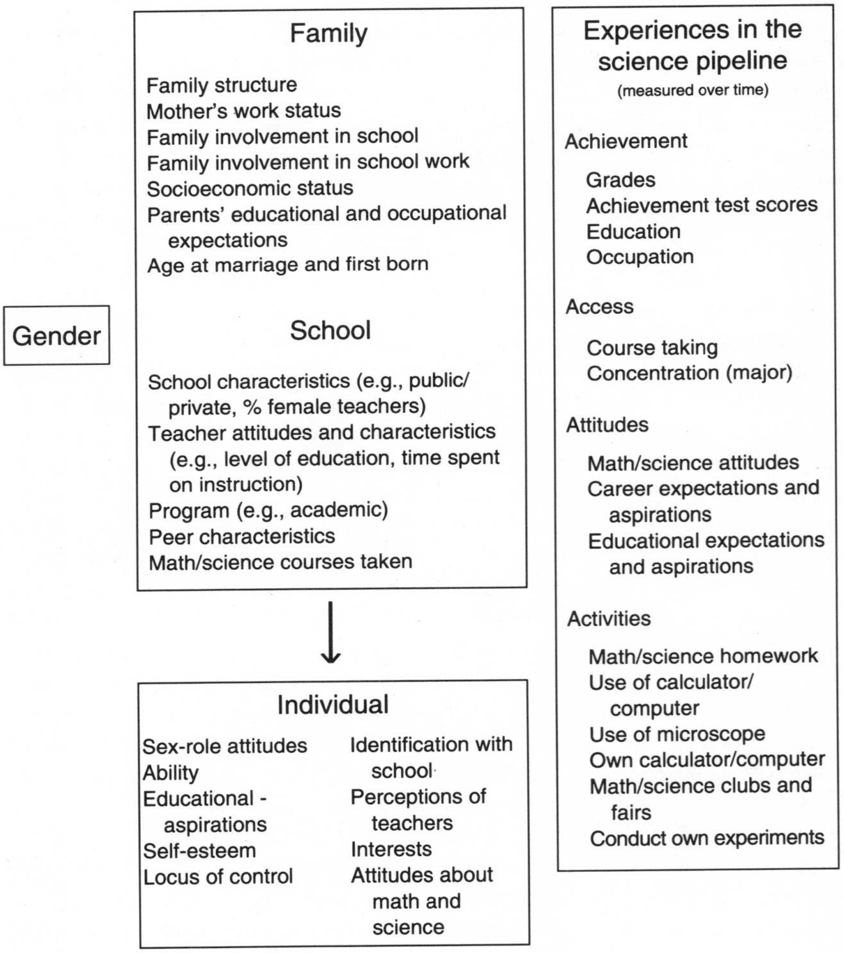

Gender

Family

Family structure
Mother's work status
Family involvement in school
Family involvement in school work
Socioeconomic status
Parents' educational and occupational
    expectations
Age at marriage and first born

School

School characteristics (e.g., public/
    private, % female teachers)
Teacher attitudes and characteristics
    (e.g., level of education, time spent
    on instruction)
Program (e.g., academic)
Peer characteristics
Math/science courses taken

Individual

Sex-role attitudes	Identification with
Ability	school
Educational -	Perceptions of
aspirations	teachers
Self-esteem	Interests
Locus of control	Attitudes about
	math and
	science

Experiences in the science pipeline
(measured over time)

Achievement

Grades
Achievement test scores
Education
Occupation

Access

Course taking
Concentration (major)

Attitudes

Math/science attitudes
Career expectations and
    aspirations
Educational expectations
    and aspirations

Activities

Math/science homework
Use of calculator/
    computer
Use of microscope
Own calculator/computer
Math/science clubs and
    fairs
Conduct own experiments

FIGURE 1-1   Model Predicting Lost Talent in the Sciences

these experiences, regardless of the family, school, and individual resources a student might have. Another important aspect of the effect of gender on science achievement is that the effect of resources might be different for girls and boys. (Both interactions and separate analyses for males and females are used to address this issue.) That is, girls may be less able to convert their family, school, and individual resources into science success than their male peers. Thus gender interacts with resources such that resources have different effects for girls and boys. This effect, together with the direct effect of gender on science outcomes, can be classified as the cost of being in the female status. These effects represent gender inequality and discrimination since they involve differences in outcomes that are dependent only on the gender status, regardless of individual qualifications.

Gender can also indirectly affect experiences in the sciences by influencing important determinants of science experiences—resources on the family, school, and individual level. Gender differences in status and power are legitimatized by cultural beliefs and sex-role socialization that define science as a male realm and contribute to the unequal channeling of key resources. Young women then come to agree with these beliefs and develop individual and personality characteristics that conform to them. Thus the model shows family and school resources preceding individual resources.

In sum, the model reflects two ways in which gender per se can affect experiences in the sciences—a direct effect and an effect vis-à-vis its interaction with resources. Both are effects of gender status that occur in spite of individual talents and resources. The model also shows how gender can indirectly affect science experiences by affecting the level of resources allocated to young girls and boys—resources that are critical for science achievement. A variety of statistical techniques will be used to assess the model. Descriptive statistics will be used to show levels of resources and types of science experiences for young women and men. Multivariate statistical models (including Analysis of Variance and logistic regression) for the total sample and for subsamples of women and men will be used to show the effect of gender and resources on science experiences. (See the Appendix for detailed information on the measurement and analysis plan.)

DATA SETS. The empirical analysis in this research will focus on available longitudinal data sets involving large nationally representative samples. These data sets allow assessment of the factors in our lost talent model and cover the years from grade 7 through early adulthood, during which youths might travel through critical education and early occupation segments of the science pipeline. The longitudinal nature of the data allows for clear assumptions about time ordering of life events and the straightforward creation of trajectories, or over-time patterns of experience. The data sets are ideal for testing the model of gender and lost talent in the sciences.

Three data sets are used. The first, High School and Beyond (HSB) contains data that were first collected in 1980 under the auspices of the National Center for Educational Statistics (NCES, 1993). Base-year data collected in the spring of 1980 from approximately 58,000 high school sophomores and seniors were obtained from a multistage stratified cluster sample from 1,015 high schools. They were interviewed again two, four, and six years later, providing information on high school experiences as well as early postsecondary and work experiences. HSB offers excellent measures of resource variables as well as science experiences. The sophomore cohort is of special interest since it is at this time that women begin falling out of the sciences. Given this and a need for parsimony, the causal model will be applied only to the HSB sophomore cohort. Only those individuals who participated in all phases of the study were included in these analyses ($N = 11,683$). Note that those who dropped out of high school between grades 10 and 12 are not included in the sample. However, all analyses include weights that control for sample attrition and nonresponse. Important descriptive information on the nature of young women's and men's experiences in the sciences will be provided for all data sets.

The High School and Beyond data also include information from the teachers and principals at the students' high schools. We use data from the supplemental 1984 "Administrator and Teacher Survey" to provide information on teachers (gender, training, ratings, time spent on instruction, and influence on curriculum, content, and teaching technique) and schools (number of years of math and science required). Although the respondents were no longer in high school in 1984, the NCES argues that these data are still valuable since these school characteristics are fairly stable over time. The data come from a probability sample of 532 of the original 1,015 schools in the High School and Beyond survey. One principal from each school and up to 30 randomly selected teachers from each school were surveyed. The final samples included 402 principals and 10,370 teachers. Given the subsample of schools represented, we restrict our study of these data to descriptive analyses. Important information on teachers and schools is also included in the student component of the High School and Beyond survey (see the Appendix).

The second data set, the National Educational Longitudinal Study (NELS), was begun in 1987–88 with a nationally representative sample of

26,200 eighth graders from 1,000 schools (National Center for Education Statistics, 1992). They were interviewed again two years later. Like the HSB, the NELS was collected under the auspices of the National Center for Educational Statistics. Its design is similar to that used for the HSB. The NELS data are valuable for studying transitions from middle school to high school.

The HSB and NELS data represent the best large-scale, nationally representative information on the high school and posthigh school years in the United States. They are two of the chief policy instruments of the U.S. Department of Education.

The third data set used in this research is the Longitudinal Study of American Youth (LSAY), conducted by the Public Opinion Laboratory of Northern Illinois University and funded by the National Science Foundation (Public Opinion Laboratory, 1992). Beginning in 1987 information was collected yearly from 60 seventh grades and 60 tenth grades in a national probability sample of 52 middle schools and 52 high schools. The survey has a special focus on students' attitudes toward science and math. In this research, only the seventh-grade cohort is analyzed (given the tenth-grade HSB cohort analysis). The data used here include the years 1987 through 1990, which represent grades 7 through 10 for this seventh-grade cohort. The LSAY data set will provide important information on experiences in the science pipeline during the middle school years and the first year of high school. It provides more detail on math and science experiences than any other data set.

The three nationally representative longitudinal data sets provide excellent measures of multiple science experiences and resources for critical years in the formation of young scientists. Descriptive and causal information gleaned from these data sets are used to provide insights into the complexities of these science experiences for women and explanations for the exiting of female talent from the sciences.

SCIENCE EXPERIENCES IN
SCHOOL AND BEYOND

Science Experiences in Middle School and Early
High School: Findings from the LSAY and NELS

What are the science experiences of boys and girls in the middle school and early high school years? Answers to this question come from the LSAY and NELS data sets.

Figures 2-1 through 2-4 present data on experiences involving science achievement, access, attitudes, and activities, respectively, for the LSAY sample. Figures 2-5 through 2-8 present this information for the NELS sample. Tables including percentages and tests for significance are presented in the Appendix. Only differences that are statistically significant will be noted in this discussion. Recall that the LSAY students were in seventh grade in the 1987 school year and that the NELS students were in eighth grade in the 1988 school year.

Figure 2-1 shows the percent of girls and boys in the LSAY sample who scored in the top quartile on standardized math and science exams in the four-year study period, and the percent getting mostly A's in math and science in ninth grade (1989). Several patterns are clear from this figure. In each of the four years, boys are more likely than girls to score in the top quartile on the standardized science exams. There are no significant gender differences in math scores in the first three years, but in 1990 (tenth grade) boys are more likely to score in the top quartile on the standardized math exam as well. There are also no significant gender differences in math and science grades in 1989 (ninth grade). Differences in standardized science scores are fairly stable over the four-year period, with the percentage of boys usually exceeding the percentage of girls by 5 percentage points or more. Thus these results suggest that gender differences in science achievement (as measured by standardized exams) occur before differences in math achievement. They are already present in seventh grade and continue into tenth grade. By tenth grade, boys score higher than girls on both science and math exams.

Figure 2-5 shows how well the NELS sample of youth is doing in math and science achievement. This information suggests that in eighth-grade boys are not only more likely to be scoring higher than girls on standardized science exams, as is indicated by the LSAY sample as well, but they are also more likely to be in high-ability math and science courses (especially science), and slightly more likely to be getting better grades in math and science courses. Gender differences on standardized math exams are significant here, but too small to be meaningful. Note that at the same time that the girls are scoring lower in math and science, they are earning much higher GPAs than the boys. In tenth grade, there are no important differences by gender in math and science grades, and it is the young women who are more likely to say that they work hard in math and science and who expect to hold a professional job at age 30.

These findings showing males getting better math and science grades than females in eighth grade but no gender differences in grades in ninth and tenth grades are at odds with other work that suggests that young

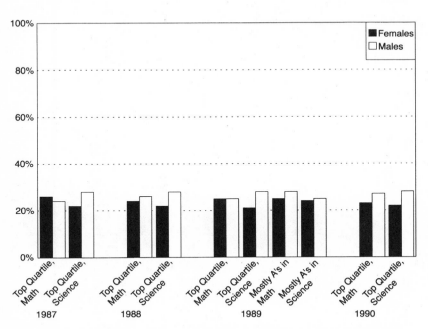

FIGURE 2-1 Involvement in the Sciences: Achievement in Math and Science (LSAY)

women get higher grades than do young men in math classes (DeBoer, 1984a). Both the time difference between the studies (DeBoer studied individuals who graduated from college in the mid to late 1970s) and the small, nonrandom sample used by DeBoer could help explain these inconsistencies.

Information on access to science in the LSAY data is provided in Figure 2-2. In general the results suggest that from seventh through tenth grade, girls tend to be at least as likely (if not more likely) as boys to have access to science as measured by enrollment in various math and science courses. There are a few exceptions. Boys are slightly more likely to be enrolled in algebra in eighth grade (1988), and they are more likely to be in high-ability science classes in ninth grade (1989). However, girls are more likely to be in the high-ability math classes in seventh grade (1987) and in the high-ability science classes in tenth grade (1990).

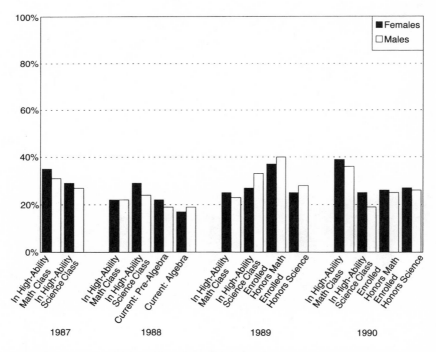

FIGURE 2-2 Involvement in the Sciences: Access to Math and Science (LSAY)

Information on access to science in the NELS cohort (Figure 2-6) shows greater gender differences during these middle school and early high school years than did the LSAY sample, with the differences favoring males. Both samples show boys more likely to be in algebra in eighth grade (these differences are very small, however). The NELS survey also asked about other courses (e.g., biology and computer education), and found boys more likely to be enrolled in these. This trend continues in tenth grade, when boys in the NELS sample are more likely than girls to be taking trigonometry, precalculus, calculus, chemistry, physics, and computer education (gender differences in algebra are very small, however). Thus, although the LSAY showed few gender differences in the middle and early high school years in terms of who takes high-ability math and science courses and who enrolls in honors math and science, the NELS sample shows that there *are* gender differences in enrollment in many advanced math and science courses. These differences are small, however, except in science and computer education classes.

Since the LSAY has considerable information on math and science attitudes, these results are presented separately by year in Figures 2-3A–2-3D.

(Text continued on page 32)

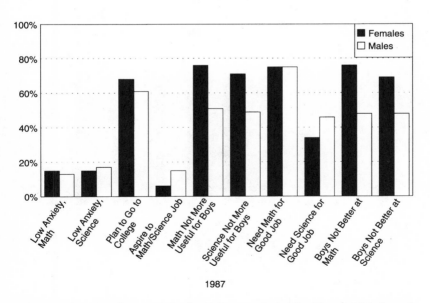

1987

FIGURE 2-3A   Involvement in the Sciences: Attitudes Toward Math and Science, 1987 (LSAY)

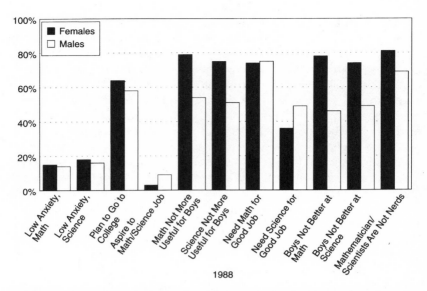

FIGURE 2-3B   Involvement in the Sciences: Attitudes Toward Math and Science, 1988 (LSAY)

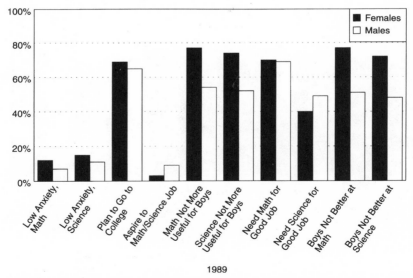

FIGURE 2-3C   Involvement in the Sciences: Attitudes Toward Math and Science, 1989 (LSAY)

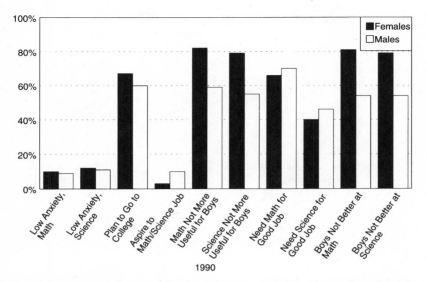

FIGURE 2-3D   **Involvement in the Sciences: Attitudes Toward Math and Science, 1990 (LSAY)**

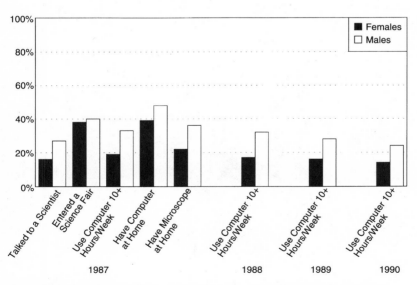

FIGURE 2-4   **Involvement in the Sciences: Activities and Resources (LSAY)**

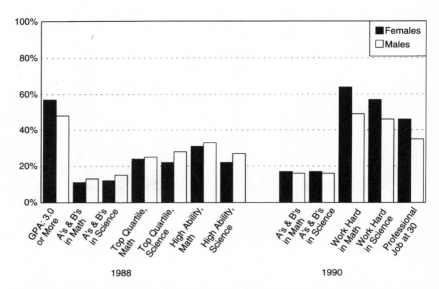

FIGURE 2-5 **Involvement in the Sciences: Achievement in Math and Science (NELS Eighth-Grade Cohort)**

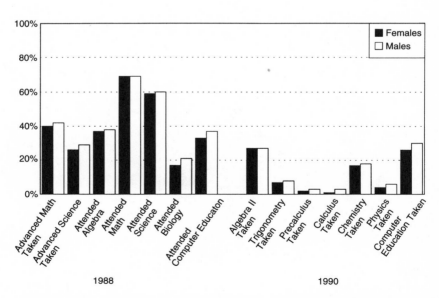

FIGURE 2-6 **Involvement in the Sciences: Access to Math and Science (NELS Eighth-Grade Cohort)**

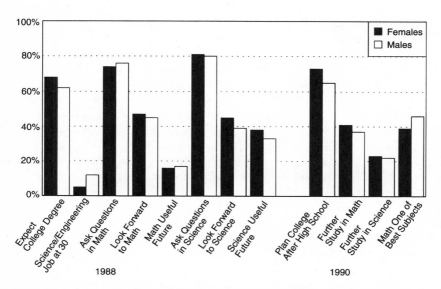

FIGURE 2-7   Involvement in the Sciences: Attitudes Toward Math and Science (NELS Eighth-Grade Cohort)

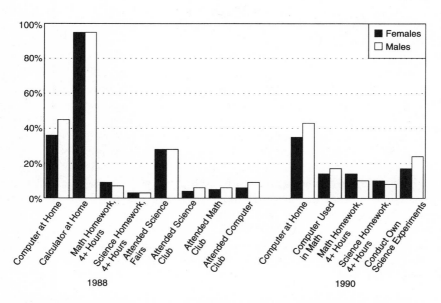

FIGURE 2-8   Involvement in the Sciences: Activities in Math and Science (NELS Eighth-Grade Cohort)

In their seventh-grade year (Figure 2-3A), girls do not differ much from boys in their anxiety about math and science, or in their belief that math knowledge is needed in getting good jobs. However, girls have less positive attitudes in two areas: aspirations for a math or science job, and attitudes about needing science knowledge for good jobs. Over twice as many boys as girls (15% versus 6%) aspire to a math or science occupation. And boys are more likely than girls to believe that knowledge of science is important for good jobs (46% versus 34%). In terms of attitudes about math and science being more useful for boys, or boys being better than girls in math and science, a majority of girls (but not always a majority of boys) disagree with these statements. Thus in seventh grade girls are not more anxious than boys about math and science, and are actually much less likely to believe that boys are better in these areas or that these areas are more useful for boys. They are also more likely to be planning on attending a four-year college. However, already at this age, these girls are much less likely to aspire to a math or science job, or to think that science knowledge is important for getting a good job.

Patterns of response for the attitudes measured in 1988 during the LSAY cohort's eighth-grade year are similar to those shown in the seventh-grade year (Figure 2-3B). Attitudes about math and science among the young women and men in the NELS cohort also show a similar pattern (Figure 2-7). However, in eighth grade the young women in the NELS cohort are *more* likely than the young men to say that science will be useful in their future. Thus even though young women may be less likely than young men to agree with the general statement that "It is important to know science for a good job" (as shown in the LSAY sample), when asked about their *own* future (as shown in the NELS sample), they are actually more likely than young men to say that it will be useful. Both the questioning about one's self and the questioning about a general future as opposed to an occupation may explain the finding in the NELS sample. When these questions are asked about math, young men and women are in agreement on both items. An additional LSAY measure of attitudes in 1988 shows that girls are more likely than boys to disagree with the statement that mathematicians and scientists are "nerds." This, together with the fact that they are not any more anxious about math and science or more likely to think that these areas are a male domain suggests girls are more positive than boys on a number of math and science attitudes in eighth grade. In eighth grade, young women in the NELS sample are actually more likely than young boys to look forward to science class.

Patterns of attitudes in the LSAY cohort in ninth and tenth grades (Figures 2-3C and 2-3D, respectively), show an amazing consistency with those of the earlier years. Interestingly, even though the young men and women in the LSAY sample show no differences in anxieties about math and science, in the NELS sample boys are more likely than girls to feel that math is one of their best subjects (Figure 2-7). Several changes do occur between seventh and tenth grade, however. For example, although there were no significant gender differences in earlier years, in tenth grade girls become significantly less likely than boys to believe that they need math knowledge for a good job. However, compared to seventh grade, by tenth grade girls become slightly more likely to believe that they need science knowledge for a good job, but they still are less likley than boys to believe this. Both boys and girls in the LSAY cohort became more convinced at some point between seventh and tenth grade that boys were not better at math and science and that these areas of study were not more useful for boys. Girls, however, were consistently much more likely to support these claims.

Are there gender differences in terms of math and science activities during these early years? Figures 2-4 and 2-8 present information on these activities in the LSAY and NELS samples, respectively. The figures reveal that, as with standardized achievement test scores, girls' and boys' activities in math and science show a consistent advantage on the part of boys. In seventh grade, the LSAY boys are more likely to have talked to a scientist, used a computer for 10 or more hours a week, have a computer in the home, and have a microscope in the home. The NELS sample suggests that these differences persist in eighth grade. More boys than girls belong to computer, math, and science clubs. One of the biggest differences in both samples is in the percent of young boys and girls who have a computer at home. Even in tenth grade, boys are more likely to have a computer in their home. They are also more likely to have conducted their own science experiment. It is the girls, however, who are spending more time on math and science homework in tenth grade.

This examination of two nationally representative samples of youth in middle school and early high school suggests that in these years there are some gender differences in access to math and science and in attitudes about math and science, but that these differences are minimal and sometimes favor girls. However, in two other areas of the sciences—achievement and activities—there is much more evidence of gender differences in these early years. What happens as the high school years continue?

Science Experiences in High School and Beyond: Findings from the HSB

SOPHOMORE COHORT. To examine science experiences in the high school and post–high school years, we turn to the HSB samples of youth who were sophomores and seniors in 1980. Figures 2-9 through 2-12 show the science experiences of the sophomore cohort of the HSB sample in areas involving achievement, access, attitudes, and activities. Figures 2-13 through 2-16 show these experiences for the senior cohort.

Results shown in Figure 2-9 on achievement suggest that in the high school years and the years immediately following young women are more likely than young men to have higher overall achievement as measured by GPA, attendance at a postsecondary school, and rates of college graduation. However, when the area of achievement is math or science, young women tend to achieve at a lower level than young men. The exception to this trend is in tenth-grade math classes. This represents a change from eighth grade (NELS), where boys are slightly more likely to be getting A's and B's in math. Here young women are more likely to be getting A's and B's. However, in the same sophomore year of high school, they are less likely to score in the top quartile on standardized math exams. The difference on standardized science exams is even larger (over 10 percentage points). By the senior year of high school, gender differences on standardized math and science exams have increased, although young women continue to get better grades in general than young men. The increase in gender differences on standardized achieve-

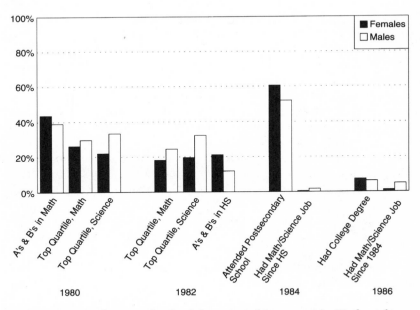

FIGURE 2-9 **Involvement in the Sciences: Achievement in Math and Science (HSB Sophomore Cohort)**

ment exams between tenth and twelfth grade also represents a long-term increase from seventh grade. The LSAY cohort showed small but significant gender differences on these science, but not math, exams. By the senior year these differences have grown considerably.

In the post-high school years, young women are more likely than young men to attend college, but they are less likely to have had a math or science job since high school. This difference in the likelihood of holding a math or science job increases in the period between 1984 (two years out of high school) and 1986 (four years out of high school).

Young women's and men's access to math and science in the HSB sophomore cohort is shown in Figure 2-10. Here it can be seen that the young people have very similar course-taking patterns in math and science in their sophomore year of high school (1980). However, in that same year, young men are more likely than young women to plan on taking two or more years of math or science in eleventh and twelfth grades. These sophomore-year gender differences in anticipated course taking show up as gender differences in actual course taking in the senior year of high school (1982). By then, young men are more likely than

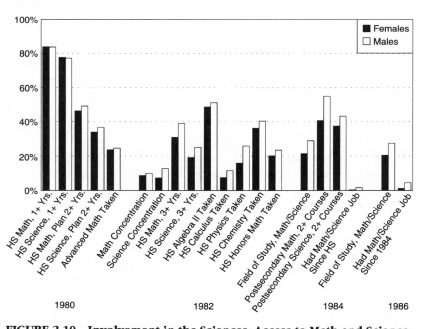

FIGURE 2-10   Involvement in the Sciences: Access to Math and Science (HSB Sophomore Cohort)

young women to have a math or science concentration, to have completed three or more years of math or science, and to have taken particular courses in math and science such as algebra II, calculus, physics, chemistry, or honors math. The gender differences are most extreme among those who reported taking a physics course, with 26 percent of young men but only 16 percent of young women having done so. The two years of postsecondary experiences—1984 and 1986—show a similar gender pattern in access to math and science. In 1984 young men are more likely than young women to have taken two or more postsecondary courses in math or science and to have chosen math or science as a field of study (these percentages are for those who attended postsecondary school). The field of study trend is similar in 1986.

These findings on young people's access to math and science in high school and beyond, when taken together with their access in the middle school years, suggest a long-term trend of increasing gender differences. Increasingly, it is young men who take math and science courses and major in math and science. In seventh grade, girls are *more* likely than boys to be in high-ability math classes and equally likely to be in high-ability science classes. In eighth grade, there are no significant gender differences on participation in high-ability or honors math and science classes, but there are small differences in taking advanced courses. By tenth grade, a small male advantage on math and science course taking emerges, and by twelfth grade, it has increased.

Information on the HSB sophomore cohort's attitudes toward math and science is presented in Figure 2-11. Results show that in their sophomore year young women have more negative attitudes toward math and science than do young men on all but one indicator. This is in contrast to the middle school years, where young women and men have similar attitudes on math and science items except for those dealing with occupations. Young women in the HSB sample are less likely than young men to see math as being useful in their future and to report positive attitudes about math class (at ease, not tense, not scared, or don't dread). In addition, they are slightly less than half as likely to report math or science as an expected field of study in college (17% versus 31%). However, young women are equally likely to state that math is interesting. They are more likely to expect to earn a four +-year college degree and to hold a professional job at age 30. These tenth-grade attitudinal results for the HSB sophomore cohort are somewhat inconsistent with those for the tenth grade in the LSAY sample, where young women are more likely than young men to have low math and science anxiety (Figure 2-3D). They are also more likely than boys to disagree with statements such as math (or science) is more useful for boys. Both the 10-year difference in measurement times (1980 for the HSB and 1990 for the LSAY) and the difference in the wording of items could be potential explanations for this divergence.

Figure 2-11 also shows that although young women in their senior year of high school continue to be more likely than young men to expect to earn a four +-year college degree, this trend is reversed in 1984 and 1986, when young people are two and four years out of high school, respectively. Young women do, however, continue to be more likely to expect a professional job at age 30 in these post–high school years.

Results for the math and science activities of the HSB sophomore cohort are presented in Figure 2-12. In their sophomore year of high school, young women are less likely to have a pocket calculator in the home, but by their senior year they are as likely as young men to have one. However, in the same year, they are less likely to have a micro/mini computer in their home. A large number of questions on the use of computers were included in the 1984 HSB survey. The answers suggest that two years out of high school, young women are more likely than young men to have ever used a pocket calculator or to have used a hand calculator in high school. They are also slightly more likely to have ever used a

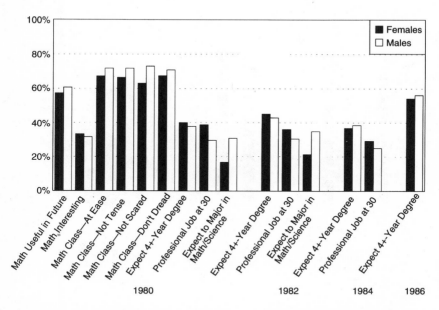

FIGURE 2-11   Involvement in the Sciences: Attitudes Toward Math and Science (HSB Sophomore Cohort)

computer terminal or to have used a computer terminal or micro computer on the job. However, young men are more likely than young women to report that they have used a computer terminal in high school or in education in general. They are also more likely to have ever used a micro computer or to have used one in education in general.

The long-term trend in gender differences in science activities is an interesting one. Earlier we noted that gender differences in science activities that favor males are present in seventh grade but diminish somewhat between seventh and tenth grades. Findings from the sophomore HSB cohort suggest that this early trend continues in some areas. In the post–high school years, women most likely begin entering the service and white-collar professions that employ a large number of females. These jobs often involve the use of terminals and word processors. However, young women in the post–high school years continue to be less likely to have used computers in education or in general.

SENIOR COHORT. Science experiences for the senior cohort of the HSB study are shown in Figures 2-13 through 2-16. Measures for the four areas of involvement in the science pipeline are very similar for the sopho-

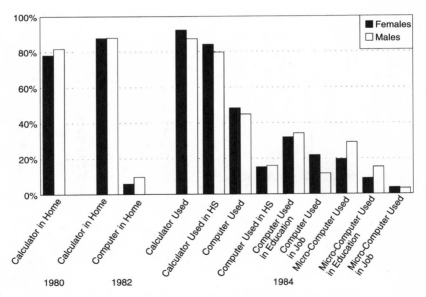

FIGURE 2-12 **Involvement in the Sciences: Activities in Math and Science (HSB Sophomore Cohort)**

more and senior cohorts. Of special interest, then, is whether the two cohorts had similar experiences. Of additional concern is the information the senior cohort provides on what happens to students six years out of high school (the sophomore cohort is followed four years out of high school). One of the interesting observations coming from the comparison of the math and science achievement of the two cohorts in their senior year of high school (1982 for the sophomore cohort, 1980 for the senior cohort) is that young women in the sophomore cohort (see Figure 2-9) are more likely than those in the senior cohort to score in the top quartile on standardized math exams (Figure 2-13). The math and science achievement experiences of the senior cohort also show that although gender differences in college attendance rates are absent in the early post–high school years, they appear in the sixth year out of high school, with young men being more likely than young women to have attended college in the most recent two-year period.

Figure 2-14 shows the senior year experiences in course taking for the senior cohort to be quite similar to those observed for the senior year of the sophomore cohort (see Figure 2-10). The results also suggest that four years out of high school, young men are taking far more postsecondary courses in math or science than are young women. This is espe-

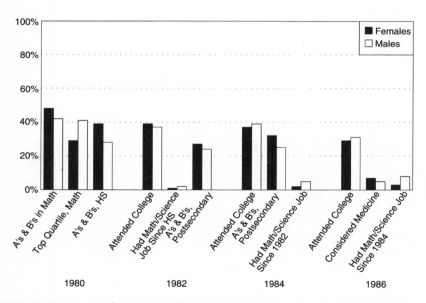

FIGURE 2-13   Involvement in the Sciences: Achievement in Math and Science (HSB Senior Cohort)

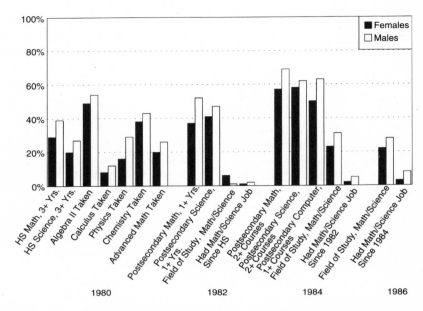

FIGURE 2-14   Involvement in the Sciences: Access to Math and Science (HSB Senior Cohort)

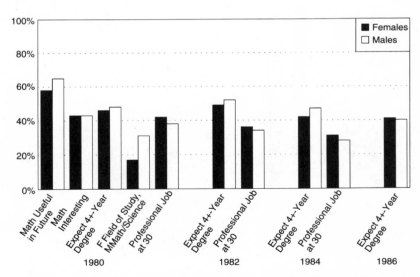

FIGURE 2-15   Involvement in the Sciences: Attitudes Toward Math and Science (HSB Senior Cohort)

40

cially true in science. Interestingly, young women are more likely than young men to major in math or science two years out of high school. However, when young people are asked about their majors four years and six years out of high school, it is young men who are more likely to be majoring in these areas. As with the sophomores, gender differences in percentages holding a job in math or science increase after high school—the 1 percentage point difference in 1982 increases to 3 percentage points in 1984 and 5 in 1986.

The senior cohort's attitudes about math and science are shown in Figure 2-15. As with the sophomore cohort (see Figure 2-11), these data show that young women and men are almost equally likely to see math as interesting, but that young men are more likely to report that it will be useful in their future. Comparisons between the two cohorts show that in their senior year of high school, the young men and women in the sophomore cohort are more likely than those in the senior cohort to expect to concentrate in math or science in college. Gender differences in the two cohorts are similar, with young men being considerably more likely to have this expectation. While young women in the sophomore cohort are *more* likely than their male peers to expect a four +-year de-

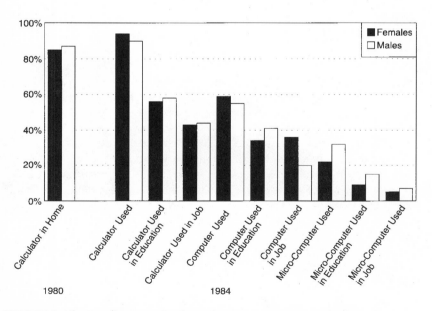

**FIGURE 2-16   Involvement in the Sciences: Activities in Math and
Science (HSB Senior Cohort)**

gree in their sophomore and senior years and equally likely to expect this degree in the two post–high school years, young women in the senior cohort are *less* likely than young men to expect this degree in three of the four years.

The senior cohort's activites in math and science are presented in Figure 2-16. Here we see that the trend that the sophomore cohort experienced earlier (see Figure 2-12) continues in the post–high school years. Young women are more likely than young men to have ever used calculators or computers and to have used them on the job. However, young men are more likely to report having used calculators, computers, and micro computers in education and to have ever used micro computers or to have used them in occupational settings.

Patterns of Experiences in the Sciences:
Trajectories

The above descriptions provide interesting "snapshots" of the typical, or average, science experiences of male and female youth at various points in time in the middle school, high school, and post–high school years. However, a better way to understand science experiences is to follow particular groups of men and women in order to describe their over-time experiences in the science pipeline. We can think of these over-time experiences as being science trajectories. (The Appendix provides details on how science trajectories are created in three areas of science experience: achievement, access, and attitudes. There were not enough data points to create trajectories for activities.) The importance of these trajectories is that they show patterns of "ins" and "outs" in the science pipeline. To be considered "in" the pipeline, a student has to place in the top quartile of a score that represents a number of measures. For example, to be considered "in" the achievement trajectory in 1980, a student had to place in the top quartile on a score that included data on 1980 math grades, standardized math score, and standardize science score. This approach to describing science experiences is unique and differs substantially from the more traditional technique of looking at average experiences of young women and men in various school years.

Earlier we suggested that many of the gender differences in science begin after eighth grade and show up in tenth grade. Accordingly, it is the experiences of the HSB sophomore cohort that are used in analyses involving trajectories.

Figures showing the percent of young women and men following various science trajectories are presented in Table 2-1. The ordering of the trajectories shown here roughly represents a continuum ranging from a pattern where young people are "out" of the science pipeline in each of the four years of the survey to a pattern where they exit from the sciences at increasingly later years to a pattern where they are "in" during each of the four survey years. What do these patterns tell us about over-time experiences in the science pipeline? Looking across all three areas of science, one first notes the broad similarity in the male and female patterns. Although there are gender differences, which are larger in some areas than others, the similarities are greater than the differences. Very few students of either gender stay in the sciences over the 1980–86 period. In most cases (except for females in the area of achievement), the most common pattern is "out throughout," where students are not in the pipeline in any year. Percentages here are large, ranging from about 30 percent to 49 percent. In the areas of achievement and access, the second most common trajectory involves a series of entries and exits, with the student ending up out of the sciences in 1986. Many more students show this haphazard pattern of experiences than a clear exit at one point, as shown in the trajectories "left after 1980," "left after 1982," and "left after 1984." An exception to these trends occurs in the area of attitudes. Here the second most common trajectory shows a series of entries into and exits from the sciences, with the student ending up *in* the pipeline. When those who stayed in the attitude pipeline throughout are combined with those who ended up in the pipeline, this group becomes very large (38% for females and 40% for

TABLE 2-1 **Over-Time Experiences (Trajectories) in the Sciences by Gender (HSB Sophomore Cohort)***

TRAJECTORY	*ACHIEVEMENT*		*ACCESS*		*ATTITUDES†*	
	Females	*Males*	*Females*	*Males*	*Females*	*Males*
Out Throughout	30.1%	35.8%	49.1%	42.4%	46.0%	37.6%
In and Out, Out 1986	35.3%	29.6%	21.3%	20.4%	1.6%	2.6%
Left After 1980	2.2%	2.2%	7.1%	6.3%	12.1%	15.1%
Left After 1982	.9%	1.5%	4.1%	3.8%	1.9%	4.1%
Left After 1984	8.0%	10.2%	3.8%	5.0%	—	—
In 1986, but Not Throughout	19.1%	14.6%	11.8%	15.3%	34.3%	33.2%
In Throughout	4.5%	6.2%	3.0%	6.9%	4.0%	7.5%
N	5,298	4,565	3,623	3,176	3,448	2,685

* Trajectories for activities are not presented since there were insufficient measures at some time points.

† Given the small number of attitudes measured in the 1986 survey, attitude trajectories are created for 1980–84. Some categories change; e.g., "in 1986, but not throughout," should be "in 1984, but not throughout," and "in and out, out 1986," should be "in and out, out 1984."

males). When compared to the two other areas of science, many more young people (both female and male) end up in the attitude pipeline than in the achievement or access pipelines.

When contrasting the three areas of science experiences, Table 2-1 suggests that although there are some similarites in patterns, there are considerable differences in achievement, access, and attitude trajectories. These different patterns across areas of science suggest that we cannot think of a single science pipeline. For both young men and women, the three science trajectories show substantially different patterns for 1980–86. For example, young people are more likely to exit early from the access and attitude pipelines and later from the achievement pipeline. Patterns of experience in all three areas include a considerable number of people who enter and exit. But in achievement and access, this coming and going is more likely to result in an exit, while in attitudes, it is more likely to end up with an entrance. A final difference of note is that for both young women and men, the science pipeline that they are most likely *never* to enter is that involving access.

In spite of the overall similarity in broad patterns of science experiences for males and females, Table 2-1 shows that gender is an important factor in understanding variations in these experiences. In each of the areas of science, males are more likely than females to be in the sciences throughout the survey period. As with the overall patterns, gender differences vary with area of science. The difference in the percent of males and females who stay in the science pipeline throughout is largest in regard to access and attitudes and slightly smaller for achievement. Interestingly, it is the area of access that young women are least likely to stay in throughout, and it is the area of achievement that young men are the least likely to stay in throughout. In fact, if one adds the percent of young men and women who follow the "in throughout" trajectory to the percent who enter and exit but end up in, it is young women who represent the largest group in the achievement pipeline.

Consider the other end of the trajectory continuum—the youth who are never in the science pipeline during the survey period. In two of the three areas of science—access and attitudes—young women are more likely than young men to show this pattern. It is young men, however, who are more likely never to enter the achievement pipeline.

What can we say about the science experiences of young women? Young women have their most successful experiences, overall, in the attitude pipeline. Over one-third (38%) end up in the science attitude pipeline two years after high school (1984). Fewer women end up in the achievement and access pipelines. This is not to say that all women experience positive science attitudes. In fact, nearly one-half (46%) of the young women are not in the attitude pipeline in any sample year. Exits are more likely to occur after the sophomore year than after the senior year.

It is in the area of access to science that young women are the least likely to have positive experiences. Only 14.8% of women are in the access pipeline throughout or ended up in the pipeline. Nearly 50 percent are never in the access pipeline, and over 77 percent are out for good

TABLE 2-2 Over-Time Experiences (Trajectories) in Areas of the Sciences for Females with Positive Experiences in a Third Area (HSB Sophomore Cohort)

IN ATTITUDE PIPELINE THROUGHOUT

	Achievement	*Access*
Out Throughout	4.0%	5.6%
In and Out, Out 1986	24.6%	8.0%
Left After 1980	0.0%	2.0%
Left After 1982	0.0%	1.6%
Left After 1984	38.8%	17.8%
In 1986, but Not Throughout	14.8%	36.7%
In Throughout	17.8%	28.3%

IN ACHIEVEMENT PIPELINE THROUGHOUT

	Access	*Attitudes*
Out Throughout	9.7%	22.6%
In and Out, Out 1986*	25.8%	1.4%
Left After 1980	.7%	13.3%
Left After 1982	10.2%	5.8%
Left After 1984	15.8%	NR†
In 1986, but Not Throughout*	19.3%	46.9%
In Throughout	18.6%	10.0%

IN ACCESS PIPELINE THROUGHOUT

	Achievement	*Attitudes*
Out Throughout	0.0%	9.1%
In and Out, Out 1986*	15.0%	0.0%
Left After 1980	0.0%	6.3%
Left After 1982	0.0%	6.7%
Left After 1984	34.8%	NR
In 1986, but Not Throughout*	16.3%	48.7%
In Throughout	33.4%	29.2%

* 1984 for attitudes.
† Not relevant. This category does not exist for this variable.

following their sophomore year of high school. A permanent exit is most likely to occur for young women after their sophomore year than after any other year.

More women are continuously in the achievement pipeline over the survey years than in the access or attitude pipelines (although the difference between the percent "in throughout" in achievement and in attitudes is small). Exiting from this area occurs later than from the other two, with 1984 (two years out of high school) being the year with the largest number of young women exiting.

To what extent do young women's experiences in the three areas of science overlap? Table 2-2 provides some insight into answering this question. Here, three groups of women are studied—those who are in the pipeline throughout in the areas of achievement, access, and attitudes. For each group, experiences in the other two areas of science are provided. Interestingly, Table 2-2 shows that there is not considerable overlap between the three dimensions of science experiences. No more than one-third of young women who are in one area of the sciences throughout the six-year period are in another area throughout that time. The greatest overlap occurs among those who remain in the access pipeline. Among this group of young women, 33 percent are in the achievement pipeline throughout, and 29 percent are in the attitude pipeline throughout. Although those with high access are well represented in the high-achievement group, the reverse is not true. Among the group of young women who stay in the achievement pipeline throughout, only 18 percent are in the access pipeline throughout. The smallest overlap is between achievement and attitudes. Only 10 percent of girls who are in the achievement pipeline throughout are in the attitude pipeline as well. Conversely, only 17 percent of young women who remain highly positive about science in their attitude, experience high achievement throughout the survey period.

Science Trajectories: How Much Lost Talent?

What do these findings suggest about lost talent? How many young women (and men) with signs of science talent (e.g., scoring in the top quartile on measures of achievement, access, or attitudes in at least one survey year) have exited the sciences by the final survey year? The findings add a layer of complexity to our understanding of women's experiences in the science pipeline. Although, as noted above, the area of science where young women are least likely to have positive experiences is access, it is in the area of science achievement that there is the largest drain of women showing evidence of talent. Almost half of the young women in the sample (46%) who have shown signs of talent in achievement have exited the pipeline by 1986. Although a good number of the young men who have shown signs of talent also exit by 1986, the number is smaller (43%). Thus, the talented young women are 7 percent more likely than their male counterparts to exit the science achievement pipeline. Although young women are more likely than young men to end up in the science achievement pipeline in 1986, talented young women exit the achievement pipeline at a faster rate than do talented young men. There is less lost talent among young women in the area of science access, but a considerable number still show unfulfilled promise here (36% of those who show promise were out of the pipeline by 1986). The number is very similar for young men. The amount of talent loss is smallest in the area of attitudes, and here it is young *men* who suffer the greatest risk (21% versus 16%).

3

SCIENCE RESOURCES

Who Has More Science Resources—
Young Men or Young Women?

One of the main assumptions of this research is that critical family, school, and individual resources are needed in order to succeed in science. Do young women have different amounts of these resources than young men? Table 3-1 presents a list of resources that theory and research suggest might affect science experiences. Let us first consider family resources. Here we see a number of significant differences between males and females, and in all but one case, the differences favor the males. The young men in the sample are more likely to come from a high-SES family, have their father in the household, have a father with a high-status occupation, have a pocket calculator in their home, have a father who keeps track of their progress in school, have parents who attend PTA meetings, and have parents who attend parent-teacher conferences. They are much less likely than the young women to have ever been married or had a child. It is here where the largest gender differences exist. Young women are more than twice as likely as young men to have been married or have had a child by the time they are two years out of high school. Only one family resource difference favors females—they are more likely than males to have parents who know where they are and what they are doing. When looking at these gender differences in resources, it is important to keep in mind that one consequence of using a large sample like HSB is that even small differences are sometimes significant. Thus gender differences in some of these resources (e.g., mother's work status, father's occupation, and a father who keeps track of progress in school) are statistically significant, but the size of the difference is so small that it is most likely not very meaningful.

When considering gender differences in school resources, remember that the school resources available in the HSB data tend to be general

TABLE 3-1 Means (and Standard Deviations) for Family, School, and Individual Resources by Gender (HSB Sophomore Cohort)

	Total	*Females*	*Males*
Demographic Characteristics			
1980			
Rural Residence			
(1 = Yes; 0 = No)	.32 (.47)	.32 (.47)	.33 (.47)
Race—African American			
(1 = African American;			
0 = Other)	.12 (.32)	.13 (.33)*	.11 (.32)*
Race—Hispanic			
(1 = Hispanic; 0 = Other)	.14 (.34)	.12 (.33)*	.15 (.36)*
Family Resources			
1980			
SES Quartile	2.48 (1.12)	2.42 (1.11)*	2.54 (1.12)*
Number of Siblings	2.94 (1.76)	2.95 (1.76)	2.94 (1.76)
Father Lives in Household			
(1 = True; 0 = False)	.74 (.44)	.72 (.45)*	.76 (.43)*
Mother Worked When Respondent Was in			
Elementary School			
(1 = True; 0 = False)	.62 (.49)	.63 (.48)*	.62 (.49)*
Mother's Occupation			
(1 = Technical, managerial, professional;			
0 = Other)	.25 (43)	.25 (.43)	.26 (.44)
Mother's Education			
(1 = At least some college; 0 = Other)	.26 (.44)	.26 (.44)	.27 (.44)
Father's Occupation			
(1 = Technical, managerial, professional;			
0 = Other)	.29 (.46)	.28 (.45)*	.30 (.46)*
Father's Education			
(1 = At least some college; 0 = Other)	.33 (.47)	.33 (.47)	.34 (.47)
Mother Monitors Schoolwork			
(1 = Yes; 0 = No)	.89 (.32)	.89 (.32)	.89 (.32)
Father Monitors Schoolwork			
(1 = Yes; 0 = No)	.76 (.43)	.76 (.43)	.76 (.43)
Mother's Educational Expectations			
(1 = College education or more;			
0 = Other)	.58 (.49)	.58 (.49)	.57 (.50)
Pocket Calculator in Home			
(1 = True; 0 = False)	.80 (.40)	.78 (.41)*	.82 (.39)*
1982			
Mother Keeps Track of Progress in School			
(1 = True; 0 = False)	.88 (.33)	.88 (.33)	.87 (.33)
Father Keeps Track of Progress in School			
(1 = True; 0 = False)	.76 (.43)	.75 (.44)*	.77 (.42)*

(continued on next page)

TABLE 3-1   *(continued)*

	Total	*Females*	*Males*

Family Resources (continued)

1982 (continued)

Parents Know Where Student is,

What Student Does

(1 = True; 0 = False)	.79 (.41)	.86 (.35)*	.72 (.45)*

How Often Parents Attend PTA Meetings

(1 = Never; 2 = Once in a while; 3 = Often)	1.26 (.54)	1.25 (.53)*	1.28 (.56)*

How Often Parents Attend
Parent-Teacher Conferences

(1 = Never; 2 = Once in a while; 3 = Often)	1.49 (.65)	1.47 (.64)*	1.52 (.66)*

1984

Ever Married

(1 = Yes; 0 = No)	.14 (.35)	.21 (.41)*	.08 (.27)*

Had Child

(1 = Yes; 0 = No)	.12 (.32)	.16 (.38)*	.07 (.25)*

School Resources

1980

School Type

(1 = Private; 0 = Public)	.09 (.29)	.10 (.30)	.09 (.28)

Program

(1 = Academic; 0 = Other)	.32 (.47)	.34 (.47)*	.31 (.46)*

Percent of Teachers Considered Excellent[P]

	27.18 (17.69)	27.72 (17.92)*	26.64 (17.42)*

Teacher Influence on Curriculum, Content,
and Teaching Techniques[T]

(Scale from low to high: 3 to 18)	13.96 (2.51)	13.90 (2.55)	14.01 (2.40)

Percent of Class Time Teachers Spend
on Instruction[T]

(1 = 0–2% to 9 = over 30%)	8.61 (1.42)	8.59 (1.47)	8.63 (1.36)

Percent Female Teachers in Sample[T]

	.45 (.50)	.48 (.50)*	.43 (.50)*

Teachers' Education[T]

(1 = HS to 8 = Doctorate)	5.48 (.93)	5.46 (.91)	5.47 (.95)

Female Math/Science Teacher in Sample[T]

(1 = Yes; 0 = No)	.13 (.33)	.13 (.34)	.12 (.33)

Number of Years of Math Required
for Graduation[P]

	1.64 (.74)	1.66 (.77)*	1.62 (.71)*

Number of Years of Science Required
for Graduation[P]

	1.46 (.65)	1.47 (.66)	1.45 (.64)

Rate School on Teacher Interest
in Students

(1 = Good, excellent; 0 = Poor, fair)	.54 (.50)	.54 (.50)	.53 (.50)

Closest Sophomore Friend At School
Gets Good Grades

(1 = True; 0 = False)	.81 (.39)	.84 (.37)*	.78 (.42)*

TABLE 3-1 *(continued)*

	Total	*Females*	*Males*
School Resources *(continued)*			
1980 *(continued)*			
Is Interested in School			
(1 = True; 0 = False)	.65 (.48)	.70 (.46)*	.61 (.40)*
Attends Classes Regularly			
(1 = True; 0 = False)	.91 (.28)	.92 (.27)*	.90 (.30)*
Plans to Go to College			
(1 = True; 0 = False)	.63 (.48)	.67 (.47)*	.60 (.49)*
Friends' Feelings About Students			
with Good Grades			
(1 = Think well of; 0 = Other)	.35 (.48)	.39 (.49)*	.31 (.46)*
1982			
Program (1 = Academic; 0 = Other)	.38 (.49)	.39 (.49)	.38 (.48)
Rate School on Teacher Interest in Students			
(1 = Good, excellent; 0 = Poor, fair)	.63 (.48)	.62 (.48)	.64 (.48)
Closest Senior Friend at School			
Gets Good Grades			
(1 = True; 0 = False)	.87 (.34)	.91 (.29)*	.83 (.38)*
Is Interested in School			
(1 = True; 0 = False)	.71 (.46)	.74 (.44)*	.67 (.47)*
Attends Classes Regularly			
(1 = True; 0 = False)	.92 (.28)	.93 (.25)*	.90 (.30)*
Plans to go to College			
(1 = True; 0 = False)	.70 (.46)	.74 (.44)*	.67 (.42)*
Individual Resources			
1980			
Self-Concept Scale	.02 (.73)	.08 (.74)*	−.04 (.71)*
Locus Of Control Scale	.00 (.65)	.05 (.63)*	.06 (.66)*
Work Orientation Scale	−.02 (.72)	−.09 (.69)*	.06 (.74)*
Family Orientation Scale	.00 (.63)	.03 (.61)*	−.02 (.65)*
Sex-Role Attitudes			
Working Mother Is a Good Mother			
(1 = Agree; 0 = Disagree)	.18 (.39)	.21 (.41)*	.15 (.36)*
Man Should Achieve, Woman Keep House			
(1 = Disagree; 0 = Agree)	.11 (.32)	.18 (.38)*	.05 (.21)*
Woman Is Happiest in Home			
(1 = Disagree; 0 = Agree)	.08 (.28)	.12 (.32)*	.05 (.21)
Popular			
(1 = Very; 0 = Somewhat or not at all)	.77 (.42)	.77 (.42)	.76 (.43)
Amount of Dating			
(1 = Almost every day or every day;			
0 = Other)	.06 (.23)	.06 (.23)	.06 (.24)
Age Expect to Get Married	23.36 (3.40)	22.80 (3.27)*	23.97 (3.43)*

(continued on next page)

TABLE 3-1 *(continued)*

	Total	Females	Males
Individual Resources *(continued)*			
1980 *(continued)*			
Age Expect to Have First Child	24.93 (3.33)	24.64 (3.27)*	25.24 (3.38)*
Interested in School			
(1 = True; 0 = False)	.75 (.43)	.79 (.41)*	.72 (.45)*
High School Grades			
(1 = A's & B's; 0 = B's or less)	.27 (45)	.32 (.47)*	.22 (.41)*
Standardized Math Score	48.78 (9.73)	48.88 (9.50)*	49.08 (9.95)*
Standardized Science Score	50.11 (9.91)	48.87 (9.49)*	51.37 (10.18)*
Time on Homework per Week			
(1 = 3+ hours; 0 = Other)	.50 (.50)	.58 (.49)*	.42 (.49)*
Educational Expectations			
(1 = College degree or more; 0 = Other)	.41 (.49)	.42 (.49)	.40 (.49)
Educational Aspirations			
(1 = Disappointed if don't go to college; 0 = Other)	.63 (.48)	.66 (.47)*	.59 (.49)*
Occupational Expectations			
(1 = Professional job; 0 = Other)	.34 (.47)	.39 (.49)*	.33 (.46)*
1982			
Interested in School			
(1 = True; 0 = False)	.76 (.43)	.79 (.41)*	.72 (.45)*
High School Grades			
(1 = A's or A's & B's; 0 = B's or less)	.32 (.47)	.38 (.49)*	.26 (.44)*
Time on Homework per Week			
(1 = 5+ hours; 0 = Other)	.30 (.46)	.36 (.48)*	.24 (.43)*

* T-test is significant ≤ .05 level.
T Item is from Teacher Survey.
P Item is from Principal Survey.

educational resources (e.g., teacher interest in students, peers' interest in school and grades) rather than specific science resources (e.g., math and science teachers who encourage them). The gender differences in school resources show a different pattern than did the gender differences in family resources. Now it is young women who have the advantage. Table 3-1 shows that the females are more likely than the males to be in an academic program. They are also more likely to be in schools that have more teachers who are considered excellent, more female teachers, and more years of math and science required. In addition, the female students are more likely than their male counterparts to have friends in their sophomore and senior years who get good grades, are interested in school, attend classes regularly, plan to go to college, and think well of students with good grades. The young men have an advantage on only two resources. Males are more likely than females to be attending schools where teachers have a greater influence on curriculum, content, and teaching techniques, and where teachers spend more time on instruction. Both of these differences are small. The largest differences in school resources occur in the area of school peers. For example, in their sophomore year of high school, young women are 20 percent more likely than young men to have friends who think well of students with good grades. They are 13 percent more likely to say that their closest friend at school is interested in school. These large gender differences in school peer groups continue into the senior year of high school.

A third type of resource that has potential implications for science experiences is individual resources. Are there gender differences in personality characteristics? in attitudes about education, occupation, and family? in behaviors both in and out of school? The answer to these questions is: it depends. If we are asking about differences involving certain personality characteristics, future family expectations, and math and science achievement, it is males who are more likely to have the characteristics that nurture science achievement. Table 3-1 shows that males are more likely than females to have an internal locus of control (i.e., to feel that their efforts have consequences) and to score higher on work orientation and lower on family orientation. Males expect to marry and have their first child later than females. They also score higher on standardized math and especially science exams.

On the other hand, if we are asking about individual resources involving self-concept, sex-role attitudes, general school achievement and activities, or attitudes about general educational and occupational roles (current and future), it is young women who have the edge over young men. Relative to males, the females have a higher self-concept and more progressive sex-role attitudes. Note that these sex-role attitudes are considered a resource only for women—women with more androgynous sex-role attitudes tend to achieve more than those with more traditional attitudes. Differences among males do not show a similar trend. The females also express more interest in school, have higher GPAs, and spend more time on homework in both their sophomore and senior years. They also are more likely to have high educational aspirations and expectations for a professional job. Some of these gender differences in individual resources favoring females are very large. For example, young women are 31 percent more likely than young men to be getting A's and

B's in their sophomore and senior years of high school, and 28 percent more likely to be spending three or more hours a week on homework in their sophomore year.

This examination indicates that there are considerable gender differences in resources that have been shown to be important for positive science experiences and that the group with the advantage varies with the type of resource being considered. Young men have more resources in the home. They also have more personality resources. Their greater orientation to work and weaker orientation to family along with their higher math and science test scores give them potential advantages in the science pipeline. On the other hand, young women have a distinct advantage in having more general school resources, the chief of which is peer groups who emphasize education. The young women also have the advantage of higher self-concepts and higher commitment to and achievement in school as well as higher educational aspirations and occupational expectations. But how important are these resources for experiences in the science pipeline? Do they work in similar ways for young women and men? Next we turn our attention to the connection between resources and science experiences.

Women's Resources and Science Experiences

Before taking a complex look at the causal role of gender and resources in science experiences, it is important to ask a more simple question about the role of resources for women. Do women in the various science trajectories have different levels of family, school, and individual resources? Although the answer does not deal with the causal impact of gender and resources on science experiences, it will help us in creating a resource portrait for women with diverse experiences in the science pipeline. It will provide valuable insights into the unique characteristics of women who fight the odds and stay in science.

Tables 3-2 through 3-4 provide information on the family, school, and individual resources of women in the science achievement, science access, and science attitude trajectories. Tables 3-5 through 3-7 will present further information on the intersection between a particular kind of individual resource—science resources—and science trajectory. Together they allow us to see whether young people with different trajectories in one area of science (e.g., achievement) have varying levels of resources in other areas (e.g., access, attitudes, and activities).

An overview of these six tables suggests that women who stay in the science pipeline (in each area of science) have distinct resource advantages that are often considerable. In general, as one looks from the far left column (representing women who were out of the sciences throughout the survey period) to the far right column (representing women who were in the sciences throughout the survey period), a clear pattern of increasing resources emerges. The more resources the young women have, the more time they are likely to spend in the sciences. However, at times the procession from lower to higher resources is not so linear. The clearest deviation comes for those who left the science pipeline late. Interestingly, these late-leavers sometimes have more resources than those young women who stay in science. This is especially noticeable in the area of access to science. Here, the late-leavers sometimes have more family resources than other groups. They are more likely than all others to come from a family with high SES and to have mothers and fathers with high education and job status. For ease of presentation, the discussion below will mainly focus on the differences in resources of young women who follow the "in throughout" and the "out throughout" trajectories.

FAMILY RESOURCES. Two family demographic characteristics are clearly related to science trajectories—residence and race. Rural residence shows a clear pattern in each area of science—women who are "out throughout" are more likely to come from rural areas than those who are "in throughout." There is some variation across areas of science. Rural women are more likely to stay in the science achievement pipeline than the other two. They are also more likely to stay out of the science attitude pipeline than the other two.

Young Hispanic women are much more likely to be found in the "out" trajectory than in the "in" trajectory in each area of science. The extreme is greatest in the area of achievement, where the percent Hispanic is four times greater in the "out" trajectory than in the "in" trajectory. The situation for young African American women is more complex. They, like the Hispanic women, are very underrepresented in the science achievement pipeline. The percent of African American women in the "out throughout" science achievement trajectory is seven times greater than the percent in the "in throughout" trajectory. The difference in access is much smaller. In the area of science attitudes, there is an interesting turnaround in that the young African American women are more likely to be continuously in the pipeline than continuously out. However, the number of African American women who are in and out of the pipeline and who end up out of the pipeline is high.

A clear pattern associating greater resources with a greater likelihood of staying in the science pipeline emerges when we look at socioeconomic status. Young women who continuously pursue science are much

(Text continued on page 62)

TABLE 3-2 Means (and Standard Deviations) for Family, School, and Individual Resources of Females in Science Achievement Trajectories (HSB Sophomore Cohort)

	Out Throughout	*In and Out, Out 1986*
Demographic Characteristics		
1980		
Rural Residence		
(1 = Yes; 0 = No)	.38 (.49)	.27 (.45)
Race—African American		
(1 = African American; 0 = Other)	.14 (.35)	.14 (.35)
Race—Hispanic		
(1 = Hispanic; 0 = Other)	.16 (.37)	.11 (.32)
Family Resources		
1980		
SES Quartile	1.85 (.93)	2.64 (1.08)
Number of Siblings	4.40 (1.81)	3.83 (1.75)
Father Lives in Household		
(1 = True; 0 = False)	.66 (.47)	.73 (.45)
Mother Worked When Respondent was		
in Elementary School		
(1 = True; 0 = False)	.64 (.48)	.65 (.48)
Mother's Occupation		
(1 = Technical, managerial, professional; 0 = Other)	.11 (.31)	.23 (.42)
Mother's Education		
(1 = At least some college; 0 = Other)	.09 (.29)	.30 (.46)
Father's Occupation		
(1 = Technical, managerial, professional; 0 = Other)	.14 (.34)	.34 (.47)
Father's Education		
(1 = At least some college; 0 = Other)	.19 (.39)	.39 (.49)
Mother Monitors Schoolwork		
(1 = Yes; 0 = No)	.85 (.36)	.90 (.31)
Father Monitors Schoolwork		
(1 = Yes; 0 = No)	.67 (.47)	.78 (.41)
Mother's Educational Expectations		
(1 = College education or more; 0 = Other)	.37 (.47)	.68 (.47)
Pocket Calculator in Home		
(1 = True; 0 = False)	.68 (.47)	.80 (.40)
1982		
Mother Keeps Track of Progress in School		
(1 = True; 0 = False)	.83 (.38)	.88 (.32)
Father Keeps Track of Progress in School		
(1 = True; 0 = False)	.66 (.47)	.75 (.44)

Left After 1980	Left After 1982	Left After 1984	In 1986, but Not Throughout	In Throughout
.42 (.49)	.24 (.43)	.32 (.47)	.34 (.47)	.33 (.47)
.02 (.14)	.02 (.14)	.02 (.13)	.14 (.34)	.02 (.14)
.05 (.22)	.04 (.21)	.04 (.19)	.10 (.30)	.04 (.20)
2.17 (.91)	2.57 (.93)	3.15 (.96)	2.60 (1.07)	3.18 (.94)
4.33 (1.62)	3.59 (1.55)	3.53 (1.47)	3.67 (1.70)	3.37 (1.52)
.70 (.46)	.68 (.47)	.83 (.38)	.77 (.42)	.87 (.33)
.67 (.47)	.64 (.48)	.53 (.50)	.61 (.49)	.57 (.50)
.19 (.39)	.16 (.37)	.28 (.45)	.24 (.43)	.33 (.47)
.25 (.43)	.17 (.38)	.42 (.49)	.28 (.45)	.54 (.50)
.25 (.43)	.45 (.50)	.47 (.50)	.31 (.46)	.49 (.50)
.23 (.42)	.43 (.50)	.51 (.50)	.35 (.48)	.54 (.50)
.81 (.39)	.79 (.40)	.94 (.24)	.91 (.29)	.95 (.21)
.72 (.45)	.68 (.47)	.89 .31)	.78 (.41)	.86 (.35)
.42 (.49)	.47 (.50)	.88 (.33)	.60 (.49)	.87 (.33)
.84 (.37)	.94 (.25)	.93 (.25)	.82 (.38)	.92 (.28)
.86 (.35)	.71 (.45)	.90 (.30)	.92 (.27)	.93 (.26)
.71 (.45)	.48 (.50)	.83 (.38)	.78 (.41)	.85 (.36)

(continued on next page)

TABLE 3-2 *(continued)*

	Out Throughout	*In and Out, Out 1986*
Family Resources *(continued)*		
1982 *(continued)*		
Parents Know Where Student Is, What Student Does		
(1 = True; 0 = False)	.81 (.39)	.87 (.34)
How Often Parents Attend PTA Meetings		
(1 = Never; 2 = Once in a while; 3 = Often)	1.17 (.42)	1.31 (.58)
How Often Parents Attend		
Parent-Teacher Conferences		
(1 = Never; 2 = Once in a while; 3 = Often)	1.41 (.59)	1.48 (.66)
1984		
Ever Married		
(1 = Yes; 0 = No)	.37 (.48)	.13 (.34)
Had Child		
(1 = Yes; 0 = No)	.33 (.47)	.08 (.26)
School Resources		
1980		
School Type		
(1 = Private; 0 = Public)	.05 (.21)	.13 (.34)
Program		
(1 = Academic; 0 = Other)	.14 (.35)	.41 (.49)
Percent of Teachers Considered Excellent[P]	25.51 (16.81)	28.60 (18.02)
Teacher Influence on Curriculum,		
Content, and Teaching Techniques[T]		
(Scale from low to high: 3 to 18)	13.57 (2.74)	13.90 (2.52)
Percent of Class Time Teachers Spend on Instruction[T]		
(1 = 0–2% to 9 = over 30%)	8.57 (1.46)	8.57 (1.50)
Percent Female Teachers in Sample[T]	.49 (.50)	.44 (.50)
Teachers' Education[T]		
(1 = HS; 8 = Doctorate)	5.52 (.96)	5.50 (.90)
Female Math/Science Teacher in Sample[T]		
(1 = Yes; 0 = No)	.40 (.49)	.35 (.48)
Number of Years of Math Required for Graduation[P]	1.54 (.66)	1.66 (.72)
Number of Years of Science Required for Graduation[P]	1.47 (.93)	1.48 (.70)
Rate School on Teacher Interest in Students		
(1 = Good, excellent; 0 = Poor, fair)	.48 (.50)	.55 (.50)
Closest Sophomore Friend at School		
· Gets Good Grades		
(1 = True; 0 = False)	.79 (.41)	.86 (.35)
· Is Interested in School		
(1 = True; 0 = False)	.59 (.49)	.74 (.44)
· Attends Classes Regularly		
(1 = True; 0 = False)	.88 (.32)	.94 (.23)

Left After 1980	Left After 1982	Left After 1984	In 1986, but Not Throughout	In Throughout
.80 (.40)	.80 (.40)	.88 (.33)	.90 (.31)	.91 (.28)
1.13 (.39)	1.04 (.26)	1.29 (.57)	1.27 (.55)	1.23 (.51)
1.31 (.54)	1.18 (.49)	1.45 (.65)	1.53 (.68)	1.54 (.67)
.43 (.49)	.44 (.50)	.08 (.27)	.09 (.29)	.03 (.17)
.29 (.46)	.28 (.45)	.02 (.15)	.09 (.29)	.00 (.05)
.08 (.27)	.06 (.24)	.15 (.36)	.12 (.32)	.16 (.36)
.32 (.47)	.48 (.50)	.67 (.47)	.38 (.48)	.70 (.46)
29.99 (19.67)	23.98 (11.18)	29.00 (19.25)	28.16 (18.97)	28.16 (18.16)
13.95 (2.13)	15.13 (1.60)	14.26 (2.42)	13.97 (2.49)	14.46 (2.24)
8.27 (2.02)	8.33 (1.84)	8.58 (1.50)	8.71 (1.22)	8.55 (1.67)
.57 (.50)	.74 (.44)	.49 (.50)	.49 (.50)	.52 (.50)
5.19 (1.03)	5.74 (.85)	5.53 (.77)	5.46 (.94)	5.39 (.85)
.48 (.50)	.60 (.49)	.42 (.49)	.43 (.50)	.45 (.50)
1.49 (.58)	1.70 (.64)	1.48 (.67)	1.64 (.80)	1.76 (.74)
1.35 (.59)	1.39 (.53)	1.34 (.65)	1.47 (.69)	1.63 (.64)
.68 (.47)	.55 (.50)	.65 (.48)	.56 (.50)	.66 (.47)
.79 (.41)	.77 (.42)	.90 (.30)	.88 (.32)	.90 (.30)
.60 (.49)	.74 (.44)	.85 (.36)	.75 (.43)	.87 (.33)
.95 (.21)	.99 (.10)	.98 (.15)	.93 (.25)	.98 (.14)

(continued on next page)

TABLE 3-2   *(continued)*

	Out Throughout	*In and Out, Out 1986*
School Resources		
1980		
· Plans to Go to College		
(1 = True; 0 = False)	.49 (.50)	.75 (.43)
Friends' Feelings About Student with Good Grades		
(1 = Think well of; 0 = Other)	.29 (.45)	.42 (.49)
1982		
Program (1 = Academic; 0 = Other)	.12 (.32)	.44 (.50)
Rate School on Teacher Interest in Students		
(1 = Good, excellent; 0 = Poor, fair)	.53 (.50)	.62 (.49)
Closest Senior Friend at School		
· Gets Good Grades		
(1 = True; 0 = False)	.87 (.33)	.92 (.27)
· Is Interested in School		
(1 = True; 0 = False)	.63 (.48)	.78 (.42)
· Attends Classes Regularly		
(1 = True; 0 = False)	.89 (.31)	.94 (.23)
· Plans to Go to College		
(1 = True; 0 = False)	.51 (.50)	.81 (.39)
Individual Resources		
1980		
Self-Concept Scale	.20 (.76)	.03 (.73)
Locus of Control Scale	−.19 (.62)	.12 (.59)
Work Orientation Scale	−.14 (.72)	−.03 (.61)
Family Orientation Scale	−.03 (.63)	.05 (.59)
Sex-Role Attitudes		
· Working Mother Is a Good Mother		
(1 = Agree; 0 = Disagree)	.21 (.41)	.22 (.42)
· Man Should Achieve, Woman Keep House		
(1 = Disagree; 0 = Agree)	.13 (.34)	.19 (.40)
· Woman Is Happiest in Home		
(1 = Disagree; 0 = Agree)	.06 (.23)	.14 (.34)
Popular (1 = Very; 0 = Somewhat or not at all)	.74 (.44)	.78 (.41)
Amount of Dating		
(1 = Almost every day or every day; 0 = Other)	.08 (.27)	.05 (.22)
Age Expect to Get Married	22.30 (3.65)	23.06 (2.97)
Age Expect to Have First Child	23.95 (3.62)	25.00 (2.93)
Interested in School		
(1 = True; 0 = False)	.69 (.46)	.83 (.38)
High School Grades		
(1 = A's or A's & B's; 0 = B's or less)	.12 (.32)	.32 (.47)
Standardized Math Score	42.80 (7.23)	48.47 (8.32)

Left After 1980	Left After 1982	Left After 1984	In 1986, but Not Throughout	In Throughout
.45 (.50)	.68 (.47)	.89 (.31)	.76 (.43)	.87 (.34)
.33 (.47)	.45 (.50)	.49 (.50)	.40 (.49)	.57 (.50)
.19 (.39)	.37 (.48)	.85 (.35)	.44 (.50)	.82 (39)
.71 (.45)	.57 (.50)	.76 (.43)	.62 (.49)	.77 (.42)
.86 (.34)	.85 (.36)	.95 (.21)	.91 (.29)	.94 (.23)
.52 (.50)	.77 (.42)	.84 (.36)	.80 (.40)	.85 (.36)
.95 (.22)	.98 (.15)	.96 (.19)	.94 (.23)	.97 (.17)
.43 (.50)	.76 (.43)	.88 (.32)	.82 (.39)	.91 (.29)
−.02 (.71)	.16 (.75)	−.08 (.71)	.06 (.72)	−.04 (.67)
.15 (.56)	.25 (.67)	.46 (.48)	.08 (.61)	.43 (.48)
−.04 (.60)	−.31 (.75)	−.13 (.62)	−.02 (.64)	−.14 (.72)
.09 (.58)	.07 (.60)	.08 (.63)	.07 (.60)	.12 (.59)
.30 (.46)	.16 (.36)	.24 (.42)	.21 (.41)	.21 (.41)
.20 (.40)	.15 (.36)	.32 (.47)	.17 (.38)	.28 (.45)
.12 (.33)	.09 (.29)	.23 (.42)	.12 (.32)	.26 (.44)
.87 (.34)	.69 (.46)	.84 (.37)	.81 (.39)	.83 (.38)
.13 (.33)	.00 (.00)	.01 (.10)	.04 (.20)	.04 (.19)
21.62 (3.01)	22.35 (3.62)	23.70 (2.80)	22.85 (3.02)	23.61 (2.71)
23.87 (3.09)	24.89 (3.19)	25.71 (2.64)	24.77 (3.02)	25.74 (2.70)
.77 (.42)	.78 (.42)	.90 (.30)	.82 (.39)	.91 (.28)
.47 (.50)	.71 (.45)	.85 (.36)	.31 (.46)	.89 (.32)
56.94 (5.36)	58.80 (5.33)	60.68 (5.12)	48.57 (8.48)	60.61 (4.55)

(continued on next page)

TABLE 3-2 *(continued)*

	Out Throughout	In and Out, Out 1986
Individual Resources		
1980		
Standardized Science Score	43.79 (7.84)	48.83 (8.42)
Time on Homework per Week		
(1 = 3+ hours; 0 = Other)	.44 (.50)	.62 (.49)
Educational Expectations		
(1 = College degree or more; 0 = Other)	.13 (.34)	.51 (.50)
Educational Aspirations		
(1 = Disappointed if don't go to college; 0 = Other)	.46 (.50)	.75 (.43)
Occupational Expectations		
(1 = Professional job; 0 = Other)	.22 (.41)	.45 (.50)
1982		
Interested in School		
(1 = True; 0 = False)	.67 (.47)	.83 (.38)
High School Grades		
(1 = A's or A's & B's; 0 = B's or less)	.16 (.37)	.35 (.48)
Time on Homework per Week		
(1 = 5+ hours; 0 = Other)	.22 (.42)	.37 (.48)

[T] Item is from Teacher Survey.
[P] Item is from Principal Survey.

more likely than other women to have families who are high on the SES scale, to have a mother with a college education and a professional job, and to have a father with a college education and a professional job. As with many of the other resources, these differences are largest in science achievement. For example, only 9 percent of women who are out of the science achievement pipeline throughout the survey years have a mother with a professional occupation, whereas 54 percent of women who are in the science achievement pipeline throughout have a mother with a professional occupation. Even in the area of science attitudes, where differences in resources tend to be smallest, women who stay are twice as likely as those who stay out to have a mother with some college education and a father with some college education.

Interestingly, even though young women who pursue science are much more likely than other women to have well-educated mothers with professional jobs, they are *less* likely to have a mother who had worked

Left After 1980	Left After 1982	Left After 1984	In 1986, but Not Throughout	In Throughout
57.64 (6.02)	59.69 (5.23)	60.05 (5.39)	48.74 (8.55)	60.32 (5.31)
.60 (.49)	.58 (.49)	.84 (.37)	.63 (.48)	.80 (.40)
.27 (.44)	.25 (.44)	.86 (.35)	.43 (.50)	.83 (.38)
.45 (.50)	.57 (.49)	.88 (.33)	.73 (.45)	.89 (.31)
.38 (.49)	.41 (.49)	.69 (.46)	.42 (.49)	.58 (.49)
.64 (.48)	.79 (.41)	.89 (.31)	.82 (.38)	.92 (.27)
.59 (.49)	.63 (.48)	.82 (.39)	.36 (.48)	.90 (.29)
.37 (.48)	.20 (.40)	.59 (.49)	.39 (.49)	.68 (.47)

during their elementary school years. These differences in mother's work status are much smaller than many of the other differences in resources, but nevertheless the pattern suggests that it is not work per se (after all, the work motivations, environments, and satisfactions are diverse), but education and high-status jobs that function as resources for young women in science.

Tables 3-2 through 3-3 also make it clear that family structure is associated with young women's science experiences. In all three areas of science, young women who stay in the sciences are more likely than those who stay out to have a father living in the household and to have fewer siblings. The differences in family structure are largest in the area of science achievement. Eighty-seven percent of young women who maintain high science achievement have fathers in the household, while only 66 percent of those who never experience high science achievement have fathers in the household.

(Text continued on page 70)

TABLE 3-3 **Means (and Standard Deviations) for Family, School, and Individual Resources of Females in Science Access Trajectories (HSB Sophomore Cohort)**

	Out Throughout	*In and Out, Out 1986*
Demographic Characteristics		
1980		
Rural Residence		
(1 = Yes; 0 = No)	.32 (.47)	.32 (.47)
Race—African American		
(1 = African American; 0 = Other)	.10 (.29)	.14 (.35)
Race—Hispanic		
(1 = Hispanic; 0 = Other)	.11 (.32)	.10 (.30)
Family Resources		
1980		
SES Quartile	2.28 (1.05)	2.84 (1.10)
Number of Siblings	3.91 (1.72)	3.67 (1.70)
Father Lives in Household		
(1 = True; 0 = False)	.75 (.43)	.76 (.43)
Mother Worked When Respondent Was in Elementary School		
(1 = True; 0 = False)	.61 (.49)	.60 (.49)
Mother's Occupation		
(1 = Technical, managerial, professional; 0 = Other)	.17 (.37)	.25 (.43)
Mother's Education		
(1 = At least some college; 0 = Other)	.19 (.39)	.37 (.48)
Father's Occupation		
(1 = Technical, managerial, professional; 0 = Other)	.25 (.43)	.38 (.39)
Father's Education		
(1 = At least some college; 0 = Other)	.27 (.45)	.48 (.50)
Mother Monitors Schoolwork		
(1 = Yes; 0 = No)	.88 (.33)	.93 (.26)
Father Monitors Schoolwork		
(1 = Yes; 0 = No)	.74 (.44)	.80 (.40)
Mother's Educational Expectations		
(1 = College education or more; 0 = Other)	.45 (.50)	.75 (.43)
Pocket Calculator in Home		
(1 = True; 0 = False)	.78 (.42)	.83 (.38)
1982		
Mother Keeps Track of Progress in School		
(1 = True; 0 = False)	.85 (.35)	.90 (.30)
Father Keeps Track of Progress in School		
(1 = True; 0 = False)	.71 (.45)	.81 (.39)

Left After 1980	Left After 1982	Left After 1984	In 1986, but Not Throughout	In Throughout
.32 (.47)	.32 (.47)	.24 (.43)	.31 (.46)	.22 (.42)
.16 (.36)	.08 (.27)	.05 (.21)	.16 (.37)	.08 (.27)
.12 (.33)	.05 (.22)	.04 (.19)	.08 (.27)	.04 (.21)
2.41 (1.10)	2.96 (1.02)	3.31 (.94)	2.63 (1.10)	3.09 (1.01)
3.98 (1.76)	3.55 (1.65)	3.48 (1.38)	3.59 (1.80)	3.35 (1.56)
.79 (.41)	.78 (.42)	.87 (.34)	.73 (.44)	.88 (.33)
.58 (.49)	.62 (.48)	.63 (.48)	.64 (.48)	.54 (.50)
.16 (.37)	.29 (.45)	.33 (.47)	.21 (.41)	.28 (.45)
.24 (.43)	.48 (.50)	.53 (.50)	.34 (.47)	.44 (.50)
.29 (.46)	.44 (.50)	.52 (.50)	.37 (.48)	.48 (.50)
.29 (.45)	.51 (.50)	.64 (.48)	.36 (.48)	.52 (.50)
.90 (.30)	.92 (.28)	.95 (.22)	.90 (.30)	.96 (.19)
.79 (.41)	.84 (.37)	.90 (.30)	.76 (.42)	.88 (.32)
.56 (.50)	.91 (.29)	.90 (.31)	.76 (.42)	.95 (.22)
.74 (.44)	.86 (.34)	.92 (.27)	.83 (.38)	.93 (.26)
.89 (.31)	.92 (.27)	.92 (.27)	.90 (.30)	.95 (.21)
.68 (.47)	.78 (.41)	.86 (.34)	.79 (.41)	.87 (.33)

(continued on next page)

TABLE 3-3 *(continued)*

	Out Throughout	*In and Out, Out 1986*
Family Resources *(continued)*		
1982 *(continued)*		
Parents Know Where Student Is, What Student Does		
(1 = True; 0 = False)	.85 (.35)	.86 (.35)
How Often Parents Attend PTA Meetings		
(1 = Never; 2 = Once in a while; 3 = Often)	1.20 (.47)	1.34 (.60)
How Often Parents Attend Parent-Teacher Conferences		
(1 = Never; 2 = Once in a while; 3 = Often)	1.44 (.62)	1.51 (.69)
1984		
Ever Married		
(1 = Yes; 0 = No)	.23 (.42)	.08 (.27)
Had Child		
(1 = Yes; 0 = No)	.13 (.34)	.06 (.24)
School Resources		
1980		
School Type		
(1 = Private; 0 = Public)	.07 (.25)	.16 (.37)
Program		
(1 = Academic; 0 = Other)	.25 (.43)	.50 (.50)
Percent of Teachers Considered Excellent[P]	25.95 (.15.91)	31.08 (20.17)
Teacher Influence on Curriculum, Content, and Teaching Techniques[T]		
(Scale from low to high: 3 to 18)	13.79 (2.51)	14.16 (2.38)
Percent of Class Time Teachers Spend on Instruction[T]		
(1 = 0–2% to 9 = over 30%)	8.63 (1.40)	8.74 (1.10)
Percent Female Teachers in Sample[T]	.45 (.50)	.47 (.50)
Teachers' Education[T]		
(1 = HS; 8 = Doctorate)	5.46 (.93)	5.56 (.87)
Female Math/Science Teacher in Sample[T]		
(1 = Yes; 0 = No)	.36 (.48)	.39 (.49)
Number of Years of Math Required for Graduation[P]	1.54 (.67)	1.64 (.76)
Number of Years of Science Required for Graduation[P]	1.36 (.61)	1.52 (.70)
Rate School on Teacher Interest in Students		
(1 = Good, excellent; 0 = Poor, fair)	.51 (.50)	.58 (.49)
Closest Sophomore Friend at School		
· Gets Good Grades		
(1 = True; 0 = False)	.82 (.38)	.88 (.33)
· Is Interested in School		
(1 = True; 0 = False)	.68 (.47)	.79 (.41)
· Attends Classes Regularly		
(1 = True; 0 = False)	.92 (.27)	.96 (.20)

Left After 1980	Left After 1982	Left After 1984	In 1986, but Not Throughout	In Throughout
.81 (.39)	.89 (.31)	.94 (.25)	.86 (.34)	.97 (.16)
1.22 (.46)	1.29 (.59)	1.34 (.56)	1.26 (.49)	1.34 (.64)
1.37 (.59)	1.54 (.64)	1.51 (.60)	1.43 (.65)	1.51 (.65)
.19 (.40)	.05 (.22)	.01 (.12)	.12 (.32)	.03 (.18)
.16 (.36)	.03 (.18)	.01 (.09)	.09 (.29)	.04 (.19)
.08 (.26)	.22 (.42)	.18 (.39)	.11 (.32)	.21 (.47)
.41 (.49)	.63 (.48)	.82 (.38)	.40 (.49)	.79 (.41)
25.37 (19.10)	32.26 (21.33)	32.40 (18.76)	27.21 (17.21)	29.66 (22.77)
14.19 (2.43)	14.89 (2.36)	14.24 (2.45)	13.72 (2.64)	14.13 (2.46)
8.57 (1.47)	8.02 (2.19)	8.39 (1.79)	8.57 (1.47)	8.35 (1.90)
.57 (.50)	.36 (.48)	.56 (.50)	.44 (.50)	.40 (.49)
5.49 (.99)	5.64 (.67)	5.39 (.82)	5.48 (.90)	5.57 (.68)
.48 (.50)	.29 (.45)	.46 (.50)	.38 (.48)	.37 (.48)
1.57 (.56)	1.63 (.79)	1.64 (.65)	1.66 (.76)	1.73 (.76)
1.43 (.78)	1.48 (.75)	1.41 (.61)	1.46 (.88)	1.49 (.57)
.53 (.50)	.64 (.48)	.74 (.44)	.57 (.50)	.71 (.45)
.84 (.36)	.90 (.30)	.93 (.26)	.87 (.34)	.89 (.31)
.72 (.45)	.78 (.41)	.86 (.35)	.72 (.45)	.88 (.32)
.95 (.22)	.94 (.24)	.98 (.13)	.94 (.24)	.98 (.13)

(continued on next page)

TABLE 3-3 *(continued)*

	Out Throughout	*In and Out, Out 1986*
School Resources		
1980		
· Plans to Go to College		
(1 = True; 0 = False)	.62 (.49)	.82 (.39)
Friends' Feelings About Student with Good Grades		
(1 = Think well of; 0 = Other)	.36 (.48)	.45 (.50)
1982		
Program (1 = Academic; 0 = Other)	.21 (.40)	.60 (.49)
Rate School on Teacher Interest in Students		
(1 = Good, excellent; 0 = Poor, fair)	.57 (.49)	.64 (.48)
Closest Senior Friend at School		
· Gets Good Grades		
(1 = True; 0 = Fales)	.89 (.31)	.91 (.28)
· Is Interested in School		
(1 = True; 0 = False)	.68 (.47)	.82 (.39)
· Attends Classes Regularly		
(1 = True; 0 = False)	.92 (.26)	.95 (.22)
· Plans to Go to College		
(1 = True; 0 = False)	.65 (.48)	.83 (.37)
Individual Resources		
1980		
Self-Concept Scale	.13 (.71)	−.01 (.68)
Locus of Control Scale	.01 (.61)	.19 (.55)
Work Orientation Scale	−.11 (.66)	−.04 (.60)
Family Orientation Scale	.04 (.62)	.07 (.60)
Sex-Role Attitudes		
· Working Mother Is a Good Mother		
(1 = Agree; 0 = Disagree)	.20 (.40)	.19 (.39)
· Man Should Achieve, Woman Keep House		
(1 = Disagree; 0 = Agree)	.14 (.34)	.22 (.41)
· Woman Is Happiest in Home		
(1 = Disagree; 0 = Agree)	.08 (.27)	.15 (.36)
Popular (1 = Very; 0 = Somewhat or not at all)	.77 (.42)	.82 (.39)
Amount of Dating		
(1 = Almost every day or every day; 0 = Other)	.06 (.24)	.03 (.18)
Age Expect to Get Married	22.33 (3.28)	23.37 (2.97)
Age Expect to Have First Child	24.23 (3.31)	25.17 (2.99)
Interested in School		
(1 = True; 0 = False)	.77 (.42)	.85 (.36)

Left After 1980	Left After 1982	Left After 1984	In 1986, but Not Throughout	In Throughout
.73 (.44)	.87 (.33)	.86 (.35)	.75 (.43)	.90 (.30)
.35 (.48)	.46 (.50)	.51 (.50)	.40 (.49)	.56 (.50)
.35 (.48)	.78 (.42)	.87 (.33)	.52 (.50)	.93 (.25)
.52 (.50)	.78 (.42)	.75 (.43)	.64 (.48)	.76 (.43)
.88 (.32)	.94 (.24)	.98 (.14)	.89 (.31)	.94 (.24)
.74 (.44)	.83 (.37)	.87 (.34)	.77 (.42)	.89 (.31)
.89 (.31)	.99 (.12)	.97 (.16)	.95 (.23)	.98 (.14)
.74 (.44)	.91 (.29)	.93 (.26)	.80 (.40)	.89 (.32)
.04 (.70)	− .17 (.70)	.10 (.70)	.02 (.69)	− .20 (.77)
.10 (.60)	.26 (.56)	.40 (.49)	.17 (.60)	.51 (.51)
− .02 (.57)	− .14 (.65)	.02 (.53)	− .03 (.57)	− .11 (.65)
.02 (.58)	.04 (.56)	.08 (.57)	.01 (.59)	.12 (.69)
.17 (.38)	.23 (.42)	.27 (.45)	.25 (.43)	.30 (.46)
.15 (.35)	.28 (.45)	.28 (.45)	.22 (.41)	.32 (.47)
.12 (.33)	.26 (.44)	.19 (.39)	.14 (.34)	.20 (.40)
.80 (.40)	.82 (.39)	.78 (.42)	.74 (.44)	.79 (.40)
.04 (.20)	.01 (.11)	.03 (.16)	.04 (.20)	.01 (.09)
23.21 (3.07)	23.79 (2.58)	23.87 (2.30)	23.09 (3.06)	24.65 (3.05)
25.12 (3.03)	25.54 (2.50)	26.08 (2.32)	25.00 (3.03)	26.30 (2.74)
.85 (.36)	.88 (.32)	.94 (.24)	.83 (.38)	.92 (.27)

(continued on next page)

TABLE 3-3 *(continued)*

	Out Throughout	In and Out, Out 1986
Individual Resources		
1980		
High School Grades		
(1 = A's or A's & B's; 0 = B's or less)	.24 (.43)	.50 (.50)
Standardized Math Score	47.12 (8.72)	51.64 (9.11)
Standardized Science Score	47.63 (8.94)	51.88 (8.71)
Time on Homework per Week		
(1 = 3+ hours; 0 = Other)	.54 (.50)	.68 (.47)
Educational Expectations		
(1 = College degree or more; 0 = Other)	.23 (.42)	.64 (.48)
Educational Aspirations		
(1 = Disappointed if don't go to college; 0 = Other)	.56 (.50)	.83 (.38)
Occupational Expectations		
(1 = Professional job; 0 = Other)	.28 (.45)	.50 (.50)
1982		
Interested in School		
(1 = True; 0 = False)	.73 (.45)	.84 (.37)
High School Grades		
(1 = A's or A's & B's; 0 = B's or less)	.26 (.44)	.51 (.50)
Time on Homework per Week		
(1 = 5+ hours; 0 = Other)	.25 (.43)	.47 (.50)

[T] Item is from Teacher Survey.

[P] Item is from Principal Survey.

Differences in family involvement and support are also strongly associated with science experiences. Women who stay involved in each area of science are more likely than those who stay out to have mothers and fathers who monitor their homework and social activities, keep track of their progress in school, attend PTA meetings and parent-teacher conferences, and have high educational expectations for their children. It is not just mothers who make a difference here. Women who pursue science clearly have fathers who are more involved as well. Even though the young women report less involvement on the part of their fathers than their mothers, the level of the father's involvement is highly related to the level of the young woman's science involvement. For example, seventy-eight percent of the young women who stay out of the science

Left After 1980	Left After 1982	Left After 1984	In 1986, but Not Throughout	In Throughout
.29 (.45)	.64 (.48)	.75 (.44)	.47 (.50)	.86 (.34)
47.92 (8.85)	57.19 (7.38)	59.30 (6.00)	51.87 (8.92)	59.80 (6.34)
48.88 (9.46)	55.54 (8.61)	56.96 (7.39)	51.67 (8.53)	58.80 (7.42)
.61 (.49)	.82 (.39)	.88 (.33)	.67 (.47)	.87 (.33)
.46 (.50)	.82 (.38)	.93 (.25)	.55 (.50)	.97 (.17)
.73 (.44)	.92 (.28)	.96 (.19)	.80 (.40)	.97 (.17)
.54 (.50)	.59 (.49)	.71 (.45)	.54 (.50)	.79 (.41)
.77 (.42)	.91 (.28)	.94 (.24)	.89 (.31)	.95 (.23)
.28 (.45)	.64 (.48)	.74 (.44)	.52 (.50)	.84 (.37)
.32 (.47)	.60 (.49)	.70 (.46)	.45 (.50)	.79 (.40)

attitude pipeline report that their fathers monitor their homework. This figure is 95 percent for those who stay in the science attitude pipeline.

Homes in which young women are most likely to succeed in science are much more likely than other homes to have a pocket calculator. Calculators are especially important for science achievement. Young women who stay in the science achievement pipeline are 26 percent more likely than those who stay out to have a pocket calculator in the home.

Some of the most striking differences between women who maintain excellence in science and other women involve experiences in the family of procreation. Women who pursue science are very unlikely to have married or had a child by 1984 (four years out of high school). As

(Text continued on page 78)

TABLE 3-4 Means (and Standard Deviations) for Family, School, and Individual Resources of Females in Science Attitude Trajectories (HSB Sophomore Cohort)

	Out Throughout	*In and Out, Out 1984*
Demographic Characteristics		
1980		
Rural Residence		
(1 = Yes; 0 = No)	.46 (.50)	.45 (.50)
Race—African American		
(1 = African American; 0 = Other)	.08 (.27)	.24 (.43)
Race—Hispanic		
(1 = Hispanic; 0 = Other)	.11 (.31)	.08 (.27)
Family Resources		
1980		
SES Quartile	2.48 (1.04)	2.29 (1.03)
Number of Siblings	3.80 (1.69)	4.17 (1.78)
Father Lives in Household		
(1 = True; 0 = False)	.78 (.42)	.70 (.46)
Mother Worked When Respondent Was in Elementary School		
(1 = True; 0 = False)	.63 (.48)	.59 (.46)
Mother's Occupation		
(1 = Technical, managerial, professional; 0 = Other)	.21 (.41)	.24 (.43)
Mother's Education		
(1 = At least some college; 0 = Other)	.23 (.42)	.16 (.36)
Father's Occupation		
(1 = Technical, managerial, professional; 0 = Other)	.28 (.45)	.20 (.40)
Father's Education		
(1 = At least some college; 0 = Other)	.30 (.46)	.35 (.48)
Mother Monitors Schoolwork		
(1 = Yes; 0 = No)	.90 (.30)	.91 (.28)
Father Monitors Schoolwork		
(1 = Yes; 0 = No)	.78 (.41)	.80 (.40)
Mother's Educational Expectations		
(1 = College education or more; 0 = Other)	.57 (.50)	.73 (.44)
Pocket Calculator in Home		
(1 = True; 0 = False)	.81 (.39)	.67 (.47)
1982		
Mother Keeps Track of Progress in School		
(1 = True; 0 = False)	.88 (.33)	.93 (.25)
Father Keeps Track of Progress in School		
(1 = True; 0 = False)	.75 (.43)	.83 (.38)

Left After 1980	Left After 1982	In 1984, but Not Throughout	In Throughout
.30 (.46)	.34 (.47)	.24 (.43)	.28 (.45)
.10 (.31)	.10 (.30)	.12 (.33)	.10 (.29)
.09 (.28)	.03 (.16)	.08 (.27)	.06 (.24)
2.75 (1.03)	3.03 (1.06)	2.94 (1.04)	3.26 (.98)
3.74 (1.77)	3.63 (1.63)	3.59 (1.65)	3.42 (1.44)
2.75 (1.03)	.87 (.33)	.76 (.42)	.86 (.34)
.65 (.48)	.64 (.48)	.61 (.49)	.59 (.49)
.31 (.46)	.36 (.48)	.34 (.47)	.33 (.47)
.35 (.48)	.42 (.49)	.41 (.49)	.58 (.49)
.38 (.49)	.48 (.50)	.51 (.50)	.57 (.50)
.36 (.48)	.47 (.50)	.43 (.49)	.61 (.49)
.93 (.25)	.99 (.08)	.93 (.25)	.96 (.20)
.82 (.38)	.92 (.27)	.84 (.37)	.95 (.23)
.82 (.38)	.91 (.29)	.81 (.39)	.99 (.09)
.88 (.32)	.91 (.29)	.85 (.36)	.93 (.26)
.89 (.32)	.98 (.14)	.90 (.30)	.91 (.28)
.78 (.42)	.83 (.37)	.79 (.41)	.83 (.37)

(continued on next page)

TABLE 3-4 *(continued)*

	Out Throughout	*In and Out, Out 1984*
Family Resources *(continued)*		
1982 *(continued)*		
Parents Know Where Student Is, What Student Does		
(1 = True; 0 = False)	.88 (.33)	.89 (.31)
How Often Parents Attend PTA Meetings		
(1 = Never; 2 = Once in a while; 3 = Often)	1.24 (.53)	1.28 (.55)
How Often Parents Attend Parent-Teacher Conferences		
(1 = Never; 2 = Once in a while; 3 = Often)	1.49 (.66)	1.55 (.66)
1984		
Ever Married		
(1 = Yes; 0 = No)	.18 (.38)	.20 (.40)
Had Child		
(1 = Yes; 0 = No)	.09 (.28)	.10 (.30)
School Resources		
1980		
School Type		
(1 = Private; 0 = Public)	.09 (.29)	.11 (.31)
Program		
(1 = Academic; 0 = Other)	.32 (.47)	.44 (.50)
Percent of Teachers Considered Excellent[P]	27.37 (17.76)	30.14 (17.55)
Teacher Influence on Curriculum, Content, and Teaching Techniques[T]		
(Scale from low to high: 3 to 18)	13.82 (2.48)	14.54 (2.00)
Percent of Class Time Teachers Spend on Instruction[T]		
(1 = 0–2% to 9 = over 30%)	8.52 (1.64)	8.95 (.61)
Percent Female Teachers in Sample[T]	.48 (.50)	.41 (.49)
Teachers' Education[T]		
(1 = HS; 8 = Doctorate)	5.45 (.92)	4.98 (.93)
Female Math/Science Teacher in Sample[T]		
(1 = Yes; 0 = No)	.39 (.49)	.37 (.48)
Number of Years of Math Required for Graduation[P]	1.44 (.67)	1.51 (.67)
Number of Years of Science Required for Graduation[P]	1.58 (.75)	1.63 (.74)
Rate School on Teacher Interest in Students		
(1 = Good, excellent; 0 = Poor, fair)	.55 (.50)	.60 (.49)
Closest Sophomore Friend at School		
· Gets Good Grades		
(1 = True; 0 = False)	.85 (.35)	.86 (.35)
· Is Interested in School		
(1 = True; 0 = False)	.74 (.44)	.78 (.41)
· Attends Classes Regularly		
(1 = True; 0 = False)	.95 (.23)	.92 (.28)

Left After 1980	Left After 1982	In 1984, but Not Throughout	In Throughout
.85 (.35)	.96 (.20)	.88 (.32)	.94 (.25)
1.25 (.49)	1.18 (.43)	1.30 (.56)	1.41 (.62)
1.48 (.66)	1.49 (.66)	1.47 (.64)	1.52 (.61)
.16 (.37)	.10 (.30)	.08 (.27)	.02 (.15)
.07 (.26)	.03 (.17)	.05 (.23)	.01 (.07)
.13 (.34)	.20 (.40)	.15 (.36)	.23 (.42)
.53 (.50)	.51 (.50)	.53 (.50)	.77 (.42)
26.44 (15.92)	29.25 (16.57)	29.64 (18.19)	28.25 (16.12)
14.06 (2.60)	14.42 (1.74)	13.96 (2.54)	15.31 (1.95)
8.59 (1.53)	9.00 (.00)	8.58 (1.52)	8.85 (.80)
.47 (.50)	.37 (.48)	.49 (.50)	.49 (.50)
5.44 (.98)	5.93 (.60)	5.52 (.84)	5.63 (.64)
.39 (.49)	.37 (.48)	.40 (.49)	.37 (.48)
1.50 (.63)	1.22 (.46)	1.42 (.64)	1.41 (.74)
1.55 (.68)	1.37 (.66)	1.64 (.73)	1.69 (.82)
.66 (.47)	.55 (.50)	.60 (.49)	.64 (.48)
.88 (.32)	.93 (.25)	.88 (.32)	.94 (.24)
.82 (.39)	.72 (.45)	.79 (.41)	.81 (.39)
.94 (.23)	.89 (.31)	.95 (.23)	.99 (.10)

(continued on next page)

TABLE 3-4   *(continued)*

	Out Throughout	In and Out, Out 1984
School Resources		
1980		
· Plans to Go to College		
(1 = True; 0 = False)	.72 (.45)	.71 (.46)
Friends' Feelings About Student with Good Grades		
(1 = Think well of; 0 = Other)	.39 (.49)	.28 (.45)
1982		
Program (1 = Academic; 0 = Other)	.32 (.47)	.42 (.49)
Rate School on Teacher Interest in Students		
(1 = Good, excellent; 0 = Poor, fair)	.63 (.48)	.55 (.50)
Closest Senior Friend at School		
· Gets Good Grades		
(1 = True; 0 = False)	.91 (.29)	.98 (.14)
· Is Interested in School		
(1 = True; 0 = False)	.75 (.43)	.80 (.40)
· Attends Classes Regularly		
(1 = True; 0 = False)	.93 (.25)	.99 (.12)
· Plans to Go to College		
(1 = True; 0 = False)	.76 (.43)	.66 (.47)
Individual Resources		
1980		
Self-Concept Scale	.10 (.71)	−.06 (.74)
Locus of Control Scale	.09 (.56)	−.06 (.62)
Work Orientation Scale	−.08 (.63)	.08 (.51)
Family Orientation Scale	.06 (.62)	−.22 (.80)
Sex-Role Attitudes		
· Working Mother Is a Good Mother		
(1 = Agree; 0 = Disagree)	.19 (.39)	.40 (.49)
· Man Should Achieve, Woman Keep House		
(1 = Disagree; 0 = Agree)	.17 (.38)	.29 (.45)
· Woman Is Happiest in Home		
(1 = Disagree; 0 = Agree)	.11 (.31)	.10 (.30)
Popular (1 = Very; 0 = Somewhat or not at all)	.80 (.40)	.80 (.40)
Amount of Dating		
(1 = Almost every day or every day; 0 = Other)	.05 (.22)	.03 (.18)
Age Expect to Get Married	22.60 (2.99)	22.93 (3.74)
Age Expect to Have First Child	24.54 (2.98)	24.97 (3.30)
Interested in School		
(1 = True; 0 = False)	.82 (.38)	.84 (.37)

Left After 1980	Left After 1982	In 1984, but Not Throughout	In Throughout
.83 (.37)	.65 (.48)	.81 (.39)	.99 (.31)
.48 (.50)	.43 (.50)	.48 (.50)	.44 (.50)
.55 (.50)	.78 (.41)	.63 (.48)	.90 (.30)
.68 (.47)	.81 (.40)	.69 (.46)	.72 (.45)
.94 (.23)	.92 (.27)	.93 (.25)	.88 (.32)
.78 (.42)	.85 (.35)	.82 (.38)	.83 (.38)
.96 (.19)	.94 (.23)	.95 (.22)	.98 (.13)
.78 (.41)	.81 (.39)	.88 (.33)	.88 (.33)
−.12 (.63)	−.06 (.73)	−.03 (.73)	−.08 (.71)
.28 (.55)	.28 (.46)	.26 (.61)	.52 (.44)
−.06 (.58)	−.14 (.68)	−.02 (.61)	−.19 (.71)
.08 (.57)	.01 (.77)	.04 (.60)	.06 (.57)
.25 (.43)	.25 (.43)	.21 (.41)	.28 (.45)
.26 (.44)	.25 (.43)	.25 (.43)	.34 (.47)
.19 (.39)	.28 (.45)	.19 (.40)	.20 (.47)
.84 (.36)	.78 (.41)	.80 (.40)	.73 (.44)
.04 (.20)	.04 (.20)	.03 (.17)	.00 (.06)
23.56 (2.77)	23.64 (2.58)	23.68 (2.97)	24.82 (2.68)
25.53 (2.64)	26.00 (2.57)	25.53 (2.90)	26.50 (2.53)
.89 (.31)	.89 (.32)	.86 (.34)	.95 (.21)

(continued on next page)

TABLE 3-4 *(continued)*

	Out Throughout	*In and Out, Out 1984*
Individual Resources		
1980		
High School Grades		
(1 = A's or A's & B's; 0 = B's or less)	.30 (.46)	.44 (.50)
Standardized Math Score	48.78 (8.65)	50.27 (10.53)
Standardized Science Score	49.36 (8.60)	51.52 (8.03)
Time on Homework per Week		
(1 = 3+ Hours; 0 = Other)	.59 (.49)	.54 (.50)
Educational Expectations		
(1 = College degree or more; 0 = Other)	.35 (.48)	.45 (.50)
Educational Aspirations		
(1 = Disappointed if don't go to college; 0 = Other)	.65 (.48)	.67 (.47)
Occupational Expectations		
(1 = Professional job; 0 = Other)	.29 (.46)	.46 (.50)
1982		
Interested in School		
(1 = True; 0 = False)	.80 (.40)	.82 (.39)
High School Grades		
(1 = A's or A's & B's; 0 = B's or less)	.36 (.48)	.40 (.49)
Time on Homework per Week		
(1 = 5+ hours; 0 = Other)	.35 (.48)	.34 (.47)

[T] Item is from Teacher Survey.
[P] Item is from Principal Survey.

with most of the other contrasts, these differences are most extreme in the area of achievement. Here, those who stayed "in throughout" are 10 times more likely than those who stay "out throughout" to have married or had a child. Only 3 percent of the young women who stay in the science achievement pipeline throughout the survey period have married by 1984, and none has had a child. In contrast, 37 percent of those who stay out of the science achievement pipeline throughout have married, and 33 percent have had a child.

SCHOOL RESOURCES. Tables 3-2 through 3-4 also reveal marked differences in the school resources of women with varying science experiences. As with family resources, school resources are associated with positive science experiences. Consider, for example, the types of schools

Left After 1980	Left After 1982	In 1984, but Not Throughout	In Throughout
.45 (.50)	.75 (.43)	.51 (.50)	.70 (.46)
52.52 (9.21)	58.03 (7.49)	52.73 (9.25)	58.46 (7.55)
51.93 (8.95)	56.18 (8.01)	53.00 (8.88)	57.09 (8.95)
.76 (.43)	.75 (.44)	.72 (.45)	.91 (.28)
.78 (.41)	.91 (.29)	.68 (.47)	.96 (.20)
.88 (.33)	.94 (.23)	.86 (.35)	.96 (.20)
.74 (.44)	.81 (.39)	.60 (.49)	.92 (.27)
.82 (.39)	.94 (.25)	.89 (.31)	.93 (.25)
.44 (.50)	.40 (.49)	.54 (.50)	.74 (.44)
.47 (.50)	.62 (.49)	.51 (.50)	.75 (.43)

and programs that the young women attend. The percent of women in private schools is three times higher among those who are continuously in the science achievement and access pipelines than among those who are continuously out of them. The figure is two times higher in the area of attitudes. Likewise, those who maintain positive science experiences in each area are much more likely to be in academic (as opposed to general or vocational) programs. For example, in their sophomore year, 70 percent of young women who stay in the science achievement pipeline are in academic programs, while only 14 percent of those who stay out of the science achievement pipeline are in these programs. By their senior year of high school, this association becomes even stronger. Now 82 percent of those who stay in are in academic programs as compared to 12 percent of those who never enter. In their senior year, young women who stay in the area of achievement are 85 percent more likely to be in an academic program than in other programs. These contrasts are 77 percent in the area of science access and 64 percent in the area of science attitudes.

Teachers are another school resource that potentially affects young women's science experiences. Unfortunately, the High School and Beyond survey does not include information on math and science teachers per se. Most of the general teacher characteristics included in the Principal and Teacher Surveys show little relation to science experiences. Percent of teachers considered excellent and teacher influence on curriculum, content, and teaching techniques reveal only a modest association with type of science experience. Although the "in throughout" group is slightly higher on these resources than the "out throughout" group, the relationship is not linear. Sometimes women having other types of science experiences report even more teacher resources. Other teacher characteristics, including percent of time spent on instruction, percent of female teachers in the sample, teachers' education, and presence of a female math/science teacher in the sample, bear no clear relation to the young women's science experiences. (Note that having a female math/science teacher in the sample does not mean that the *respondent* had a female math/science teacher. It only means that the sample taken from the respondent's school included a female.)

Two school characteristics—number of years of science required for graduation and number of years of math required for graduation—show only a modest association with some of young women's science experiences. Especially in the areas of science achievement and access, women who stay involved in science are slightly more likely to be in schools with higher math and science requirements.

Two school resources that *are* important for science experiences, according to Tables 3-2 through 3-4, are teacher interest in students and school peer groups. Regardless of the area of science, women who stay in the sciences are much more likely to rate their schools high on teacher interest in students. For example, among the women who stay in the area of science achievement throughout the survey years, 66 percent rate their school high on teacher interest in students in their sophomore year of high school. Only 48 percent of the women who stay out of the science achievement pipeline give this high rating. These trends continue in the senior year of high school.

In both their sophomore and senior years of high school, young women who maintain high achievement, access, and attitudes about science have very different school friends than those who do not. Their friends are more likely to get good grades, be interested in school, attend classes regularly, plan to go to college, and think well of students with good grades than are the friends of other students. Some of the biggest differences occur in the achievement pipeline. In their sophomore year, almost twice as many young women who stay in the science achievement pipeline compared to those who stay out have friends who think well of students with good grades. Differences in friends' college plans are also extreme. For example, virtually all of the young women whose attitudes about science remain high say their closest sophomore friend plans to go to college (99%), while only 72 percent of the young women who stay disinterested in science report this about their closest friend.

INDIVIDUAL RESOURCES.   Do young women who stay in the sciences have different individual characteristics than those who do not? Tables 3-2 through 3-4 suggest that they often do. Consider personality characteristics involving self-concept, locus of control, work orientation, and family orientation. Women who remain in science, regardless of the area, have a lower self-concept than those who stay out of science. In fact, women who stay out of science have a higher self-concept than any other group of women. Perhaps women in science have internalized the negative attitudes that many young people hold toward science. However, when control over one's fate is considered (locus of control), women who stay in science are much more likely than those who stay out (as well as most women with other patterns of science experience) to think that it is their own actions and efforts, rather than fate or luck, that make a difference in what happens. Thus the ability to master what is thought to be one of the most difficult areas of the curriculum is associated with a higher degree of confidence in one's abilities.

Findings on the work and family orientation of young women with different science experiences provide unexpected results. There are no differences in the work orientation of young women who stay in or out of the science achievement and access pipelines. The highest work orientation can be found among women who do not consistently stay in or out of the sciences. In the area of attitudes, young women who stay interested in science have a lower work orientation than any other group of women. Again, the highest work orientation is not found in either the "in throughout" or "out throughout" groups. Thus women who stay involved in science apparently differ little from those who do not on general measures of orientation toward work that include questions about committment to one's work and career as well as to the idea of work in general.

Just as the young women who stay in the sciences are unexpectedly low on work orientation, they are unexpectedly high on family orientation. In the areas of achievement and access, they have a higher family orientation than any other group of women. In the area of attitudes, women who are consistently interested and consistently uninterested in science share a similarly high score on family orientation. Thus at this stage in young women's science careers (these items were measured when the respondents were sophomores), they do not seem to be putting a greater priority on work than family. It may be that later realities of post-secondary education and employment will change these attitudes or cause those who do not change them to drop out of science.

Given this relatively low work orientation and high family orienta-tion, can we expect to find conservative sex-role attitudes among women in science? No. When asked about women's role in the home and work setting, the young women who stay in the sciences are, with one ex-ception, more liberal in their attitudes than those who stay out. Some of the biggest differences in sex-role attitudes are found in responses to a question about women being happiest in the home. Young women who stay in the science achievement pipeline are over four times as likely as those who stay out to disagree with this statement. Regardless of area of science, young women who persevere in science are at least twice as likely as women who never engage in science to disagree with the state-ment "Man should achieve, woman keep house." There is less variation on responses to the statement that a working mother is a good mother. In fact, in the area of science achievement, young women who stay in science are no more likely than those who stay out to agree with this statement. However, in the areas of access and attitudes, young women who stay in science show higher support for this statement than almost any other group of women.

When it comes to dating and popularity, it appears that young women scientists date much less than do other women, but do not nec-essarily view themselves as being unpopular. The biggest differences in dating occur in the area of science access and attitudes. Here, women who remain out of the pipeline are at least five times more likely than those who remain in to say that they date almost every day or every day (6% versus 1% and 5% versus 0%, respectively). Interestingly, this differ-ence in dating behavior does not translate into lower popularity except in the area of science attitudes. In fact, young women who maintain high achievement and access tend to be among the most likely to rate them-selves as being popular. This is not the case among women who have consistently high science attitudes, however. In fact, these women are the least likely to rate themselves as popular. These results suggest an in-teresting distinction between science attitudes and behaviors (achieve-ment and access). Taking science courses and doing well in science can actually translate into feelings of popularity, while holding positive atti-tudes about science does not. Despite the popular image of scientists as

·"nerds," girls can apparently successfully compete in this field and still be popular. However, if one begins to *think* like a "nerd," this may not be the case.

Although young women who are involved in science do not necessarily have a lower orientation to family than do other women, they do have very different expectations for when they will marry and have their first child. In each area of science, women who stay involved expect to marry and have their first child at a later age than almost every other group of women. Those who stay out of the sciences often report the lowest expected ages. In most cases, women who continue to participate in the sciences expect to experience these family events approximately two years later than those who stay out.

As expected, the grades and standardized test scores of women who stay in each of the three areas of science are considerably higher than the scores of those who stay out and are among the highest of any group of women. Young women who stay in science are at least twice as likely as those who stay out to be getting A's or A's and B's. For example, only 24 percent of women who never enter the science access pipeline report these high grades, while 86 percent of those who never leave report them.

Do young women scientists spend more time on their homework than other women? Evidently, they spend *much* more. Regardless of the area of science, Tables 3-2 through 3-4 show increasing time spent on homework with increased time in the sciences. Consider the science attitude pipeline. Ninety-one percent of the young women who stay in this pipeline report that they spend three or more hours a week on homework, whereas only 59 percent of young women who stay out of this pipeline report doing this amount of homework.

Do young women with different science experiences have different aspirations and expectations about their future education and occupation? The answer is an unqualified "yes." Tables 3-2 through 3-4 present a linear progression associating increasingly high aspirations and expectations with increased time in the sciences. As with many other contrasts, some of the largest differences are between women who stay in the science achievement pipeline and those who stay out. Young women who remain in this area are over six times as likely as those who remain out to expect a college degree or more (83% versus 13%). They are almost twice as likely to aspire to go to college (89% versus 46%), and over twice as likely to expect a professional job (58% versus 22%). Differences in the educational and occupational aspirations of women with different experiences in the science access and attitudes pipelines are also very large.

An area of individual resources that is particularly relevant in the

(Text continued on page 90)

TABLE 3-5 Means (and Standard Deviations) for Selected Science Resources for Females in Science Achievement Trajectories (HSB Sophomore Cohort)

RESOURCES	Out Throughout	In and Out, Out 1986	Left After 1980
Access			
1980			
HS Math, 1+ Years	.73 (.44)	.87 (.33)	.89 (.32)
HS Science, 1+ Years	.71 (.45)	.79 (.41)	.86 (.35)
Advanced Math Taken	.13 (.33)	.23 (.42)	.34 (.47)
1982			
HS Math, 3+ Years	.10 (.30)	.27 (.44)	.26 (.44)
HS Science, 3+ Years	.05 (.21)	.17 (.37)	.12 (.33)
HS Calculus Taken	.00 (.06)	.04 (.19)	.00 (.01)
HS Physics Taken	.06 (.24)	.10 (.30)	.06 (.25)
1984			
College Math, 2+ Semesters	.00 (.00)	.35 (.48)	.00 (.00)
College Science, 2+ Semesters	.00 (.00)	.32 (.47)	.00 (.00)
1986			
Field of Study, Math/Science	.02 (.15)	.19 (.39)	.05 (.23)
Attitudes			
1980			
Math Useful in Future	.50 (.50)	.60 (.49)	.54 (.50)
Math Interesting	.30 (.46)	.32 (.46)	.44 (.50)
1982			
Expect 4+−Year Degree	.22 (.41)	.56 (.50)	.21 (.41)
1984			
Professional Job at 30	.11 (.32)	.36 (.48)	.13 (.38)
1986			
Expect 4+−Year Degree	.17 (.37)	.64 (.48)	.29 (.46)
Activities			
1980			
Calculator at Home	.68 (.47)	.80 (.40)	.84 (.37)
1982			
Calculator at Home	.79 (.41)	.90 (.30)	.91 (.28)
Computer at Home	.05 (.21)	.06 (.24)	.03 (.16)
1984			
Computer Used in HS	.11 (.31)	.14 (.35)	.22 (.42)
Micro-Computer Used	.10 (.29)	.22 (.41)	.18 (.27)

Left After 1982	Left After 1984	In 1986, but Not Throughout	In Throughout
.94 (.24)	.97 (.18)	.84 (.37)	.98 (.90)
.81 (.39)	.92 (.28)	.79 (.40)	.90 (.30)
.42 (.49)	.53 (.50)	.23 (.42)	.57 (.49)
.23 (.42)	.53 (.50)	.28 (.45)	.65 (.48)
.26 (.44)	.48 (.50)	.17 (.37)	.50 (.50)
.08 (.27)	.33 (.47)	.06 (.23)	.37 (.48)
.17 (.37)	.48 (.50)	.12 (.32)	.47 (.50)
.00 (.00)	.54 (.50)	.35 (.48)	.60 (.49)
.00 (.00)	.55 (.50)	.29 (.46)	.59 (.49)
.01 (.11)	.25 (.43)	.13 (.33)	.33 (.47)
.52 (.50)	.75 (.43)	.56 (.50)	.74 (.44)
.51 (.50)	.54 (.50)	.31 (.46)	.55 (.50)
.33 (.47)	.84 (.36)	.44 (.50)	.83 (.37)
.25 (.43)	.56 (.50)	.34 (.47)	.56 (.50)
.32 (.47)	.87 (.33)	.63 (.48)	.39 (.49)
.94 (.25)	.93 (.25)	.82 (.38)	.92 (.28)
.95 (.25)	.97 (.18)	.89 (.31)	.99 (.09)
.02 (.14)	.07 (.26)	.07 (.25)	.03 (.18)
.19 (.39)	.30 (.46)	.14 (.35)	.27 (.45)
.30 (.46)	.61 (.49)	.21 (.41)	.45 (.50)

TABLE 3-6 Means (and Standard Deviations) for Selected Science Resources for Females in Science Access Trajectories (HSB Sophomore Cohort)

RESOURCES	Out Throughout	In and Out, Out 1986	Left After 1980
Achievement			
1980			
A's and B's in Math	.36 (.48)	.53 (.50)	.50 (.50)
Standardized Math Score	47.12 (.8.72)	51.64 (9.11)	47.92 (8.85)
Standardized Science Score	47.63 (8.94)	51.88 (8.71)	48.88 (9.46)
1982			
Standardized Math Score	47.55 (7.93)	52.32 (9.21)	49.35 (8.07)
Standardized Science Score	48.05 (8.39)	52.07 (8.83)	49.00 (9.59)
1984			
Attended Postsecondary School	.47 (.50)	.95 (.21)	.53 (.50)
1988			
Had College Degree	.04 (.19)	.13 (.33)	.03 (.18)
Attitudes			
1980			
Math Useful in Future	.51 (.50)	.62 (.49)	.61 (.49)
Math Interesting	.29 (.46)	.39 (.49)	.33 (.47)
1982			
Expect 4+–Year Degree	.30 (.46)	.67 (.47)	.44 (.50)
1984			
Professional Job at 30	.20 (.40)	.38 (.49)	.27 (.44)
1986			
Expect 4+–Year Degree	.41 (.49)	.80 (.40)	.48 (.50)
Activities			
1980			
Calculator at Home	.78 (.42)	.83 (.38)	.74 (.44)
1982			
Calculator at Home	.87 (.34)	.91 (.29)	.86 (.34)
Computer at Home	.05 (.22)	.06 (.25)	.07 (.25)
1984			
Computer Used in HS	.15 (.36)	.17 (.38)	.19 (.39)
Micro-Computer Used	.16 (.37)	.26 (.44)	.21 (.41)

Left After 1982	Left After 1984	In 1986, but Not Throughout	In Throughout
.75 (.44)	.77 (.42)	.54 (.50)	.83 (.38)
57.19 (7.38)	59.30 (6.00)	51.87 (8.92)	59.80 (6.34)
55.54 (8.61)	56.96 (7.39)	51.67 (8.53)	58.80 (7.42)
58.69 (8.61)	62.59 (8.15)	52.86 (9.63)	62.13 (8.34)
55.95 (8.73)	57.64 (6.42)	52.01 (8.83)	60.16 (6.63)
.82 (.38)	1.00 (.00)	.86 (.35)	1.00 (.00)
.23 (.42)	.24 (.43)	.07 (.26)	.36 (.48)
.67 (.47)	.88 (.32)	.66 (.47)	.87 (.33)
.52 (.50)	.54 (.50)	.37 (.48)	.65 (.48)
.72 (.45)	.94 (.24)	.58 (.49)	.89 (.32)
.44 (.50)	.58 (.49)	.58 (.49)	.76 (.43)
.89 (.31)	.90 (.31)	.69 (.46)	.96 (.20)
.86 (.34)	.92 (.27)	.83 (.38)	.93 (.26)
.97 (.26)	1.00 (.06)	.89 (.31)	.99 (.10)
.08 (.27)	.10 (.30)	.04 (.09)	.08 (.27)
.34 (.47)	.30 (.46)	.15 (.36)	.40 (.49)
.37 (.48)	.45 (.50)	.23 (.42)	.40 (.49)

TABLE 3-7 Means (and Standard Deviations) for Selected Science Resources for Females in Science Attitude Trajectories (HSB Sophomore Cohort)

RESOURCES	Out Throughout	In and Out, Out 1984
Achievement		
1980		
A's and B's in Math	.43 (.49)	.47 (.50)
Standardized Math Score*	48.78 (8.65)	50.27 (10.53)
Standardized Science Score*	49.36 (8.60)	51.52 (8.03)
1982		
Standardized Math Score*	49.38 (8.62)	51.52 (7.73)
Standardized Science Score*	49.43 (8.59)	50.82 (9.73)
1984		
Attended Postsecondary School	.67 (.47)	.62 (.49)
1988		
Had College Degree	.09 (.25)	.03 (.16)
Access		
1980		
HS Math, 1+ Years	.84 (.37)	.87 (.34)
HS Science, 1+ Years	.79 (.41)	.75 (.43)
Advanced Math Taken	.20 (.40)	.28 (.45)
1982		
HS Math, 3+ Years	.22 (.41)	.28 (.45)
HS Science, 3+ Years	.13 (.34)	.20 (.40)
HS Calculus Taken	.03 (.18)	.05 (.22)
HS Physics Taken	.09 (.29)	.14 (.35)
1984		
College Math, 2+ Semesters	.23 (.42)	.33 (.47)
College Science, 2+ Semesters	.18 (.38)	.33 (.47)
1986		
Field of Study, Math/Science	.07 (.25)	.19 (.39)
Activities		
1980		
Calculator at Home	.81 (.39)	.67 (.47)
1982		
Calculator at Home	.89 (.31)	.80 (.40)
Computer at Home	.05 (.21)	.03 (.17)
1984		
Computer Used in HS	.15 (.36)	.26 (.44)
Micro-Computer Used	.22 (.42)	.26 (.44)

* With the exception of these variables, all variables are coded 1 = True; 0 = False.

Left After 1980	Left After 1982	In 1984, but Not Throughout	In Throughout
.59 (.49)	.70 (.46)	.54 (.50)	.70 (.46)
52.52 (9.21)	58.03 (7.49)	52.73 (9.25)	58.46 (7.55)
51.93 (8.95)	56.18 (8.01)	53.00 (8.88)	57.09 (8.95)
53.23 (9.08)	59.29 (8.77)	54.00 (9.92)	60.89 (9.72)
52.87 (8.33)	57.37 (7.10)	53.59 (8.66)	59.58 (.7.61)
.80 (.40)	.89 (.31)	.93 (.26)	.95 (.22)
.10 (.29)	.14 (.34)	.16 (.37)	.21 (.41)
.93 (.26)	.96 (.19)	.91 (.29)	.98 (.12)
.85 (.36)	.84 (.37)	.83 (.38)	.94 (.24)
.42 (.49)	.57 (.50)	.34 (.47)	.54 (.50)
.45 (.50)	.63 (.48)	.47 (.50)	.73 (.45)
.30 (.46)	.41 (.49)	.29 (.46)	.73 (.45)
.13 (.33)	.30 (.46)	.14 (.35)	.36 (.48)
.22 (.41)	.30 (.46)	.25 (.44)	.61 (.49)
.41 (.49)	.56 (.50)	.40 (.49)	.54 (.50)
.30 (.46)	.47 (.50)	.47 (.50)	.86 (.34)
.08 (.27)	.24 (.43)	.16 (.37)	.63 (.48)
.88 (.32)	.68 (.47)	.85 (.36)	.93 (.26)
.94 (.23)	.85 (.35)	.92 (.27)	.96 (.18)
.08 (.26)	.03 (.18)	.08 (.26)	.11 (.31)
.22 (.41)	.18 (.38)	.21 (.41)	.34 (.48)
.28 (.45)	.41 (.49)	.24 (.43)	.40 (.49)

study of women in science is science resources. Are resources in one area of science important for experiences in another? Are positive science attitudes associated with science achievement? Is high achievement possible without high access? Tables 3-5 through 3-7 allow an examination of the kinds of science resources of women in the different trajectories.

First consider the science access, attitude, and activities resources of women in the various science achievement trajectories (Table 3-5). As with our examination of other individual resources, these figures make it clear that science resources are not equally distributed among young women with different science achievement trajectories. As one looks from the far left column of Table 3-5 (representing women who are never in the science achievement pipeline) to the far right column (representing women who never leave), it is clear that women have increasing levels of science resources. As with other comparisons of resources, however, some deviations from linearity occur. Again, it is the late-leavers who often have high resources—sometimes as high or higher than those who stay in the achievement pipeline.

What are the differences in resources at the extremes of experiences in science achievement ("in throughout" versus "out throughout")? Consider access resources. Women who stay in the achievement pipeline are much more likely than those who stay out to have taken math and science courses in their sophomore and senior years of high school (1980 and 1982). They are also much more likely to be taking math and science courses and to be majoring in math and science in the two post–high school years (1984 and 1986). For example, young women who stay in the science achievement pipeline are over four times more likely to have taken advanced math in their sophomore year of high school (57% versus 13%). They are over six times more likely to have had three or more years of high school math by their senior year (65% versus 10%). None of the young women who stay out of the science achievement pipeline have had two or more years of college science or math in 1984, but approximately 60 percent of those who stay in the science achievement pipeline throughout have had these courses.

This look at women who follow different science trajectories has shown that, with few exceptions, women who spend more time in the sciences have considerably more resources than those who spend less. This is true whether one is referring to family resources, school resources, or individual resources. Sometimes unexpected patterns occur, as when it is the late-leavers who have more resources than those who stay in science. Many times the differences in resources are most extreme when comparing women who spend different amounts of time in the science *achievement* pipeline. It is in the area of individual resources where some of the most intriguing resource differences take place. Young women who stay in science may actually have lower self-concepts than women who do not, and they have unexpectedly high family orientation and low work orientation. However, these women are more likely than others to feel that they have control over their lives and are not (except for those who stay in the science attitude pipeline) more likely than others to view themselves as unpopular (even though they date less). These findings suggest that many of the popular images about people in science do not hold for these young women in their sophomore year of high school. In part, this may be an outcome of our looking at the three realms of science as opposed to some general notion of science (e.g., we find only that those women in the science *attitudes* pipeline view themselves as unpopular). In addition, attitudes and values are not stable personality characteristics. We measured them in the sophomore year of high school, when the realities of work and family are still quite distant. Others who look at these attitudes and values at different times will most likely find considerable variation. In the next chapter we consider whether the variations observed here involve causal relationships.

4

GENDER AND RESOURCES

Of critical importance in an understanding of young women's experiences in the sciences is the causal process. Of special import in this causal process is a discovery of the role that gender per se plays in affecting science experiences. That is, when other important predictors of science experiences (family, school, and individual resources) are taken into account, does the fact of being a female or a male still have an impact on what happens in the science arena? A second important question about the role of gender has to do with the interaction between gender and resources. Do resources have different effects on the science experiences of young men and young women? That is, do some resources make more of a difference for one gender than the other? Do they sometimes work in opposite directions? A third important issue in trying to understand the role of gender in affecting science experiences involves connecting our earlier descriptive findings with our causal findings. For example, we found that young men have more of certain family resources than do young women. If our causal analyses show that these resources have an important causal impact on science experiences for young men and young women, we have acquired an important insight into why young men have more positive science experiences: they have more of the critical resources.

To answer these questions we turn to the results from multivariate models that predict science trajectories and that include gender, family resources, school resources, and individual resources. First we look at ANOVA models, which reveal how well the gender and resource variables are able to predict variation between the different types of science trajectories. Interaction terms from ANOVA models will also show whether resources have significantly different consequences for the science experiences of young men and women. Second we turn to logistic regression models, which provide information on the effect of gender and resources on the chances of being in one trajectory or another. Special reduced form models will offer details on the extent to which the effects of gender are direct or indirect (through its impact on family, school, and individual resources). Separate logistic models for males and females and subsets of females will provide information on the difference in these effects for young men and women and for women in different SES and ethnic groups.

Gender, Resources, and Variations in Science Experiences

Table 4-1 presents results from ANOVA models in which science achievement, access, and attitude trajectories are the dependent variables, and gender and resources are the independent variables. The findings show that the independent variables explain a significant amount of variation in each of the three sets of trajectories. Gender significantly predicts variation in the type of achievement and access trajectory a young person will experience, even when important differences in family, school, and individual resources are taken into account. Thus at least some of the differences between young women and men in science achievement and science access are not due to different qualifications or levels of resources, but to the pure and simple fact that one is female and one is male. In the area of science attitudes, gender per se does not affect science experiences.

The ANOVA results in Table 4-1 also show that the effect of resources on experiences in the three areas of science vary for young women and men. Several interaction terms involving gender and resources are significant in each of the equations. These results confirm our earlier prediction that the same level of resources will sometimes have different consequences for the success experienced by young women and young men in science. Resources that have different effects for males and females include SES, mother's work status, mother's and father's involvement in monitoring homework, mother's occupation, and respondent's marital status. Later examination of separate logistic regression models for young women and young men will reveal the specific ways in which the effects of these and other variables not included in the ANOVA model vary by gender.

Gender, Resources and the Odds of
Being in Different Science Trajectories

Tables 4-2, 4-3, and 4-4 present logistic regression coefficients for the odds of being in each of the trajectories (as contrasted to being in the "out throughout" trajectory) in the three areas of science. Once again, the results reveal that even with the larger number of resources in-

TABLE 4-1 ANOVA Coefficients for Models Predicting Science Trajectories (HSB Sophomore Cohort)

INDEPENDENT VARIABLES	*ACHIEVEMENT*			
	Sum of Squares	*DF*	*Mean Square*	*F*
Sex (1 = Female; 0 = Male)	40.05	1	40.05	12.17*
Race (1 = African American; 0 = Other)	9.38	1	9.38	2.85
Family				
1980				
SES Quartile	126.31	3	42.10	12.80*
Mother Worked When Respondent Was in Elementary School				
(1 = True; 0 = False)	10.41	1	10.41	3.16
Mother's Occupation				
(1 = Technical, managerial, professional; 0 = Other)	17.45	1	17.45	5.30*
Father's Occupation				
(1 = Technical, managerial, professional; 0 = Other)	18.68	1	18.68	5.68*
Mother Monitors Schoolwork				
(1 = Yes; 0 = No)	1.77	1	1.77	.54
Father Monitors Schoolwork				
(1 = Yes; 0 = No)	.05	1	.05	.01
1984				
Ever Married				
(1 = Yes; 0 = No)	252.16	1	252.16	76.64*
School				
1980				
School Type				
(1 = Private; 0 = Public)	2.17	1	2.17	.66
Program				
(1 = Academic; 0 = Other)	25.23	1	25.23	7.67*
Friends' Educational Behavior Scale†				
(4 = High; 0 = Low)	89.24	1	89.24	27.13*
Individual				
1980				
Self-Concept Scale†	6.38	1	6.38	1.94
Locus of Control Scale†	31.21	1	31.21	9.49*
Sex-Role Attitudes†				
• Working Mother Is a Good Mother				
(1 = Agree; 0 = Disagree)	13.02	1	13.02	3.96*
Amount of Dating†				
(1 = Almost every day or every day; 0 = Other)	2.80	1	2.80	.85
Standardized Math Score†	549.07	1	549.07	166.89*
Standardized Science Score†	563.71	1	563.71	171.34*

ACCESS					ATTITUDES			
Sum of Squares	DF	Mean Square	F		Sum of Squares	DF	Mean Square	F
102.11	1	102.11	31.29*		4.68	1	4.68	1.60
88.23	1	88.23	27.03		99.81	1	99.81	34.06*
35.69	3	11.90	3.65*		100.97	3	33.66	11.49*
1.46	1	1.64	.45		10.11	1	10.11	3.45
9.02	1	9.02	2.76		13.57	1	13.57	4.63*
.20	1	.20	.06		11.11	1	11.11	3.79*
.30	1	.30	.09		2.79	1	2.79	.95
.29	1	.29	.09		9.31	1	9.31	3.18
22.98	1	22.98	7.04*		53.80	1	53.80	18.36*
6.53	1	6.53	2.00		6.51	1	6.51	2.22
126.38	1	126.38	38.72*		56.45	1	56.45	19.26*
14.12	1	14.12	4.33*		37.50	1	37.50	12.80*
.36	1	.36	.11		2.81	1	2.81	.96
1.48	1	1.48	.46		31.38	1	31.38	10.71*
1.96	1	1.96	.60		.08	1	.08	.03
16.19	1	16.19	4.96*		.01	1	.01	.00
2.61	1	2.61	.80		2.05	1	2.05	.70
.20	1	.20	.06		10.87	1	10.87	3.71*

(continued on next page)

TABLE 4-1   *(continued)*

INDEPENDENT VARIABLES	ACHIEVEMENT			
	Sum of Squares	*DF*	*Mean Square*	*F*
Individual *(continued)*				
1980 *(continued)*				
Math/Science Achievement Factor Score†				
Math/Science Access Factor Score†	67.18	1	67.18	20.42
Math/Science Attitude Factor Score†	61.37	1	61.37	18.65*
Significant Gender Interactions				
Sex × Mother Monitors Schoolwork	16.89	1	16.89	5.13*
Sex × Ever Married	16.71	1	16.71	5.08*
EXPLAINED	6271.49	85	73.78	22.43*
RESIDUAL	14685.31	4464	3.29	—
Total	20956.83	4549	4.61	—

* Significant at ≤ .05.
† Covariate.

cluded in these models, gender per se often plays a role in determining which science pathway a young person will follow. Consider the effect of gender on the odds of staying in the sciences for longer periods as opposed to staying out of each area when variations in other resources are taken into account. For two of the three areas of science, the effect of gender is as predicted—being female *reduces* the odds of staying in the science access and science attitude pipelines, even when variations in resources are taken into account. That is, young women with the same qualifications as young men continue to be less likely to maintain high access to science and positive attitudes toward science. Note that in the area of science access, although the effect of gender is not significant in the equation comparing the "in throughout" and the "out throughout" trajectories, it is significant in most of the other equations. Moreover, the direction of the effect is consistent—young women are less likely then young men to stay in the science access pipeline. There is, then, a *cost* of being female when it comes to science access and attitudes.

In the area of science achievement, however, being female is not a detriment. It is, in fact, an advantage. When variations in resources are taken into account, being female actually *increases* the odds of staying in the science achievement pipeline (as opposed to staying out). In fact, the odds are increased by a factor of 6.98. When resources are taken

ACCESS				ATTITUDES			
Sum of Squares	DF	Mean Square	F	Sum of Squares	DF	Mean Square	F
71.80	1	71.80	22.00*	438.11	1	438.11	149.50*
				9.57	1	9.57	3.27
952.40	1	952.40	291.80*				
30.69	3	10.23	3.13*	28.30	3	9.43	3.22*
16.34	1	16.34	5.01*	14.35	1	14.35	4.90*
29.70	1	29.70	9.10				
4504.78	85	60.10	16.24*	2570.74	85	30.24	10.32*
11265.30	3451	3.26	—	10012.81	3417	2.93	—
15770.08	3536	4.46	—	12583.55	3502	3.59	—

into account, females also have higher odds of exiting and of having a series of ins and outs. Thus, although young women have a greater chance of staying in the science achievement pipeline than do equally qualified young men, they also have a greater chance of showing some sign of talent in science achievement but of dropping out regardless of that talent.

A Comparison of Results from
Trajectory Models and Traditional Models

This examination of young people's experiences in science has focused on a description and prediction of the over-time experiences that we have referred to as science trajectories. Our earlier discussion of past research suggested that the conventional approach is to describe and predict a single indicator of experience at one particular point in time. Even though these descriptions and predictions might be performed separately at several points, the model still focuses on describing and predicting science experience at one point in time (e.g., a researcher might use a model to predict tenth-grade science grades and then use it to predict twelfth-grade science grades). The argument presented here is that a more dynamic approach to experiences in science that looks at the paths of those experiences is needed. We also argue for multiple measures of

(Text continued on page 102)

TABLE 4-2 Logistic Regression Results for Odds of Experiencing Various Science Achievement Trajectories Versus Being Out of the Science Achievement Pipeline (HSB Sophomore Cohort)*

INDEPENDENT VARIABLES

	In and Out, Out 1986	Left After 1980
Sex		
(1 = Female; 0 = Male)	27.00 (1.06)†	8.61 (.42)†
Demographic		
1980		
Rural Residence		
(1 = Yes; 0 = No)	2.02 (.79)	
Race—African American		
(1 = African American; 0 = Other)	6.28 (.2.32)	.63 (1.24)
Race—Hispanic		
(1 = Hispanic; 0 = Other)	.13 (1.18)	
Family		
1980		
SES Quartile	.92 (.50)	1.24 (.19)
Number of Siblings	1.46 (.20)	
Father Lives in Household		
(1 = True; 0 = False)	.13 (1.03)†	
Mother Worked When Respondent Was in Elementary School		
(1 = True; 0 = False)	2.54 (.73)	.76 (.33)
Mother's Occupation		
(1 = Technical, managerial, professional; 0 = Other)	1.20 (.96)	.61 (.43)
Mother's Education		
(1 = At least some college; 0 = Other)	.13 (.93)†	
Father's Occupation		
(1 = Technical, managerial, professional; 0 = Other)	3.97 (.83)	2.74 (.44)†
Father's Education		
(1 = At least some college; 0 = Other)	2.23 (.80)	
Mother Monitors Schoolwork		
(1 = Yes; 0 = No)	.12 (1.08)†	.98 (.56)
Father Monitors Schoolwork		
(1 = Yes; 0 = No)	15.71 (1.13)†	1.28 (.43)
Mother's Educational Expectations		
(1 = College education or more; 0 = Other)	4.24 (.89)	
Pocket Calculator in Home		
(1 = True; 0 = False)	2.18 (1.01)	

Left After 1982	Left After 1984	In 1986, but Not Throughout	In Throughout
2.21 (.58)	5.17 (.39)†	2.27 (.13)†	6.98 (.47)†
1.55 (1.38)	.36 (1.27)	1.87 (.22)	.92 (1.44)
.73 (.28)	2.20 (.20)†	1.87 (.07)†	1.99 (.24)†
.50 (.45)	.88 (.34)	.73 (.12)†	.91 (.41)
.42 (.65)	1.20 (.40)	1.39 (.14)†	.49 (.52)
4.42 (.58)†	2.01 (.41)	.75 (.15)	1.55 (.52)
.63 (.80)	1.80 (.64)	.97 (.22)	.81 (.83)
1.25 (.65)	2.04 (.45)	1.06 (.16)	4.23 (.58)†

(continued on next page)

TABLE 4-2   *(continued)*

INDEPENDENT VARIABLES

	In and Out, Out 1986	Left After 1980
Family *(continued)*		
1984		
Ever Married		
(1 = Yes; 0 = No)	.02 (1.14)†	.37 (.40)†
Had Child		
(1 = Yes; 0 = No)	.01 (1.71)†	
School		
1980		
School Type		
(1 = Private; 0 = Public)	1.99 (1.06)	2.44 (.68)
Program		
(1 = Academic; 0 = Other)	1.19 (.79)	.34 (.44)†
Rate School on Teacher Interest in Students		
(1 = Good, excellent; 0 = Poor, fair)	1.10 (.79)	
Friends' Educational Behavior Scale		
(4 = High; 0 = Low)	.80 (.32)	.66 (.14)†
Friends' Feelings About Students with Good Grades		
(1 = Think well of; 0 = Other)	3.47 (.76)	
Individual		
1980		
Self-Concept Scale	.67 (.46)	.86 (.25)
Locus of Control Scale	.90 (.53)	.57 (.33)
Sex-Role Attitudes		
· Working Mother Is a Good Mother		
(1 = Agree; 0 = Disagree)	.29 (.90)	1.49 (.40)
· Man Should Achieve, Woman Keep House		
(1 = Disagree; 0 = Agree)	.22 (1.31)	
· Woman Is Happiest in Home		
(1 = Disagree; 0 = Agree)	1.54 (2.29)	
Popular (1 = Very; 0 = Somewhat or not at all)	.34 (.87)	
Amount of Dating		
(1 = Almost every day or every day; 0 = Other)	3.89 (2.08)	2.00 (.58)
Age Expect to Get Married	.90 (.25)	
Age Expect to Have First Child	1.63 (.27)	
Interested in School		
(1 = True; 0 = False)	.35 (.91)	
High School Grades		
(1 = A's or A's & B's; 0 = B's or less)	6.22 (.83)†	

Left After 1982	Left After 1984	In 1986, but Not Throughout	In Throughout
.47 (.60)	.07 (.50)†	.16 (.19)†	.05 (.65)†
2.76 (.93)	3.42 (.55)†	1.46 (.21)	3.82 (.70)†
.87 (.53)	.97 (.35)	1.14 (.15)	2.03 (.45)
1.08 (.23)	1.00 (.17)	1.19 (.06)†	.94 (.23)
.96 (.36)	1.83 (.27)†	1.17 (.09)	1.81 (.32)
1.64 (.43)	1.74 (.37)	1.18 (.10)	.63 (.44)
.22 (.73)†	.25 (.43)†	.79 (.16)	.56 (.50)
.11 (1.68)	.11 (.98)†	.63 (.28)	.18 (1.01)

(continued on next page)

TABLE 4-2   *(continued)*

INDEPENDENT VARIABLES	*In and Out, Out 1986*	*Left After 1980*
Individual (continued)		
1980 (continued)		
Standardized Math Score	1.10 (.05)†	1.27 (.03)†
Standardized Science Score	1.27 (.07)†	1.34 (.04)†
Time on Homework per Week		
(1 = 3+ hours; 0 = Other)	.07 (.85)†	
Educational Expectations		
(1 = College degree or more; 0 = Other)	1.26 (.95)	
Educational Aspirations		
(1 = Disappointed if don't go to college; 0 = Other)	.39 (.88)	
Occupational Expectations		
(1 = Professional job; 0 = Other)	.08 (.91)†	
Math/Science Access Factor Score	1.92 (.35)	1.25 (.14)
Math/Science Attitude Factor Score	1.57 (.26)	1.63 (.11)†
1982		
Math/Science Access Factor Score	.27 (.63)	
Math/Science Attitude Factor Score	1.30 (.49)	
1984		
Math/Science Access Factor Score	(63.69)‡	
Math/Science Attitude Factor Score	13.23 (.72)†	
1986		
Math/Science Access Factor Score	.11 (5.94)†	
Model Chi Square (*df*)	462 (20)†	453 (20)†

* Coefficients are antilogs of logistic coefficients. Standard errors are in parentheses.
† Significant at ≤ .05.
‡ 2.22 E⁺25 or, before antilog, 58.36.

each type of science experience. The pipeline model and the creation of science trajectories are critical to this approach. In fact, the argument has been that the two approaches will lead to very different conclusions and insights about gender and science. We have just presented some results from models predicting trajectories. What would a more traditional model have found?

Table 4-5 presents results from a traditional OLS regression model that predicts two achievement outcomes—standardized math and science scores for the HSB sophomore cohort in their senior year of high school. It is much like the models that are typically used, in which family, school, and individual factors as well as earlier math and science

Left After 1982	Left After 1984	In 1986, but Not Throughout	In Throughout
1.32 (.04)†	1.42 (.04)†	1.04 (.01)†	1.51 (.05)†
1.38 (.05)†	1.40 (.04)†	1.06 (.01)†	1.42 (.05)†
1.18 (.21)	1.32 (.14)†	1.23 (.05)†	1.35 (.18)
1.54 (.15)†	2.26 (.12)†	1.11 (.04)†	2.07 (.15)†
308 (20)†	1853 (20)†	738 (20)†	1419 (20)†

scores (from the sophomore year) are taken into account. As the R^2 suggests, the models are quite effective, explaining over 50 percent of the variation in these scores. Our earlier analysis (Table 4-2) of science achievement trajectories (which included these math and science scores as well as other achievement information for this and other years) showed that gender has an unexpected effect here. Although, as predicted, there is more lost talent among young women than young men in the science achievement pipeline, when resources are equalized, young women have a greater chance than young men of following a trajectory that involves staying in this pipeline throughout the survey pe-

(Text continued on page 108)

TABLE 4-3 Logistic Regression Results for Odds of Experiencing Various Science Access Trajectories Versus Being Out of the Science Access Pipeline (HSB Sophomore Cohort)*

INDEPENDENT VARIABLES

	In and Out, Out 1986	Left After 1980
Sex		
(1 = Female; 0 = Male)	.46 (.22)†	.82 (.38)
Demographic		
1980		
Rural Residence		
(1 = Yes; 0 = No)	1.10 (.19)	1.18 (.30)
Race—African American		
(1 = African American; 0 = Other)	3.70 (.51)†	.73 (1.18)
Race—Hispanic		
(1 = Hispanic; 0 = Other)	1.39 (.37)	1.40 (.56)
Family		
1980		
SES Quartile	.96 (.15)	1.12 (.24)
Number of Siblings	1.01 (.06)	.99 (.09)
Father Lives in Household		
(1 = True; 0 = False)	1.84 (.28)†	2.39 (.53)
Mother Worked When Respondent Was in Elementary School		
(1 = True; 0 = False)	1.17 (.19)	1.12 (.30)
Mother's Occupation		
(1 = Technical, managerial, professional; 0 = Other)	.89 (.23)	1.53 (.37)
Mother's Education		
(1 = At least some college; 0 = Other)	.80 (.23)	.81 (.40)
Father's Occupation		
(1 = Technical, managerial, professional; 0 = Other)	.98 (.23)	.72 (.39)
Father's Education		
(1 = At least some college; 0 = Other)	1.35 (.22)	1.03 (.37)
Mother Monitors Schoolwork		
(1 = Yes; 0 = No)	1.49 (.46)	.64 (.71)
Father Monitors Schoolwork		
(1 = Yes; 0 = No)	1.05 (.28)	3.04 (.62)
Mother's Educational Expectations		
(1 = College education or more; 0 = Other)	1.59 (.26)	.56 (.42)
Pocket Calculator in Home		
(1 = True; 0 = False)	.91 (.31)	.42 (.44)†

Left After 1982	Left After 1984	In 1986, but Not Throughout	In Throughout
.82 (.49)	.33 (.58)†	.41 (.27)†	.37 (.69)
.73 (.45)	.76 (.49)	1.08 (.24)	.60 (.59)
2.24 (.1.56)	25.76 (1.54)†	4.82 (.58)†	3.76 (2.51)
.77 (.93)	2.23 (1.13)	1.54 (.52)	.58 (1.70)
1.35 (.35)	1.58 (.42)	1.49 (.19)†	1.69 (.53)
1.04 (13)	.87 (.17)	.91 (.08)	.95 (.20)
.23 (.60)†	4.78 (.1.10)	.92 (.36)	2.43 (1.24)
1.50 (.46)	1.91 (.49)	1.02 (.24)	1.37 (.63)
.67 (.52)	.66 (.63)	1.08 (.27)	1.10 (.70)
.49 (.56)	1.32 (.59)	.63 (.30)	.52 (.72)
.36 (.52)†	.63 (.65)	.47 (.29)†	.17 (.87)†
1.17 (.50)	1.99 (.64)	.90 (.28)	.83 (.69)
.47 (1.14)	.56 (1.62)	.60 (.52)	.38 (1.37)
2.48 (.70)	5.49 (1.00)	2.31 (.38)†	.64 (.89)
3.41 (.81)	.19 (.87)†	1.96 (.33)†	3.51 (1.16)
.91 (.77)	3.54 (.94)	1.01 (.39)	4.18 (1.08)

(continued on next page)

TABLE 4-3 *(continued)*

INDEPENDENT VARIABLES

	In and Out, Out 1986	Left After 1980
Family		
1980		
Ever Married		
(1 = Yes; 0 = No)	.56 (.37)	2.44 (.44)†
Had Child		
(1 = Yes; 0 = No)	.25 (.63)†	.90 (.62)
School		
1980		
School Type		
(1 = Private; 0 = Public)	1.53 (.26)	1.01 (.47)
Program		
(1 = Academic; 0 = Other)	1.29 (.19)	1.55 (.31)
Rate School on Teacher Interest in Students		
(1 = Good, excellent; 0 = Poor, fair)	.96 (.19)	.96 (.32)
Friends' Educational Behavior Scale		
(4 = High; 0 = Low)	.98 (.11)	1.13 (.17)
Friends' Feelings About Students with Good Grades		
(1 = Think well of; 0 = Other)	.86 (.18)	.77 (.31)
Individual		
1980		
Self-Concept Scale	1.05 (.15)	1.38 (.23)
Locus of Control Scale	.85 (.18)	1.16 (.30)
Sex-Role Attitudes		
· Working Mother Is a Good Mother		
(1 = Agree; 0 = Disagree)	1.04 (.26)	3.14 (.38)†
· Man Should Achieve, Woman Keep House		
(1 = Disagree; 0 = Agree)	.64 (.30)	.29 (.54)†
· Woman Is Happiest in Home		
(1-Disagree; 0 = Agree)	3.11 (.34)†	1.10 (.59)
Popular (1 = Very; 0 = Somewhat or not at all)	1.37 (.27)	.70 (.40)
Amount of Dating		
(1 = Almost every day or every day; 0 = Other)	.48 (.61)	2.27 (.48)
Age Expect to Get Married	.94 (.06)	1.08 (.09)
Age Expect to Have First Child	1.00 (.06)	1.04 (.09)
Interested in School		
(1 = True; 0 = False)	1.57 (.26)	1.25 (.41)

Left After 1982	Left After 1984	In 1986, but Not Throughout	In Throughout
.17 (.91)†	.24 (1.49)	.66 (.44)	.20 (2.00)
2.06 (1.04)	.40 (2.01)	1.46 (.58)	3.45 (2.28)
3.12 (.58)†	1.15 (.62)	1.57 (.35)	2.25 (.79)
.90 (.42)	2.57 (.52)	.99 (.25)	.82 (.64)
.99 (.46)	4.81 (.57)†	.88 (.24)	1.09 (.63)
.69 (.24)	1.03 (.38)	.79 (.12)†	1.02 (.34)
.77 (.43)	.84 (.49)	.92 (.23)	2.05 (.58)
.60 (.37)	1.42 (.38)	.91 (.19)	1.33 (.53)
.66 (.40)	.53 (.49)	.72 (.23)	.50 (.59)
.37 (.63)	.61 (.73)	2.13 (.32)†	1.27 (.24)
1.18 (.61)	.15 (.78)†	.24 (.42)†	.84 (.79)
4.27 (.64)†	.66 (.79)	1.95 (.43)	1.18 (.97)
1.21 (.58)	.25 (.77)	.52 (.30)†	1.61 (.85)
8.18 (.99)†	.22 (1.22)	1.52 (.62)	1.68 (1.74)
.99 (.15)	1.18 (.18)	1.09 (.07)	1.30 (.22)
.77 (.14)	1.05 (.17)	1.02 (.08)	.88 (.20)
1.76 (.67)	2.58 (.91)	1.68 (.33)	3.73 (1.07)

(continued on next page)

TABLE 4-3 *(continued)*

INDEPENDENT VARIABLES	In and Out, Out 1986	Left After 1980
Individual		
1980		
High School Grades		
(1 = A's or A's & B's; 0 = B's or less)	1.36 (.22)	.73 (.37)
Standardized Math Score	.96 (.02)	.95 (.04)
Standardized Science Score	.95 (.02)†	.93 (.03)†
Time on Homework per Week		
(1 = 3+ hours; 0 = Other)	1.02 (.19)	1.41 (.33)
Educational Expectations		
(1 = College degree or more; 0 = Other)	1.79 (.28)†	2.27 (.48)
Educational Aspirations		
(1 = Disappointed if don't go to college; 0 = Other)	1.25 (.23)	1.26 (.38)
Occupational Expectations		
(1 = Professional job; 0 = Other)	1.28 (.22)	1.05 (.36)
Math/Science Achievement Factor Score	2.50 (.31)†	3.05 (.52)†
Math/Science Attitude Factor Score	1.01 (.06)	1.06 (.11)
1982		
Math/Science Achievement Factor Score	1.27 (.14)	1.13 (.22)
Math/Science Attitude Factor Score	.96 (.12)	1.29 (.19)
1984		
Math/Science Achievement Factor Score	3.76 (.23)†	1.51 (.29)
Math/Science Attitude Factor Score	1.21 (.13)	1.03 (.21)
1986		
Math/Science Achievement Factor Score	1.01 (.11)	.69 (.24)
Model Chi Square (*df*)	337 (47)†	86 (47)†

* Coefficients are antilogs of logistic coefficients. Standard errors are in parentheses.
†Significant at ≤ .05.

riod. Contrast these findings with those from the OLS regression in Table 4-5. Here we see that the traditional model yields the traditional finding—being female creates a disadvantage. In their senior year of high school, young women are significantly less likely than young men to score high on the standardized math and science exams when resources are equalized. Thus depending on whether science experiences are seen as static events that can be viewed at a single point in time with a single measure, or whether they are viewed as complex dynamic events that occur over time, one's conclusions about the effect of gender would vary widely.

Left After 1982	Left After 1984	In 1986, but Not Throughout	In Throughout
.81 (.54)	4.09 (.64)†	1.70 (.29)	1.12 (.75)
1.05 (.05)	1.06 (.06)	1.00 (.03)	.97 (.07)
.92 (.05)	.90 (.05)†	.94 (.03)†	.87 (.07)†
1.38 (.49)	3.65 (.60)†	.95 (.26)	2.10 (.62)
2.17 (.71)	1.54 (.92)	.83 (.33)	3.04 (1.08)
13.95 (.88)†	2.66 (.90)	2.04 (.30)†	2.97 (1.45)
.92 (.51)	2.77 (.61)	1.18 (.29)	7.09 (.83)†
4.76 (.75)	4.64 (.89)	2.76 (.41)†	14.38 (1.16)†
1.35 (.16)	1.55 (.19)†	1.22 (.09)†	.93 (.25)
2.49 (.29)†	2.23 (.37)†	1.16 (.16)	13.57 (.60)†
1.52 (.27)	1.16 (.36)	1.05 (.15)	3.06 (.44)
1.22 (.46)	335.98 (14.74)	1.45 (.15)†	558.76 (13.33)
1.04 (.29)	1.68 (.30)	1.97 (.16)†	1.40 (.40)
1.10 (.25)	.90 (.27)	1.55 (.09)†	2.66 (.25)†
244 (47)†	450 (47)†	372 (47)†	556 (47)†

The Influence of Gender: Direct and Indirect

What is the precise nature of the causal mechanism through which gender affects science experiences? Tables 4-6 through 4-8 help answer this question. Here, we first consider the effect of gender alone on the odds of following various science trajectories. Then each of the subsets of resources is added to the equation. This series of equations allows us to look at the total effect of gender (when gender alone is in the equation), the direct effect of gender (when resources are controlled), and, through comparison of these effects, the indirect effect of gender. (For an explanation of columns 1 through 4 in these tables, see the Appendix, pp. 200 and 203).

TABLE 4-4 Logistic Regression Results for Odds of Experiencing Various Science Attitude Trajectories Versus Being Out of the Science Attitude Pipeline (HSB Sophomore Cohort)*

INDEPENDENT VARIABLES

	In and Out, Out 1984	Left After 1980	Left After 1982	In 1984, but Not Throughout	In Throughout
Sex					
(1 = Female; 0 = Male)	.64 (.70)	1.69 (.25)†	2.51 (.97)	1.37 (.20)	.14 (.93)†
Demographic					
1980					
Rural Residence					
(1 = Yes; 0 = No)	.11 (.74)†	.73 (.22)	.08 (.99)†	.66 (.17)†	.18 (.77)†
Race—African American					
(1 = African American; 0 = Other)	.01 (4.58)	.77 (.54)	.44 (1.88)	.53 (.49)	1.32 (1.62)
Race—Hispanic					
(1 = Hispanic; 0 = Other)	.73 (1.35)	1.67 (.43)	.04 (2.19)	.82 (.37)	1.20 (1.74)
Family					
1980					
SES Quartile	.39 (.51)	.95 (.17)	.21 (.62)†	.89 (.14)	.17 (.73)†
Number of Siblings	1.28 (.18)	1.06 (.07)	1.35 (.24)	1.06 (.05)	1.07 (.22)
Father Lives in Household					
(1 = True; 0 = False)	2.61 (1.24)	.94 (.34)	1.82 (1.33)	.65 (.26)	14.45 (1.61)
Mother Worked When Respondent Was in Elementary School					
(1 = True; 0 = False)	.67 (.60)	1.56 (.22)†	2.50 (.78)	.89 (.18)	4.85 (.86)
Mother's Occupation					
(1 = Technical, managerial, professional; 0 = Other)	1.08 (.69)	1.26 (.27)	9.22 (1.00)†	1.50 (.20)†	8.87 (.92)†
Mother's Education					
(1 = At least some college; 0 = Other)	15.29 (.86)†	.88 (.29)	.22 (1.06)	1.29 (.21)	4.94 (1.04)
Father's Occupation					
(1 = Technical, managerial, professional; 0 = Other)	2.24 (.69)	.94 (.26)	1.51 (.88)	1.20 (.21)	13.39 (1.15)†
Father's Education					
(1 = At least some college; 0 = Other)	.54 (.73)	.87 (.26)	3.56 (1.02)	1.13 (.20)	2.87 (.92)
Mother Monitors Schoolwork					
(1 = Yes; 0 = No)	.35 (1.23)	2.80 (.50)†	3341.4 (27.12)	2.22 (.40)†	2.50 (1.88)

TABLE 4-4 *(continued)*

INDEPENDENT VARIABLES

	In and Out, Out 1984	Left After 1980	Left After 1982	In 1984, but Not Throughout	In Throughout
Family *(continued)*					
1980 *(continued)*					
Father Monitors Schoolwork					
(1 = Yes; 0 = No)	1.45 (1.01)	.78 (.34)	2.77 (1.71)	.81 (.26)	.83 (1.49)
Mother's Educational Expectations					
(1 = College education or more;					
0 = Other)	1.82 (1.02)	.75 (.32)	247.00 (4.33)	.99 (.24)	19.41 (1.48)†
Pocket Calculator in Home					
(1 = True; 0 = False)	5.96 (1.52)	1.27 (.37)	3.86 (1.90)	.79 (.28)	.92 (1.46)
1984					
Ever Married					
(1 = Yes; 0 = No)	.20 (1.71)	.72 (.38)	.50 (2.04)	.38 (.37)†	.78 (2.38)
Had Child					
(1 = Yes; 0 = No)	1.87 (1.85)	1.11 (.51)	.00 (31.70)	1.12 (.51)	2.36 (3.19)
School					
1980					
School Type					
(1 = Private; 0 = Public)	3.41 (.75)	.61 (.34)	.19 (1.10)	1.74 (.24)†	1.05 (.88)
Program					
(1 = Academic; 0 = Other)	.33 (.62)	1.24 (.22)	.23 (.95)	1.12 (.18)	.75 (.82)
Rate School on Teacher					
Interest in Students					
(1 = Good, excellent;					
0 = Poor, fair)	3.98 (.72)†	1.27 (.22)	1.06 (.92)	1.19 (.17)	1.40 (.87)
Friends' Educational Behavior Scale					
(4 = High; 0 = Low)	.80 (.28)	1.19 (.12)	1.54 (.41)	1.05 (.09)	4.47 (.57)†
Friends' Feelings About Student					
with Good Grades					
(1 = Think well of; 0 = Other)	1.68 (.62)	1.31 (.21)	6.24 (.89)†	1.09 (.17)	3.48 (.74)
Individual					
1980					
Self-Concept Scale	.44 (.56)	.87 (.17)	.30 (.71)	.85 (.14)	1.23 (.62)
Locus of Control Scale	.99 (.63)	.60 (.21)†	.57 (.86)	.93 (.16)	.76 (.72)
Sex-Role Attitudes					
• Working Mother Is a Good Mother					
(1 = Agree; 0 = Disagree)	2.11 (.67)	.88 (.17)	18.86 (.96)†	1.50 (.23)	10.62 (.93)†

(continued on next page)

TABLE 4-4 *(continued)*

INDEPENDENT VARIABLES

	In and Out, Out 1984	Left After 1980	Left After 1982	In 1984, but Not Throughout	In Throughout
Individual *(continued)*					
1980 *(continued)*					
· Man Should Achieve, Woman Keep House					
(1 = Disagree; 0 = Agree)	2.81 (.92)	1.30 (.33)	.10 (1.43)	.66 (.29)	1.91 (1.01)
· Woman Is Happiest in Home					
(1 = Disagree; 0 = Agree)	.73 (1.03)	.48 (.35)†	.69 (1.07)	.93 (.30)	.85 (1.10)
Popular (1 = Very;					
0 = Somewhat or not at all)	.17 (.84)†	.48 (.30)†	.18 (1.40)	.48 (.22)†	.46 (1.25)
Amount of Dating					
(1 = Almost every day					
or every day; 0 = Other)	.88 (1.78)	3.27 (.51)†	.95 (2.21)	.38 (.62)	19.48 (1.73)
Age Expect to Get Married	.69 (.17)†	1.12 (.07)	1.09 (.24)	1.07 (.05)	1.18 (.28)
Age Expect to Have First Child	1.47 (.17)†	.93 (.06)	1.42 (.23)	.94 (.05)	.76 (.29)
Interested in School					
(1 = True; 0 = False)	5.99 (1.05)	1.88 (.31)†	1.19 (1.38)	1.42 (.25)	8.93 (1.34)
High School Grades					
(1 = A's or A's & B's;					
0 = B's or less)	4.09 (.82)	.54 (.26)†	1.49 (.89)	1.42 (.21)	2.25 (.94)
Standardized Math Score	1.04 (.07)	.97 (.03)	1.05 (.11)	1.00 (.02)	1.02 (.11)
Standardized Science Score	1.17 (.06)†	.94 (.02)†	.96 (.07)	1.00 (.02)	.92 (.08)
Time on Homework per Week					
(1 = 3⁺ hours; 0 = Other)	.64 (.64)	.75 (.23)	.41 (.85)	1.11 (.18)	4.26 (.96)
Educational Expectations					
(1 = College degree or more;					
0 = Other)	5.36 (1.02)	2.45 (.33)†	165.53 (2.50)†	1.91 (.24)†	32.59 (2.29)
Educational Aspirations					
(1 = Disappointed if don't					
go to college; 0 = Other)	1.73 (.92)	1.01 (.30)	1.87 (2.16)	.97 (.23)	.29 (1.85)
Occupational Expectations					
(1 = Professional Job;					
0 = Other)	1.48 (.57)	8.32 (.22)†	25.21 (.94)†	4.19 (.18)†	504.81 (1.18)†
Math/Science Access Factor Score	1.14 (.30)	.88 (.10)	1.67 (.37)	1.06 (.08)	2.33 (.40)†
Math/Science Achievement					
Factor Score	.22 (1.09)	4.98 (.38)†	4.14 (1.30)	1.09 (.30)	13.33 (1.61)
1982					
Math/Science Access Factor Score	.90 (.30)	1.26 (.11)†	1.26 (.38)	1.09 (.08)	2.09 (.33)†
Math/Science Achievement					
Factor Score	1.41 (.44)	1.12 (.16)	1.17 (.54)	1.16 (.13)	1.11 (.53)
1984					
Math/Science Access Factor Score	.68 (.43)	.93 (.14)	2.55 (.47)†	1.55 (.11)†	1.48 (.43)

TABLE 4-4   *(continued)*

INDEPENDENT VARIABLES

	In and Out, Out 1984	Left After 1980	Left After 1982	*In 1984, but Not Throughout*	*In Throughout*
Individual (continued)					
1984 (continued)					
Math/Science Achievement					
Factor Score	1.41 (.32)	1.11 (.12)	1.37 (.59)	1.31 (.09)†	3.29 (.41)†
Model Chi Square (*df*)	106 (48)†	298 (48)†	188 (48)†	495 (48)†	462 (48)†

* Coefficients are antilogs of logistic coefficients. Standard errors are in parentheses.
† Significant at ≤ .05.

In the area of science achievement, we discovered above (Table 4-2) that the direct effect of gender on the odds of having a science trajectory that involved staying in the sciences was *positive,* involving a female advantage. However, Table 4-6 shows that the total effect of gender is *negative.* When gender alone is considered, females are less likely to stay in the science achievement pipeline. How can we understand a total effect that is negative and a direct effect that is positive? The paths through which gender can indirectly affect science experiences are the key here. Thus, even though young women in general are less likely to stay in the science achievement pipeline than are young men, young women who have the same resources as young men are actually *more* likely to stay in the area of science achievement. Part of the reason that females in general do not follow the science achievement trajectory is that they have fewer of the important resources that affect science achievement experiences. The resources that appear to be critical here are *individual* resources, since the effect of gender does not become significant in a direction favoring females until these resources are equalized (column 4 under "in throughout" in Table 4-6). Some of the most important individual resources are standardized math and science scores and science attitudes, those that we discovered earlier are often highly skewed to the advantage of males.

TABLE 4-5   OLS Regression Coefficients for Models Predicting Senior Math and Science Scores (HSB Sophomore Cohort)*

INDEPENDENT VARIABLES

	Math	*Science*
Sex		
(1 = Female; 0 = Male)	− 2.52 (.32)†	− 2.11 (.25)†
Demographic		
1980		
Rural Residence		
(1 = Yes; 0 = No)	−.39 (.30)	−.14 (.24)
Race—African American		
(1 = African American; 0 = Other)	−1.21 (.69)	−3.00 (.55)†
Race—Hispanic		
(1 = Hispanic; 0 = Other)	−1.77 (.52)†	−.96 (.42)†
Family		
1980		
SES Quartile	.40 (.22)	.16 (.18)
Number of Siblings	.15 (.09)	−.11 (.07)
Father Lives In Household		
(1 = True; 0 = False)	−.11 (.42)	.42 (.34)
Mother Worked When Respondent Was in Elementary School		
(1 = True; 0 = False)	.04 (.30)	−.17 (.24)
Mother's Occupation		
(1 = Technical, managerial, professional; 0 = Other)	−.21 (.34)	.21 (.27)
Mother's Education		
(1 = At least some college; 0 = Other)	.36 (.38)	−.15 (.30)
Father's Occupation		
(1 = Technical, managerial, professional; 0 = Other)	.20 (.35)	−.72 (.28)†
Father's Education		
(1 = At least some college; 0 = Other)	.02 (.36)	.27 (.29)
Mother Monitors Schoolwork		
(1 = Yes; 0 = No)	.92 (.60)	1.04 (.48)†
Father Monitors Schoolwork		
(1 = Yes; 0 = No)	−1.13 (.43)†	−.82 (.34)†
Mother's Educational Expectations		
(1 = College education or more; 0 = Other)	−.63 (.41)	.31 (.32)
Pocket Calculator in Home		
(1 = True; 0 = False)	.26 (.45)	.87 (.36)†
School		
1980		
School Type		
(1 = Private; 0 = Public)	.54 (.44)	−.29 (.35)

TABLE 4-5 *(continued)*

INDEPENDENT VARIABLES

	Math	*Science*
School *(continued)*		
1980 *(continued)*		
Program		
(1 = Academic; 0 = Other)	.16 (.32)	.63 (.26)†
Rate School on Teacher Interest in Students		
(1 = Good, excellent; 0 = Poor, fair)	.03 (.30)	.23 (.24)
Friends' Educational Behavior Scale		
(4 = High; 0 = Low)	.00 (.15)	.08 (.12)
Friends' Feelings About Students with Good Grades		
(1 = Think well of; 0 = Other)	−.05 (.29)	.01 (.23)
Individual		
1980		
Self-Concept Scale	.32 (.22)	−.04 (.17)
Locus of Control Scale	1.17 (.26)†	1.41 (.21)†
Work Orientation Scale	−1.23 (.22)†	−.77 (.18)†
Family Orientation Scale	.31 (.24)	−.23 (.19)
Sex-Role Attitudes		
· Working Mother Is a Good Mother		
(1 = Agree; 0 = Disagree)	.34 (.38)	−.52 (.30)†
· Man Should Achieve, Woman Keep House		
(1 = Disagree; 0 = Agree)	−.21 (.49)	.54 (.39)
· Woman Is Happiest in Home		
(1 = Disagree; 0 = Agree)	−.47 (.50)	−.00 (.40)
Popular		
(1 = Very; 0 = Somewhat or not at all)	−.30 (.37)	−.77 (.29)†
Amount of Dating		
(1 = Almost every day or every day; 0 = Other)	.60 (.75)	−1.70 (.60)†
Age Expect to Get Married	−.04 (.08)	−.05 (.06)
Age Expect to Have First Child	.04 (.08)	.16 (.06)†
Interested in School		
(1 = True; 0 = False)	−.17 (.40)	−.25 (.32)
High School Grades		
(1 = A's & B's; 0 = B's or less)	2.00 (.33)†	1.38 (.26)†
Standardized Math Score	.47 (.02)†	.12 (.02)†
Standardized Science Score	.09 (.03)†	.47 (.02)†
Time on Homework per Week		
(1 = 3+ hours; 0 = Other)	.05 (.31)	−.02 (.25)
Educational Expectations		
(1 = College degree or more; 0 = Other)	1.58 (.44)†	1.32 (.35)†
Educational Aspirations		
(1 = Disappointed if don't go to college;		
0 = Other)	1.04 (.38)†	.21 (.31)

(continued on next page)

TABLE 4-5   *(continued)*

INDEPENDENT VARIABLES	*Math*	*Science*
Individual *(continued)*		
1980 (continued)		
Occupational Expectations		
(1 = Professional Job; 0 = Other)	−.41 (.34)	.19 (.27)
Math/Science Access Factor Score	.67 (.12)†	.11 (.10)
Math/Science Attitude Factor Score	.42 (.10)†	−.15 (.08)
R^2	.52	.58

* Coefficients are antilogs of logistic coefficients. Standard errors are in parentheses.
† Significant at # .05*

Causal mechanisms in the area of science access (see Table 4-7) are different than for science achievement. Consider the odds of having access to science throughout the study period versus being out throughout. When only gender is in the equation, females are significantly less likely than males to be "in throughout." This trend continues even when different levels of family and school resources are taken into account. However, when variation in individual resources is controlled, there is no longer a difference between males and females in the odds of maintaining access. Why is this true? It is neither discrimination nor the effect of gender per se that keeps women out of the science access pipeline, but rather inequalities in individual (not family or school) resources. Once these different levels of resources are taken into account and one essentially compares equally qualified young women and men, they are equally likely to stay in the sciences throughout the study period. Women's deficits in key individual resources involving standardized science scores, occupational expectations, and science attitudes and achievement are the main explanations for gender differences in the odds of maintaining science access.

It is the case, however, that when less extreme sets of science access experiences are considered, females often have lower odds of spending time in the access pipeline as compared to males, even when their different resources are accounted for. Regardless of resources, females have lower odds than do males of being in three of the five remaining science access trajectories. That is, they are more likely than their equally qualified male counterparts to remain out of science access than to have experiences in science access. In the case of the popular "in"-and-out" pattern, which ends by exiting, when only gender is considered females are less likely than males to be in this trajectory (Table 4-7). And taking into account the family, school, and individual resources of the young men and women does not change this likelihood. A consideration of each of the sets of resources does lower the difference in male and female odds a bit, but the difference remains significant when all are considered. Thus when young women have similar family resources (e.g., mothers with high educational expectations), school resources (e.g., being in an academic program and having interested teachers), and individual resources (e.g., high science scores, high educational expectations, and high levels of science achievement and attitudes), their odds of having at least some experiences in the science access pipeline are increased, but they are still not as high as those of equally qualified young men.

These gender differences in science access trajectories suggest that the unequal treatment that disadvantages females is often a factor in differential access to science (as in the gender effects that remain significant regardless of equal resources). At other times it is not differential treatment but different resources (as in the "in throughout" equation, where gender was not significant when individual resources were controlled). This situation is in contrast to the science achievement process, where differential treatment sometimes works to the advantage of females and where much of the effect of gender is indirect through different levels of resources. In addition, a comparison of the two causal processes suggests greater losses of talented young women in the area of science achievement (where young women are more likely than young men to have participated and then left) than in the area of science access (where young women are less likely than young men to have had any kind of experience).

An examination of the causal process leading to experiences in science attitudes illuminates a third kind of interplay between gender, resources, and science trajectories. The process shown in Tables 4-4 and 4-8 suggests that gender is less important as a causal explanation for variation in science attitudes than for science achievement and access. Although being female does decrease the odds of staying in the science attitude pipeline throughout the study period (even when resources are considered), it is significant in only one of the other science attitude trajectory equations. And in this equation (looking at the odds of leaving after 1980 as opposed to never having been in), it is females who have

(Text continued on page 122)

TABLE 4-6 Sequential Logistic Regression Results for Odds of Experiencing Various Science Achievement Trajectories Versus Being Out of the Science Achievement Pipeline (HSB Sophomore Cohort)*

INDEPENDENT VARIABLES	*IN AND OUT, OUT 1986*			
	1	*2*	*3*	*4*
Sex				
(1 = Female; 0 = Male)	1.02 (.19)	1.97 (.25)†	1.64 (.26)†	27.00 (1.06)†
Demographic				
1980				
Rural Residence				
(1 = Yes; 0 = No)		1.52 (.25)	1.48 (.26)	2.02 (.79)
Race—African American				
(1 = African American; 0 = Other)		1.25 (.65)	1.99 (.64)	6.28 (2.32)
Race—Hispanic				
(1 = Hispanic; 0 = Other)		.33 (.36)†	.28 (.38)†	.13 (1.18)
Family				
1980				
SES Quartile		1.27 (.17)	1.21 (.18)	.92 (.50)
Number of Siblings		.89 (.07)	.92 (.07)	1.46 (.20)
Father Lives in Household				
(1 = True; 0 = False)		.85 (.37)	.88 (.38)	.13 (1.03)†
Mother Worked When Respondent Was in Elementary School				
(1 = True; 0 = False)		1.21 (.24)	1.12 (.24)	2.54 (.73)
Mother's Occupation (1 = Technical, managerial, professional; 0 = Other)		.83 (.33)	.87 (.34)	1.20 (.96)
Mother's Education (1 = At least some college; 0 = Other)		1.14 (.32)	1.03 (.33)	.13 (.93)†
Father's Occupation (1 = Technical, managerial, professional; 0 = Other)		1.17 (.31)	1.08 (.32)	3.97 (.83)
Father's Education (1 = At least some college; 0 = Other)		2.43 (.30)†	2.50 (.30)†	2.23 (.80)
Mother Monitors Schoolwork (1 = Yes; 0 = No)		.95 (.46)	.95 (.47)	.12 (1.08)†
Father Monitors Schoolwork (1 = Yes; 0 = No)		1.12 (.32)	.99 (.34)	15.71 (1.13)†
Mother's Educational Expectations (1 = College education or more; 0 = Other)		4.63 (.25)†	3.74 (.26)†	4.24 (.89)

	LEFT AFTER 1980				IN THROUGHOUT		
1	**2**	**3**	**4**	**1**	**2**	**3**	**4**
1.73 (.20)†	1.80 (.21)†	1.81 (.22)†	8.61 (.42)†	.73 (.12)†	.90 (.14)	1.23 (.18)	7.00 (.47)†
	.23 (.78)	.23 (.79)	.63 (1.24)		.36 (.48)†	.21 (.52)†	.92 (.24)
	1.46 (.12)†	1.47 (.12)†	1.24 (.19)		3.06 (.09)†	2.89 (.12)†	1.99 (.24)†
	1.08 (.21)	1.04 (.21)	.76 (.33)		.67 (.15)†	.66 (.18)†	.91 (.41)
	1.07 (.26)	.99 (.26)	.61 (.43)		1.44 (.17)†	1.03 (.20)	.49 (.52)
	.99 (.26)	.93 (.26)	2.74 (.44)†		1.17 (.16)	1.05 (.20)	1.55 (.52)
	.72 (.32)	.71 (.32)	.98 (.56)		2.80 (.34)†	1.44 (.39)	.81 (.83)
	1.01 (.26)	1.03 (.26)	1.28 (.43)		1.23 (.20)	1.41 (.25)	4.23 (.58)†

(continued on next page)

TABLE 4-6   *(continued)*

INDEPENDENT VARIABLES	IN AND OUT, OUT 1986			
	1	**2**	**3**	**4**

Family *(continued)*

1980 *(continued)*

Pocket Calculator in Home
   (1 = True; 0 = False) | | .77 (.36) | .72 (.38) | 2.18 (1.01)

1984

Ever Married
   (1 = Yes; 0 = No) | | .14 (.33)† | .15 (.34)† | .02 (1.14)†

Had Child
   (1 = Yes; 0 = No) | | .19 (.46)† | .23 (.47)† | .01 (1.71)†

School

1980

School Type
   (1 = Private; 0 = Public) | | | 1.71 (.40) | 1.99 (1.06)

Program
   (1 = Academic; 0 = Other) | | | 1.59 (.26) | 1.20 (.79)

Rate School on Teacher Interest in Students
   (1 = Good, excellent; 0 = Poor, fair) | | | .94 (.24) | 1.10 (.79)

Friends' Educational Behavior Scale
   (4 = High; 0 = Low) | | | 1.33 (.12)† | .80 (.32)

Friends' Feelings About Students
with Good Grades
   (1 = Think well of; 0 = Other) | | | 1.39 (.25) | 3.47 (.76)

Individual

1980

Self-Concept Scale | | | | .67 (.46)

Locus of Control Scale | | | | .90 (.53)

Sex-Role Attitudes
   • Working Mother Is a Good Mother
     (1 = Agree; 0 = Disagree) | | | | .29 (90)

   • Man Should Achieve, Woman Keep House
     (1 = Disagree; 0 = Agree) | | | | .22 (1.31)

   • Woman Is Happiest in Home
     (1 = Disagree; 0 = Agree) | | | | 1.54 (2.29)

Popular (1 = Very; 0 = Somewhat
   or not at all) | | | | .34 (.87)

Amount of Dating (1 = Almost every day
   or every day; 0 = Other) | | | | 3.89 (2.08)

Age Expect to Get Married | | | | .90 (.25)

Age Expect to Have First Child | | | | 1.63 (.27)

	LEFT AFTER 1980				IN THROUGHOUT			
	1	*2*	*3*	*4*	*1*	*2*	*3*	*4*
			.96 (.24)	.38 (.40)†			.09 (.41)†	.05 (.65)†
			1.43 (.39)	2.44 (.68)			1.51 (.28)	3.82 (.70)†
			1.92 (.23)†	.34 (.44)†			8.09 (.18)†	2.03 (.45)
			.92 (.09)	.66 (.14)†			1.76 (.10)†	.94 (.23)
				.86 (.25)				1.81 (.32)
				.57 (.33)				.62 (.44)
				1.49 (.40)				.56 (.50)
				2.00 (.58)				.18 (1.01)

(continued on next page)

TABLE 4-6 *(continued)*

INDEPENDENT VARIABLES	*IN AND OUT, OUT 1986*			
	1	*2*	*3*	*4*
Individual *(continued)*				
1980 *(continued)*				
Interested in School				
(1 = True; 0 = False)				.35 (.91)
High School Grades				
(1 = A's or A's & B's; 0 = B's or less)				6.22 (.83)†
Standardized Math Score				1.10 (.05)
Standardized Science Score				1.22 (.07)†
Time on Homework per Week				
(1 = 3+ hours; 0 = Other)				.07 (.85)†
Educational Expectations				
(1 = College degree or more; 0 = Other)				
Educational Aspiratiions				
(1 = Disappointed if don't go				
to college; 0 = Other)				.39 (.88)
Occupational Expectations				
(1 = Professional job; 0 = Other)				.08 (.91)†
Math/Science Access Factor Score				1.92 (.35)
Math/Science Attitude Factor Score				1.57 (.26)
1982				
Math/Science Access Factor Score				.27 (.63)
Math/Science Attitude Factor Score				1.30 (.49)
1984				
Math/Science Access Factor Score				2.22E + 25 (63.69)
Math/Science Attitude Factor Score				13.23 (.72)†
1986				
Math/Science Access Factor Score				.11 (.90)†
Model Chi Square	.01	203.10†	16.71†	369.50†

* Coefficients are antilogs of logistic coefficients. Standard errors are in parentheses.

† Significant at ≤ .05.

the higher odds. This suggests that young women are more likely than young men to have shown an early interest in science but then left (as opposed to staying out altogether). Although this gives women an edge in science exposure, it also shows more lost talent on their part (even when resources are equalized).

Returning to the critical role of gender in affecting odds of maintaining positive science attitudes, Table 4-8 shows an interesting causal

	LEFT AFTER 1980				IN THROUGHOUT			
1	*2*	*3*	*4*	*1*	*2*	*3*	*4*
			1.27 (.03)†				1.51 (.05)†
			1.34 (.04)†				1.42 (.05)†
1.26 (.95)							
			1.25 (.14)				1.35 (.18)
			1.63 (.11)†				2.07 (.15)†
7.50†	23.49†	8.74	413.64†	6.56†	380.61†	351.39†	680.86†

sequence. Gender is significant in this equation when no other resources are considered. Odds for females are significantly lower than odds for males by a factor of .66. Gender loses significance when family and school resources are controlled, but regains significance (although the size of the effect is diminished) when individual resources are controlled. Thus it appears that young men and women with equal family

(Text continued on page 136)

TABLE 4-7 Sequential Logistic Regression Results for Odds of Experiencing Various Science Access Trajectories Versus Being Out of the Science Access Pipeline (HSB Sophomore Cohort)*

INDEPENDENT VARIABLES	IN AND OUT, OUT 1986			
	1	2	3	4
Sex				
(1 = Female; 0 = Male)	.58 (.14)†	.67 (.16)†	.59 (.17)†	.46 (22)
Demographic				
1980				
Rural Residence				
(1 = Yes; 0 = No)		1.17 (.16)	1.21 (.17)	1.10 (.19)
Race—African American				
(1 = African American; 0 = Other)		2.23 (.42)†	1.22 (.42)	3.70 (.51)†
Race—Hispanic				
(1 = Hispanic; 0 = Other)		.83 (.31)	.82 (.31)	1.39 (.37)
Family				
1980				
SES Quartile		1.04 (.12)	1.05 (.12)	.96 (.15)
Number of Siblings		1.10 (.05)	1.01 (.05)	1.01 (.06)
Father Lives in Household				
(1 = True; 0 = False)		1.90 (.25)†	1.90 (.25)†	1.84 (.28)†
Mother Worked When Respondent Was in Elementary School				
(1 = True; 0 = False)		1.10 (.16)	1.09 (.17)	1.17 (.19)
Mother's Occupation (1 = Technical, managerial, professional; 0 = Other)		.99 (.20)	.98 (.20)	.89 (.23)
Mother's Education (1 = At least some college; 0 = Other)		.89 (.20)	.83 (.20)	.80 (.23)
Father's Occupation (1 = Technical, managerial, professional; 0 = Other)		1.14 (.20)	1.04 (.20)	.98 (.23)
Father's Education (1 = At least some college; 0 = Other)		1.78 (.19)†	1.77 (.19)†	1.35 (.22)
Mother Monitors Schoolwork				
(1 = Yes; 0 = No)		1.82 (.38)	1.75 (.38)	1.49 (.46)

124

	LEFT AFTER 1980				IN THROUGHOUT		
1	**2**	**3**	**4**	**1**	**2**	**3**	**4**
1.28 (.27)	1.16 (.29)	1.07 (.30)	.82 (.38)	.30 (.19)†	.39 (.23)†	.23 (.27)†	.37 (.69)
	1.10 (.26)	1.11 (.26)	1.18 (.30)		.64 (.25)	.62 (.28)	.60 (.59)
	.34 (1.10)	.40 (.49)	.73 (1.18)		.90 (.61)	1.27 (.68)	3.77 (2.51)
	1.03 (.48)	1.08 (.48)	1.40 (.56)		.48 (.53)	.59 (.61)	.58 (1.70)
	1.04 (.20)	1.09 (.20)	1.12 (.24)		1.02 (.20)	1.13 (.22)	1.69 (.53)
	.93 (.08)	.92 (.08)	.99 (.09)		.97 (.08)	.93 (.09)	.95 (.20)
	2.30 (.49)	2.27 (.49)	2.39 (.53)		2.64 (.40)†	2.44 (.43)†	2.43 (1.24)
	.97 (.26)	.96 (.27)	1.12 (.30)		.88 (.24)	.87 (.27)	1.37 (.63)
	1.23 (.32)	1.20 (.32)	1.53 (.37)		1.44 (.27)	1.39 (.30)	1.10 (.70)
	.84 (.35)	.81 (.35)	.81 (.40)		1.01 (.30)	1.03 (.33)	.52 (.72)
	.70 (.33)	.62 (.34)	.72 (.39)		.81 (.30)	.63 (.33)	.17 (.87)†
	1.41 (.32)	1.37 (.32)	1.03 (.37)		1.55 (.30)	1.75 (.33)	.83 (.69)
	.74 (.61)	.75 (.63)	.64 (.71)		1.60 (.67)	.92 (.78)	.38 (1.37)

(continued on next page)

TABLE 4-7 *(continued)*

INDEPENDENT VARIABLES	IN AND OUT, OUT 1986			
	1	*2*	*3*	*4*

Family *(continued)*

1980 *(continued)*

Father Monitors Schoolwork

(1 = Yes; 0 = No) | | .88 (.23) | .86 (.23) | 1.05 (.28)

Mother's Educational Expectations

(1 = College education or more;

0 = Other) | | 3.62 (.18)† | 3.14 (.18)† | 1.59 (.26)

Pocket Calculator in Home

(1 = True; 0 = False) | | 1.10 (.27) | .98 (.28) | .91 (.31)

1984

Ever Married

(1 = Yes; 0 = No) | | .36 (.31)† | .40 (.31)† | .56 (.37)

Had Child

(1 = Yes; 0 = No) | | .28 (.48)† | .28 (.49)† | .25 (.63)†

School

1980

School Type

(1 = Private; 0 = Public) | | | 1.30 (.24) | 1.53 (.26)

Program

(1 = Academic; 0 = Other) | | | 1.68 (.16)† | 1.29 (.19)

Rate School on Teacher Intrerest

in Students

(1 = Good, excellent;

0 = Poor, fair) | | | 1.06 (.16) | .96 (.19)

Friends' Educational Behavior Scale

(4 = High; 0 = Low) | | | 1.27 (.09)† | .98 (.11)

Friends' Feelings About Students

with Good Grades

(1 = Think well of; 0 = Other) | | | .88 (.16) | .86 (.18)

Individual

1980

Self-Concept Scale | | | | 1.05 (.15)

Locus of Control Scale | | | | .85 (.18)

Sex-Role Attitudes

· Working Mother Is a Good Mother

(1 = Agree; 0 = Disagree) | | | | 1.04 (.26)

· Man Should Achieve,

Woman Keep House

(1 = Disagree; 0 = Agree) | | | | .64 (.30)

· Woman Is Happiest in Home

(1 = Disagree; 0 = Agree) | | | | 3.11 (.34)†

LEFT AFTER 1980				IN THROUGHOUT			
1	*2*	*3*	*4*	*1*	*2*	*3*	*4*
	3.41 (.56)*	.35 (.56)*	3.04 (.62)		.90 (.38)	.69 (.44)	.64 (.89)
	1.75 (.28)*	1.53 (.29)	.56 (.42)		27.85 (.51)†	16.89 (.55)†	3.51 (1.16)
	.45 (.38)*	.39 (.39)*	.42 (.44)†		1.45 (.45)	1.60 (.50)	4.18 (1.08)
	1.41 (.36)	1.53 (.36)	2.44 (.44)†		.17 (.75)†	.29 (.80)	.21 (2.00)
	.80 (.54)	.74 (.54)	.90 (.62)		.28 (.84)	.24 (.88)	3.45 (2.28)
		1.06 (.42)	1.01 (.47)			1.00 (.37)	2.25 (.79)
		1.81 (.27)*	1.55 (.31)			4.06 (.27)†	.82 (.64)
		1.04 (.27)	.96 (.32)			2.55 (.27)†	1.09 (.63)
		1.12 (.14)	1.13 (.17)			1.52 (.16)†	1.02 (.34)
		.78 (.27)	.77 (.31)			1.81 (.26)†	2.05 (.58)
			1.38 (.23)				1.33 (.53)
			1.16 (.30)				.50 (.59)
			3.14 (.38)†				1.27 (.69)
			.29 (.54)†				.84 (.79)
			1.10 (.59)				1.18 (.97)

(continued on next page)

TABLE 4-7 *(continued)*

INDEPENDENT VARIABLES	IN AND OUT, OUT 1986			
	1	*2*	*3*	*4*

Individual (continued)

1980 (continued)

Popular (1 = Very; 0 = Somewhat or not at all)				1.37 (.27)
Amount of Dating (1 = Almost every day or every day; 0 = Other)				.48 (.61)
Age Expect to Get Married				.94 (.06)
Age Expect to Have First Child				1.01 (.06)
Interested in School (1 = True; 0 = False)				1.57 (.26)
High School Grades (1 = A's or A's & B's; 0 = B's or less)				1.36 (.22)
Standardized Math Score				.96 (.02)
Standardized Science Score				.95 (.02)†
Time on Homework per Week (1 = 3+ hours; 0 = Other)				1.02 (.19)
Educational Expectations (1 = College degree or more; 0 = Other)				1.79 (.28)†
Educational Aspirations (1 = Disappointed if don't go to college; 0 = Other)				1.25 (.23)
Occupational Expectations (1 = Professional job; 0 = Other)				1.28 (.22)
Math/Science Achievement Factor Score				2.50 (.31)†
Math/Science Attitude Factor Score				1.01 (.06)

1982

Math/Science Achievement Factor Score				1.27 (.14)
Math/Science Attitude Factor Score				.96 (.12)

1984

Math/Science Achievement Factor Score				3.76 (.23)†
Math/Science Attitude Factor Score				1.21 (.13)

1986

Math/Science Achievement Factor Score				1.02 (.11)
Model Chi Square	14.51†	143.25†	21.09†	157.81†

* Coefficients are antilogs of logistic coefficients. Standard errors are in parentheses.

† Significant at ≤.05.

	LEFT AFTER 1980				IN THROUGHOUT		
1	2	3	4	1	2	3	4
			.70 (.40)				1.61 (.85)
			2.64 (.69)				1.68 (1.74)
			1.08 (.09)				1.30 (.22)
			1.04 (.09)				.88 (.20)
			1.25 (.41)				3.73 (1.07)
			.73 (.37)				1.12 (.75)
			.95 (.04)				.97 (.07)
			.93 (.03)†				.87 (.07)†
			1.41 (.33)				2.10 (.62)
			2.27 (.48)				3.04 (1.08)
			1.26 (.38)				2.97 (1.45)
			1.05 (.36)				7.09 (.83)†
			3.05 (.52)†				14.38 (1.16)†
			1.06 (.11)				.93 (.25)
			1.13 (.22)				13.57 (.60)†
			1.29 (.19)				3.06 (.44)†
			1.51 (.29)				558.76 (13.33)
			1.03 (.21)				1.40 (.40)
			.69 (.24)				2.66 (.25)†
.88	25.35	6.25	53.96†	40.31†	168.74†	65.77†	281.51†

TABLE 4-8 Sequential Logistic Regression Results for Odds of Experiencing Various Science Attitude Trajectories Versus Being Out of the Science Attitude Pipeline (HSB Sophomore Cohort)*

INDEPENDENT VARIABLES	IN AND OUT, OUT 1984			
	1	2	3	4
Sex				
(1 = Female; 0 = Male)	.95 (.38)	1.30 (.42)	1.30 (.44)	.64 (.70)
Demographic				
1980				
Rural Residence				
(1 = Yes; 0 = No)		.23 (.53)†	.22 (.55)†	.11 (.74)†
Race—African American				
(1 = African American; 0 = Other)		.03 (4.28)	.04 (4.30)	.001 (4.58)
Race—Hispanic				
(1 = Hispanic; 0 = Other)		.96 (.98)	.96 (.98)	.73 (1.35)
Family				
1980				
SES Quartile		.72 (.41)	.77 (.42)	.39 (.51)
Number of Siblings		1.12 (.14)	1.12 (.15)	1.28 (.18)
Father Lives in Household				
(1 = True; 0 = False)		3.20 (1.06)	2.66 (1.07)	2.61 (1.24)
Mother Worked When Respondent Was in Elementary School				
(1 = True; 0 = False)		.79 (.44)	.70 (.46)	.67 (.60)
Mother's Occupation (1 = Technical, managerial, professional; 0 = Other)		1.25 (.48)	1.45 (.50)	1.08 (.69)
Mother's Education (1 = At least some college; 0 = Other)		6.15 (.55)†	5.21 (.58)†	15.29 (.86)†
Father's Occupation (1 = Technical, managerial, professional; 0 = Other)		2.55 (.52)	1.95 (.54)	2.24 (.69)
Father's Education (1 = At least some college; 0 = Other)		.63 (.55)	.70 (.57)	.54 (.73)
Mother Monitors Schoolwork (1 = Yes; 0 = No)		.49 (.99)	.43 (1.01)	.35 (1.23)
Father Monitors Schoolwork (1 = Yes; 0 = No)		1.67 (.83)	1.12 (.88)	1.45 (1.01)

	LEFT AFTER 1980				IN THROUGHOUT		
1	**2**	**3**	**4**	**1**	**2**	**3**	**4**
1.22 (.16)	1.47 (.17)†	1.32 (.18)	1.69 (.25)†	.66 (.22)†	.88 (.26)	.71 (.28)	.14 (.93)†
	.70 (.18)†	.68 (.18)†	.73 (.22)		.38 (.30)†	.31 (.33)†	.18 (.77)†
	1.01 (.41)	.98 (.42)	.77 (.54)		1.81 (.60)	2.03 (.65)	1.32 (1.62)
	1.17 (.32)	1.16 (.33)	1.67 (.43)		.68 (.67)	.79 (.73)	1.20 (1.74)
	.87 (.13)	.88 (.14)	.95 (.17)		.82 (.23)	.81 (.25)	.17 (.73)†
	1.02 (.05)	1.02 (.06)	1.06 (.07)		1.01 (.09)	1.01 (.10)	1.07 (.22)
	1.31 (.27)	1.27 (.28)	.94 (.34)		2.03 (.49)	1.87 (.55)	14.45 (1.61)
	1.30 (.17)	1.26 (.18)	1.56 (22)†		.80 (.28)	.72 (.31)	4.85 (.86)
	1.07 (.21)	1.12 (.22)	1.26 (.27)		1.56 (.30)	1.66 (.33)	8.87 (.92)†
	1.06 (.22)	1.00 (.22)	.88 (.29)		1.50 (.32)	1.22 (.35)	4.94 (1.04)
	1.15 (.21)	1.03 (.21)	.94 (.26)		2.18 (.32)†	1.63 (.35)	13.39 (1.15)†
	1.18 (.21)	1.20 (.21)	.87 (.26)		1.70 (.33)	2.18 (.38)†	2.87 (.92)
	2.09 (.43)	2.07 (.44)	2.80 (.50)†		1.96 (.78)	2.90 (.94)	2.50 (1.88)
	1.01 (.26)	.77 (.27)	.78 (.34)		1.07 (.47)	.70 (.55)	.83 (1.49)

(continued on next page)

TABLE 4-8 *(continued)*

INDEPENDENT VARIABLES	*IN AND OUT, OUT 1984*			
	1	*2*	*3*	*4*

Family *(continued)*

1980 *(continued)*

Mother's Educational Expectations

(1 = College education or more;

0 = Other)

| | | 5.53 (.66)† | 5.17 (.67)† | 1.82 (1.02) |

Pocket Calculator in Home

(1 = True; 0 = False)

| | | 6.00 (1.31) | 6.77 (1.32) | 5.96 (1.52) |

1984

Ever Married

(1 = Yes; 0 = No)

| | | .30 (1.31) | .21 (1.37)† | .20 (1.71) |

Had Child

(1 = Yes; 0 = No)

| | | .94 (1.35) | 1.71 (1.35) | 1.87 (1.85) |

School

1980

School Type

(1 = Private; 0 = Public)

| | | | 1.22 (.57) | 3.41 (.75) |

Program

(1 = Academic; 0 = Other)

| | | | .64 (.45) | .33 (.62) |

Rate School on Teacher Interest in Students

(1 = Good, excellent; 0 = Poor, fair)

| | | | 2.59 (.49)† | 3.98 (.72)† |

Friends' Educational Behavior Scale

(4 = High; 0 = Low)

| | | | 1.11 (.23) | .80 (.28) |

Friends' Feelings About Students

with Good Grades

(1 = Think well of; 0 = Other)

| | | | 2.10 (.46) | 1.68 (.62) |

Individual

1980

Self-Concept Scale

| | | | | .44 (.56) |

Locus of Control Scale

| | | | | .99 (.63) |

Sex-Role Attitudes

· Working Mother Is a Good Mother

(1 = Agree; 0 = Disagree)

| | | | | 2.11 (.67) |

· Man Should Achieve, Woman

Keep House

(1 = Disagree; 0 = Agree)

| | | | | 2.81 (.92) |

· Woman is Happiest in Home

(1 = Disagree; 0 = Agree)

| | | | | .73 (1.03) |

Popular (1 = Very; 0 = Somewhat

or not at all)

| | | | | .17 (.84)† |

132

	LEFT AFTER 1980				IN THROUGHOUT			
	1	2	3	4	1	2	3	4
		2.78 (.20)†	2.24 (.20)†	.75 (.32)		17.22 (.59)†	14.11 (.61)†	19.41 (1.48)†
		1.66 (.31)	1.62 (.32)	1.27 (.37)		2.20 (.53)	2.54 (.58)	.92 (1.46)
		.62 (.30)	.65 (.31)	.72 (.38)		.27 (.80)	.39 (.94)	.78 (2.38)
		.72 (.42)	.79 (.43)	1.11 (.51)		.68 (.94)	.63 (1.08)	2.36 (3.19)
			.74 (.27)	.61 (.34)			.88 (.38)	1.05 (.88)
			1.64 (.18)†	1.24 (.22)			2.90 (.31)†	.75 (.82)
			1.52 (.18)†	1.27 (.22)			3.12 (.32)†	1.40 (.87)
			1.28 (.10)†	1.19 (.12)			2.23 (.20)†	4.47 (.57)†
			1.41 (.17)†	1.31 (.21)			1.64 (.28)	3.48 (.74)
				.86 (.17)				1.23 (.62)
				.60 (.21)†				.76 (.72)
				.88 (.31)				10.62 (.93)†
				1.30 (.33)				1.91 (1.01)
				.48 (.35)†				.86 (1.10)
				.48 (.30)†				.46 (1.25)

(continued on next page)

TABLE 4-8 *(continued)*

INDEPENDENT VARIABLES	IN AND OUT, OUT 1984			
	1	*2*	*3*	*4*

Individuals (continued)

1980 (continued)

Amount of Dating (1 = Almost every day or every day; 0 = Other)				.88 (1.78)
Age Expect to Get Married				.69 (.17)†
Age Expect to Have First Child				1.47 (.17)†
Interested in School (1 = True; 0 = False)				5.99 (1.05)
High School Grades (1 = A's or A's & B's; 0 = B's or less)				4.09 (.82)
Standardized Math Score				1.04 (.07)
Standardized Science Score				1.17 (.06)†
Time on Homework per Week (1 = 3+ hours; 0 = Other)				.64 (.64)
Educational Expectations (1 = College degree or more; 0 = Other)				5.36 (1.02)
Educational Aspirations (1 = Disappointed if don't go to college; 0 = Other)				1.73 (.92)
Occupational Expectations (1 = Professional job; 0 = Other)				1.48 (.57)
Math/Science Achievement Factor Score				.22 (1.09)
Math/Science Access Factor Score				1.14 (.30)
1982				
Math/Science Achievement Factor Score				1.41 (.44)
Math/Science Access Factor Score				.90 (.30)
1984				
Math/Science Achievement Factor Score				1.41 (.32)
Math/Science Access Factor Score				.68 (.43)
Model Chi Square	.02	53.15†	7.11	45.57†

* Coefficients are antilogs of logistic coefficients. Standard errors are in parentheses.

† Significant at ≤.05.

	LEFT AFTER 1980				IN THROUGHOUT		
1	*2*	*3*	*4*	*1*	*2*	*3*	*4*
			3.27 (.51)†				19.48 (1.73)
			1.12 (.07)				1.18 (.28)
			.93 (.06)				.76 (.29)
			1.88 (.31)†				8.93 (1.34)
			.54 (.26)†				2.54 (.94)
			.97 (.03)				1.03 (.11)
			.93 (.02)†				.92 (.08)
			.75 (.23)				4.26 (.96)
			2.45 (.33)†				32.59 (2.29)
			1.01 (.30)				.29 (1.85)
			8.32 (.22)				504.81 (1.18)†
			4.98 (.38)†				13.33 (1.61)
			.88 (.10)				2.53 (.40)†
			1.12 (.16)				1.11 (.53)
			1.26 (.11)†				2.09 (.33)†
			1.11 (.12)				3.29 (.41)†
			.93 (.14)				1.48 (.43)
1.51	53.37†	31.64†	209.75†	3.65†	139.96†	61.86†	259.83†

and school resources do equally well on science attitudes. But this may be because of women's higher level of some individual resources, because once these are equalized, women have a lower odds than men of staying in the science pipeline.

Gender Variation in the Effect of Resources on Science Experiences

We have observed that gender sometimes interacts with resources to affect science experiences. Thus the process leading to positive science experiences varies for young women and young men. Results from separate logistic regression models presented in Table 4-9 give insight into this variation. (In the interest of parsimony, we restrict our examination here to three trajectory comparisons in the areas of achievement and access.) A careful look at the patterns of significance shown in Table 4-9 suggests that there are considerable gender differences in the process leading to positive science achievement and access experiences. For example, when levels of other resources are taken into account, a number of resources have a significant effect on the science experiences of young women but not young men—especially in the area of access to science. One of the most interesting findings is that when variation in important family, school, and individual resources is taken into account (or controlled), young African American women are *more likely* than other women to have experiences in science achievement and access (including being more likely to be in the area of achievement throughout the survey period). There is no race effect for young men. Another resource that affects the science achievement experiences of young women but not young men is school program—young women who are in academic programs increase their chances of spending at least some time in the area of science achievement. The same is not true for young men. With regard to access, other resources that affect young women's experiences but not young men's include: father's occupation, mother's and father's monitoring of homework, marital status, type of school, locus of control, sex-role attitudes about men's and women's home and work roles, and math score (more detail on the nature of these effects will be provided in chapter 5, when we focus on characteristics of women who stay in science). An important trend to note here is that *family resources have a significant impact on the science access experiences of young women but not of young men*. And, in some situations, these are *negative* effects. For example, having a father with a higher status occupation reduces the chances of a young woman having science access. Being married and having a father who monitors homework are each associated with early signs of promise that are not fulfilled.

Young women are also more likely than young men to experience the effects of individual factors on their access to science. Again, these individual factors often work to detract from science access. For example, women who have a greater internal locus of control (i.e., those who feel more in charge of their lives) and high math scores actually are less likely to stay in the science access pipeline. More time spent on homework and expectations to marry later are associated with both early access and early departure from the science access pipeline for young women but not for young men.

Table 4-9 also reveals a good number of situations in which resources have an impact on the experiences of young men, but not young women in the sciences. In the case of science achievement, this pattern is much more common that the reverse, and it is often individual resources that have a consequence for young men but not young women. Young men but not young women are more likely to have experiences in the science achievement pipeline when they go to a private school, have a positive self-concept and a greater internal locus of control, and date less. In addition, sex-role attitudes affect the science achievement experiences of young men but not young women and it is young men with less progressive sex-role attitudes who are more likely to stay in this area.

In the area of access to science, young men but not young women are more likely to have experiences in the science access pipeline when they are in an academic program and score high on the 1980 science attitude factor. However, young men but not young women who have friends who value education are less likely to have experiences in the science achievement pipeline, and young men who are more progressive on their attitudes about working mothers are more likely than other men to have early access to science but also an early departure.

Considering the large number of resources included in these models, there are relatively few instances in which a resource has a significant effect going in the same direction for both young women and young men, especially in the area of access to science. Scores on the science exam and on the science achievement factor in 1980 and 1984 are the only resources that have similar significant effects on young women and young men in the equations predicting their experiences in science access. For both groups, higher SES, friends with good grades, higher standardized math and science scores, and higher scores on the 1980 access and attitude factors have a significant and positive effect on science achievement. Early marriage detracts significantly from science achievement for young men and young women. It is interesting to note that for

(Text continued on page 144)

TABLE 4-9 Logistic Regression Results for Odds of Experiencing Various Science Trajectories Versus Being Out of the Sciences by Gender (HSB Sophomore Cohort)*

INDEPENDENT VARIABLES	ACHIEVEMENT					
	In and Out, Out 1986		Left After 1980		In Throughout	
	Female	*Male*	*Female*	*Male*	*Female*	*Male*

Demographic

1980

Rural Residence
(1 = Yes; 0 = No)
Race—African American
(1 = African American

0 = Other)	2.14 (.26)†	1.14 (.29)	1.65 (1.53)	.03 (30.60)	31.63 (1.72)†	.24 (2.94)

Race—Hispanic
(1 = Hispanic; 0 = Other)

Family

1980

SES Quartile	1.54 (.08)†	1.73 (.09)†	.93 (.26)	2.05 (30.60)	2.29 (.51)†	3.11 (.47)†

Number of Siblings
Father Lives in Household
(1 = True; 0 = False)
Mother Worked When
Respondent Was in
Elementary School

(1 = True; 0 = False)	.90 (.15)	1.04 (.15)	.82 (.45)	.86 (.79)	.29 (.72)	3.68 (.96)

Mother's Occupation
(1 = Technical, managerial,

professional; 0 = Other)	1.59 (.18)†	.89 (.19)	2.38 (.56)	.15 (1.04)	2.06 (.86)	.04 (1.10)†

Mother's Education
(1 = At least some college;
0 = Other)
Father's Occupation
(1 = Technical, managerial,

professional; 0 = Other)	1.52 (.19)†	.76 (.19)	3.93 (.57)†	.06 (1.23)†	2.79 (1.03)	.53 (.85)

Father's Education
(1 = At least some college;
0 = Other)
Mother Monitors Schoolwork

(1 = Yes; 0 = No)	1.42 (.25)	1.18 (.30)	.92 (.72)	.32 (1.23)	2.33 (1.20)	4.82 (2.75)

Father Monitors Schoolwork

(1 = Yes; 0 = No)	1.23 (.18)	1.15 (.21)	.92 (.54)	1.63 (1.04)	2.11 (.96)	3.12 (1.34)

| ACCESS | | | | | |
| In and Out, Out 1986 | | Left After 1980 | | In Throughout | |
Female	*Male*	*Female*	*Male*	*Female*	*Male*
1.08 (.26)	.73 (.38)	.85 (.40)	6.07 (1.43)	.23 (1.09)	
4.74 (.68)†	3.80 (1.05)	.71 (1.34)	0.00 (6.90)	1.26 (2.35)	2.15 (.96)
.61 (.54)	1.73 (.71)	.95 (.79)	.63 (2.16)	.05 (2.59)	
1.33 (.22)	1.03 (.29)	.65 (.31)	.93 (.90)	6.18 (1.03)	1.34 (.19)
.98 (.09)	1.08 (.11)	.85 (.13)	1.66 (.32)	1.87 (.37)	
1.96 (.39)	1.87 (.59)	2.31 (.59)	.82 (1.89)	.59 (1.76)	
1.08 (.27)	1.71 (.36)	1.60 (.41)	.26 (1.26)	2.81 (1.24)	1.56 (.33)
.76 (.32)	1.04 (.40)	.45 (.53)	1.79 (1.20)	.53 (1.23)	1.70 (.36)
.62 (.33)	.77 (.43)	.84 (.55)	2.80 (1.60)	.34 (1.43)	
.66 (.32)	1.01 (.43)	1.11 (.50)	.73 (1.75)	.02 (1.81)†	1.06 (.38)
1.00 (.30)	1.18 (.44)	1.67 (.46)	7.94 (2.27)	1.04 (1.26)	
3.95 (.65)†	.43 (.94)	.41 (.89)	.66 (2.40)	2.67 (2.00)	2.26 (.83)
.90 (.36)	1.21 (.61)	6.91 (.86)†	1.04 (1.98)	.40 (1.70)	.96 (.48)

(continued on next page)

TABLE 4-9 *(continued)*

INDEPENDENT VARIABLES	ACHIEVEMENT					
	In and Out, Out 1986		*Left After 1980*		*In Throughout*	
	Female	*Male*	*Female*	*Male*	*Female*	*Male*
Family *(continued)*						
1980 (continued)						
Mother's Educational Expectations (1 = College education or more; 0 = Other)						
Pocket Calculator in Home (1 = True; 0 = False)						
1984						
Ever Married (1 = Yes; 0 = No)	.23 (.16)†	.53 (.29)†	.42 (.44)†	2.15 (1.43)	.01 (1.05)†	.05 (10.81)
Had Child (1 = Yes; 0 = No)						
School						
1980						
School Type (1 = Private; 0 = Public)	1.53 (.26)	1.83 (.29)†	4.84 (.86)	1.53 (1.99)	3.70 (1.20)	10.90 (1.27)
Program (1 = Academic; 0 = Other)	1.71 (.16)†	1.19 (.19)	.48 (.56)	3.31 (.94)	2.09 (.83)	1.04 (.25)
Rate School on Teacher Interest in Students (1 = Good, excellent; 0 = Poor, fair)						
Friends' Educational Behavior Scale (4 = High; 0 = Low)	1.29 (.07)†	1.27 (.07)†	.65 (.20)†	.42 (.38)†	.57 (.47)	1.25 (.37)
Friends' Feelings About Students with Good Grades (1 = Think well of; 0 = Other)						
Individual						
1980						
Self-Concept Scale	.93 (.10)	1.28 (.12)†	1.03 (.32)	1.84 (.66)	1.29 (.58)	2.04 (.68)
Locus of Control Scale	1.03 (.12)	1.52 (.13)†	1.10 (.42)	.39 (.85)	.22 (.82)	1.07 (.88)

ACCESS					
In and Out, Out 1986		*Left After 1980*		*In Throughout*	
Female	*Male*	*Female*	*Male*	*Female*	*Male*
2.10 (.42)	1.92 (.43)	1.78 (.51)	.58 (2.03)	73.21 (2.62)	
.73 (.41)	.59 (.62)	.43 (.57)	20.94 (2.33)	2.93 (1.83)	
.57 (.48)	.75 (1.33)	4.38 (.52)†	.83 (2.86)	.08 (3.60)	
1.77 (.82)	.09 (1.63)	2.51 (.79)	3.79 (2.58)	.02 (117.14)	.14 (1.38)
2.27 (.36)†	.66 (.53)	.78 (.62)	1.22 (1.49)	4.89 (1.47)	1.16 (.47)
1.17 (.38)	1.94 (.38)	29.77 (1.62)†	.69 (1.35)	2.41 (.32)†	
.64 (.27)	1.48 (.37)	.68 (.41)	6.39 (1.64)	.53 (1.15)	
1.25 (.17)	.61 (.19)†	1.01 (.22)	1.59 (.84)	.97 (.69)	1.27 (.19)
.66 (.25)	1.80 (.36)	.73 (.38)	.67 (1.33)	1.43 (1.03)	
.61 (.22)†	2.12 (.31)†	1.19 (.28)	4.02 (1.05)	.63 (.81)	.70 (.28)
.49 (.28)†	1.61 (.35)	1.64 (.41)	5.83 (1.35)	.12 (1.03)†	1.17 (.31)

(continued on next page)

TABLE 4-9 *(continued)*

INDEPENDENT VARIABLES	ACHIEVEMENT					
	In and Out, Out 1986		*Left After 1980*		*In Throughout*	
	Female	*Male*	*Female*	*Male*	*Female*	*Male*

Individual (continued)

1980 (continued)

Sex-Role Attitudes

· Working Mother Is
Good Mother
(1 = Agree;

0 = Disagree) — 1.02 (.17), 1.17 (.21), 1.37 (.54), .46 (.84), 1.76 (.88), .12 (1.09)†

· Man Should Achieve,
Woman Keep House
(1 = Disagree; 0 = Agree)

· Woman Is Happiest in Home
(1 = Disagree; 0 = Agree)

Popular
(1 = Very; 0 = Somewhat
or not at all)

Amount of Dating
(1 = Almost every day
or every day; 0 = Other) — 1.02 (.32), .24 (.44)†, 1.92 (.65), .02 (1.79)†, .04 (1.91), .03 (2.01)

Age Expect to Get Married

Age Expect to Have First Child

Interested in School
(1 = True; 0 = False)

High School Grades
(1 = A's or B's; 0 = B's
or less)

Standardized Math Score — 1.04 (.01)†, 1.04 (.01)†, 1.31 (.04)†, 1.46 (.10)†, 1.79 (.11)†, 1.67 (.10)†

Standardized Science Score — 1.05 (.01)†, 1.04 (.01)†, 1.35 (.05)†, 1.53 (.10)†, 1.44 (.08)†, 1.62 (.11)†

Time on Homework per Week
(1 = 3+ hours; 0 = Other)

Educational Expectations
(1 = College degree or more;
0 = Other)

Educational Aspirations
(1 = Disappointed if don't
go to college; 0 = Other)

Occupational Expectations
(1 = Professional Job;
0 = Other)

Math/Science Access
Factor Score — 1.23 (.06)†, 1.41 (.06)†, 1.37 (.17), .77 (.35), 1.75 (.29), 1.58 (.41)

Math/Science Achievement
Factor Score

| | ACCESS | | | | |
| In and Out, Out 1986 | | Left After 1980 | | In Throughout | |
Female	*Male*	*Female*	*Male*	*Female*	*Male*
.76 (.35)	1.26 (.51)	1.12 (.53)	39.78 (1.54)†	.29 (1.16)	.74 (.50)
1.08 (.36)	.78 (.96)	.27 (.64)†	.06 (2.64)	.41 (1.65)	
3.45 (.41)†	2.48 (.94)	.92 (.75)	2499.87 (3.81)†	2.07 (1.43)	
.91 (.37)	2.14 (.51)	.27 (.50)†	6.05 (2.29)	1.02 (1.67)	
.70 (.66)	.13 (2.48)	2.59 (1.01)	45.26 (2.79)	2.21 (3.64)	.12 (1.31)
.95 (.09)	.94 (.11)	1.30 (.12)†	.97 (.46)	1.28 (.39)	
1.04 (.09)	1.02 (.11)	1.02 (.11)	.89 (.40)	1.01 (.35)	
1.47 (.36)	2.62 (.48)†	5.14 (.67)†	1.57 (1.49)	5.01 (1.93)	
.93 (.30)	1.33 (.45)	.90 (.48)	6.40 (1.49)	1.02 (1.67)	
.94 (.03)†	.98 (.04)	.94 (.05)	1.15 (.15)	1.09 (.15)	1.00 (.04)
.95 (.03)†	.90 (.04)†	.95 (.04)	.86 (.14)	.84 (.14)	.99 (.03)
.96 (.27)	1.76 (.34)	3.26 (.48)†	.85 (1.14)	13.94 (1.70)	
1.02 (.44)	1.50 (.49)	1.21 (.61)	2.01 (1.98)	.44 (2.52)	
1.57 (.34)	1.00 (.44)	2.03 (.51)	.17 (1.67)	1023.88 (3.67)	
.99 (.29)	1.56 (.41)	.94 (.44)	.86 (1.40)	5.28 (1.42)	
3.31 (.43)†	6.02 (.61)†	2.37 (.70)	1.68 (2.29)	9.90 (2.33)	8.92 (.54)†

(continued on next page)

TABLE 4-9   *(continued)*

INDEPENDENT VARIABLES	ACHIEVEMENT					
	In and Out, Out 1986		Left After 1980		In Throughout	
	Female	*Male*	*Female*	*Male*	*Female*	*Male*
Individual (continued)						
1980 *(continued)*						
Math/Science Attitude Factor Score	1.11 (.04)†	1.11 (.05)†	1.22 (.13)	4.62 (.42)†	1.83 (.24)†	3.59 (.36)†
1982						
Math/Science Achievement Factor Score						
Math/Science Attitude Factor Score						
1984						
Math/Science Achievement Factor Score						
Math/Science Attitude Factor Score						
1986						
Math/Science Achievement Factor Score						
Model Chi Square (*df*)	560 (19)†	430 (19)†	287 (19)†	202 (19)†	749 (19)†	734 (19)†

* Coefficients are antilogs of logistic coefficients. Standard errors are in parentheses.
† Significant at ≤.05.

both young women and young men, high science scores detract from their chances of having access to science but contribute to their chances of being involved in the area of science achievement.

A final consideration in our examination of gender differences in the process leading to positive experiences in the sciences involves resources that have *opposite* effects for young women and young men. This is not a common occurrence. In fact, there are only two instances of opposite effects in Table 4-9. Having a father with a higher status occupation makes young women more likely to leave the science achievement pipeline after 1980 (as opposed to staying out), but it makes young men less likely to follow this path. That is, these young men are more likely to have stayed out of the science achievement pipeline than to have entered it and left early. Having a high self-concept increases the chances that a young man will experience a trajectory involving going in and out of the science access pipeline but ending up out (as opposed to staying out).

	ACCESS				
In and Out, Out 1986		**Left After 1980**		**In Throughout**	
Female	*Male*	*Female*	*Male*	*Female*	*Male*
1.06 (.08)	.69 (.13)†	.96 (.15)	.94 (.38)	1.44 (.51)	1.72 (.12)†
1.36 (.19)	1.67 (.27)	1.11 (.30)	.08 (.97)†	2.95 (.81)	
1.04 (.16)	.80 (.24)	1.36 (.25)	.90 (.89)	18.40 (.84)†	
8.59 (.48)†	3.26 (.37)†	2.09 (.39)	2.59 (1.60)	1778.02 (22.25)	
1.18 (.17)	1.87 (.25)†	1.04 (.27)	2.28 (.76)	1.98 (.74)	
.80 (.17)	1.39 (.22)	.48 (.32)†	2.13 (13.71)	1.63 (.38)	
208 (46)†	178 (46)†	116 (46)†	59 (46)†	314 (46)†	404 (19)†

This same high self-concept *decreases* the chance that a young woman will experience this in-and-out trajectory (as opposed to staying out).

In sum, an examination of the ways in which resources affect science experiences for young women and young men suggests that a *consideration of gender is often important for understanding how a resource will affect experiences in science.* This is especially true in the area of experiences in science access. In this area, a large majority of the resources that are important for success have an impact that varies by gender. In the case of science achievement, the resources that are important for success are almost as likely to have similar effects for young women and young men as they are to have different effects for young women and young men.

The evidence presented in this chapter provides strong support for the notion that gender per se is often a critical factor in determining experiences in science. When family, school, and individual resources are taken into account, gender still has a significant impact in many of the equations predicting experiences in science achievement, access, and attitudes. In the areas of access and attitudes, the gender effect often involves a *disadvantage* for young women. They are less likely than young men with equal resources to spend time in these areas. However, in the area of science achievement, when resources are equalized, it is the young woman who has the advantage of spending more time in the pipeline. Gender is also an important factor in predicting lost talent in science, especially in the area of science achievement. Thus although young women with equal resources are more likely than young men to stay in this area throughout the 6-year period examined, there is also a greater exiting of female talent than male talent.

The findings presented in this chapter also highlight the fact that the way in which resources affect science experiences varies by gender. Thus gender can have a direct impact on science experiences, but it can also indirectly affect them through its association with family, school and individual resources.

5

WHO SURVIVES IN SCIENCE?

The comparisons of predictive models for young women and young men gave us some insight into the role that gender plays in affecting experiences in science. Now we shall limit our attention to young women. Given their greater amount of lost talent (in two of the three areas of science) and lesser chances of success (in two of the three areas of science) relative to young men, what are the important variables in predicting successful science experiences for young women? Alternatively, which variables are important in predicting lost talent among young women? Thus, the first goal of this chapter is to use causal models to describe the kinds of resources (or resource deficits) that lead to the development of female science talent and to the loss of female science talent.

The second goal of this chapter is to provide insight into the science experiences of different groups of women. Gender is not the only social status that is related to science experiences. Access to important resources necessary for success in science varies by race and social class as well. It is impossible to talk about women's science experiences without recognizing these variations. Thus this chapter concludes with an examination of the science resources and science experiences (and the relation between them) of young women with different racial and social class characteristics.

Table 5-1 presents results from three of the logistic regression equations in each area of science for young women. Given the large number of resources that are taken into account, or controlled, in these models, we can conclude with considerable confidence that a causal relationship exits when a particular resource continues to be significant in predicting the odds of following one or another science trajectory. What can we conclude about the causal process behind the science experiences of young women? Several general patterns are clear. First, as we noted in

(Text continued on page 152)

TABLE 5-1 Logistic Regression Results for Females' Odds of Experiencing Various Science Trajectories Versus Being Out of the Sciences (HSB Sophomore Cohort)*

INDEPENDENT VARIABLES	ACHIEVEMENT		
	In and Out, Out 1986	*Left After 1980*	*In Throughout*
Demographic			
1980			
Rural Residence			
(1 = Yes; 0 = No)			
Race—African American			
(1 = African American; 0 = Other)	2.14 (.26)†	1.65 (1.53)	31.63 (1.72)†
Race—Hispanic			
(1 = Hispanic; 0 = Other)			
Family			
1980			
SES Quartile	1.54 (.08)†	.93 (.26)	2.29 (.51)†
Number of Siblings			
Father Lives in Household			
(1 = True; 0 = False)			
Mother Worked When Respondent Was in Elementary School			
(1 = True; 0 = False)	.90 (.15)	.82 (.45)	.29 (.72)
Mother's Occupation			
(1 = Technical, managerial, professional; 0 = Other)	1.59 (.18)†	2.38 (.56)	2.06 (.86)
Mother's Education			
(1 = At least some college; 0 = Other)			
Father's Occupation			
(1 = Technical, managerial, professional; 0 = Other)	1.52 (.19)†	3.93 (.57)†	2.79 (1.03)
Father's Education			
(1 = At least some college; 0 = Other)			
Mother Monitors Schoolwork			
(1 = Yes; 0 = No)	1.42 (.25)	.92 (.72)	2.33 (1.20)
Father Monitors Schoolwork			
(1 = Yes; 0 = No)	1.23 (.18)	.92 (.54)	2.11 (.96)
Mother's Educational Expectations			
(1 = College education or more; 0 = Other)			
Pocket Calculator in Home			
(1 = True; 0 = False)			
1984			
Ever Married			
(1 = Yes; 0 = No)	.23 (.16)†	.42 (.44)†	.01 (1.05)†
Had Child			
(1 = Yes; 0 = No)			

148

ACCESS			ATTITUDES		
In and Out, Out 1986	*Left After 1980*	*In Throughout*	*In and Out, Out 1984*	*Left After 1980*	*In Throughout*
1.08 (.26)	.85 (.40)	.23 (1.09)	.24 (1.17)	.57 (.31)	.00 (3.79)†
4.74 (.68)†	.71 (1.34)	1.26 (2.35)	.03 (4.93)	.70 (.71)	.04 (5.75)
.61 (.54)	.95 (.79)	.05 (2.59)	.07 (3.02)	.32 (.68)	1.16 (5.01)
1.33 (.22)	.65 (.31)	6.18 (1.03)	.88 (.81)	.80 (.22)	.00 (3.59)
.98 (.09)	.85 (.13)	1.87 (.37)	1.17 (.29)	1.08 (.09)	.79 (1.19)
1.96 (.39)	2.31 (.59)	.59 (1.76)	1.04 (1.89)	2.27 (.44)	179.28 (5.45)
1.08 (.27)	1.60 (.41)	2.81 (1.24)	.52 (1.01)	1.66 (.30)	184.94 (3.12)
.76 (.32)	.45 (.53)	.53 (1.23)	.12 (1.15)	.70 (.36)	5.15 (3.19)
.62 (.33)	.84 (.55)	.34 (1.43)	30.06 (1.43)†	1.19 (.38)	21.11 (3.97)
.66 (.32)	1.11 (.50)	.02 (1.81)†	1.96 (1.10)	.67 (.36)	468.31 (5.91)
1.00 (.30)	1.67 (.46)	1.04 (1.26)	.04 (1.51)†	1.56 (.37)	5.13 (4.11)
3.95 (.65)†	.41 (.89)	2.67 (2.00)	.00 (2.51)†	13.93 (1.06)†	.00 (5.57)†
.90 (.36)	6.91 (.86)†	.40 (1.70)	97.17 (1.96)†	.82 (.46)	2968.25 (4.89)
2.10 (.42)	1.78 (.51)	73.21 (2.62)	2.17 (1.34)	.66 (.49)	.00 (6.29)
.73 (.41)	.43 (.57)	2.93 (1.83)	14.52 (2.35)	1.26 (.48)	213132 (6.79)
.57 (.48)	4.38 (.52)†	.08 (3.60)	1.82 (1.60)	2.22 (.46)	.00 (82.88)
1.77 (.82)	2.51 (.79)	.02 (117.14)	.16 (2.50)	.44 (.72)	5.72 (159.43)

(continued on next page)

TABLE 5-1 *(continued)*

INDEPENDENT VARIABLES	ACHIEVEMENT		
	In and Out, Out 1986	Left After 1980	In Throughout

School

1980

School Type
  (1 = Private; 0 = Public) | 1.53 (.26) | 4.84 (.86) | 3.70 (1.20)
Program
  (1 = Academic; 0 = Other) | 1.71 (.16)† | .48 (.56) | 2.95 (.78)
Rate School on Teacher Interest in Students
  (1 = Good, excellent; 0 = Poor, fair)
Friends' Educational Behavior Scale
  (4 = High; 0 = Low) | 1.29 (.07)† | .65 (20)† | .57 (.47)
Friends' Feelings About Students with Good Grades
  (1 = Think well of; 0 = Other)

Individual

1980

Self-Concept Scale	.93 (.10)	1.03 (.32)	1.29 (.58)
Locus of Control Scale	1.03 (.12)	1.10 (.42)	.22 (.82)
Sex-Role Attitudes			
• Working Mother Is a Good Mother			
(1 = Agree; 0 = Disagree)	1.02 (.17)	1.37 (.54)	1.76 (.88)
• Man Should Achieve, Woman Keep House			
(1 = Disagree; 0 = Agree)			
• Woman Is Happiest in Home			
(1 = Disagree; 0 = Agree)			
Popular			
(1 = Very; 0 = Somewhat or not at all)			
Amount of Dating			
(1 = Almost every day or every day; 0 = Other)	1.02 (.32)	1.92 (.65)	.04 (1.91)
Age Expect to Get Married			
Age Expect to Have First Child			
Interested in School			
(1 = True; 0 = False)			
High School Grades			
(1 = A's or B's; 0 = B's or less)			
Standardized Math Score	1.04 (.01)†	1.31 (.04)†	1.79 (.11)†
Standardized Science Score	1.05 (.01)†	1.35 (.05)†	1.44 (.08)†
Time on Homework per Week			
(1 = 3+ hours; 0 = Other)			
Educational Expectations			
(1 = College degree or more; 0 = Other)			
Educational Aspirations			
(1 = Disappointed if don't go to college; 0 = Other)			

150

ACCESS			ATTITUDES		
In and Out, Out 1986	*Left After 1980*	*In Throughout*	*In and Out, Out 1984*	*Left After 1980*	*In Throughout*
2.27 (.36)†	.78 (.62)	4.89 (1.47)	.82 (1.13)	.40 (.46)†	.04 (2.64)
1.04 (.25)	1.94 (.38)	.69 (1.35)	1.42 (.97)	1.02 (.31)	.13 (2.48)
.64 (.27)	.68 (.41)	.53 (1.15)	.52 (.98)	1.33 (.32)	1.11 (2.39)
1.25 (.17)	1.01 (.22)	.97 (.69)	.26 (.59)†	1.29 (.20)	2.44 (2.69)
.66 (.25)	.73 (.38)	1.43 (1.03)	1.35 (.99)	1.38 (.28)	5.43 (3.44)
.61 (.22)†	1.19 (.28)	.63 (.81)	.15 (.89)†	.99 (.23)	.01 (2.92)
.49 (.28)†	1.64 (.41)	.12 (1.03)†	.71 (1.19)	.84 (.31)	48.65 (2.92)
.76 (.35)	1.12 (.53)	.29 (1.16)	3.30 (1.19)	.85 (.41)	7.81 (2.92)
1.08 (.36)	.27 (.64)	.41 (1.65)	10.56 (1.23)	1.71 (.37)	4.65 (3.97)
3.45 (.41)†	.92 (.75)	2.07 (1.43)	4.05 (1.59)	.81 (.44)	.05 (3.92)
.91 (.37)	.27 (.50)	1.02 (1.67)	.51 (1.55)	1.03 (.43)	.70 (4.91)
.70 (.66)	2.59 (1.01)	2.21 (3.64)	.00 (41.52)	4.26 (.65)†	267,830.20 (9.82)
.95 (.09)	1.30 (.12)†	1.28 (.39)	.72 (.26)	1.05 (.09)	1.58 (.73)
1.04 (.09)	1.02 (.11)	1.01 (.35)	1.43 (.23)	.94 (.09)	1.54 (1.21)
1.47 (.36)	5.14 (.67)†	5.01 (1.93)	5.81 (1.65)	2.51 (.47)†	.10 (4.69)
.93 (.30)	.90 (.48)	1.02 (1.67)	7.03 (1.22)	.26 (.37)†	53.72 (3.66)
.94 (.03)†	.94 (.05)	1.09 (.15)	.97 (.11)	.96 (.03)	.77 (.46)
.95 (.03)†	.95 (.04)	7.84 (.14)	1.16 (.11)	.93 (.03)†	1.17 (.30)
.96 (.27)	3.26 (.48)†	13.94 (1.70)	5.17 (1.22)	.95 (.33)	5.59 (2.77)
1.02 (.44)	1.21 (.61)	.44 (2.52)	5.60 (1.50)	3.60 (.51)†	7,133.40 (8.25)
1.57 (.34)	2.03 (.51)	1023.88 (3.67)	1.44 (1.41)	.39 (.40)†	.03 (4.96)

(continued on next page)

TABLE 5-1   *(continued)*

INDEPENDENT VARIABLES	ACHIEVEMENT		
	In and Out, Out 1986	*Left After 1980*	*In Throughout*
Individual *(continued)*			
1980 *(continued)*			
Occupational Expectations			
(1 = Professional Job; 0 = Other)			
Math/Science Access Factor Score	1.23 (.06)†	1.37 (.17)	1.75 (.29)
Math/Science Achievement Factor Score			
Math/Science Attitude Factor Score	1.11 (.04)†	1.22 (.13)	1.83 (.24)†
1982			
Math/Science Access Factor Score			
Math/Science Achievement Factor Score			
Math/Science Attitude Factor Score			
1984			
Math/Science Access Factor Score			
Math/Science Achievement Factor Score			
Math/Science Attitude Factor Score			
1986			
Math/Science Access Factor Score			
Math/Science Achievement Factor Score			
Model Chi Square (*df*)	560 (19)†	287 (19)†	749 (19)†

* Coefficients are antilogs of logistic coefficients. Standard errors are in parentheses.
† Significant at ≤05.

our comparison of male and female models, young African American women are *more* likely than other young women to have a number of experiences in the science achievement and access pipelines. Race has no effect on experiences in science attitudes. Thus, even though some of the African American women's experiences in the sciences are not continuous, the bottom line is that they are more likely than other women to have at least some science experiences.

A second general conclusion that can be made about the causal process behind women's science experiences is that the nature of the process varies with the area of science that is being examined. Of the many resources considered, only standardized science scores have a significant effect on science experiences in each of the areas, and even then, the nature of the effect varies. High science scores increase the odds of being in each of the three science achievement trajectories examined, but they reduce the chances of being in certain access and attitude trajectories that end up out of the sciences.

| | ACCESS | | | ATTITUDES | | |
	In and Out, Out 1986	Left After 1980	In Throughout	In and Out, Out 1984	Left After 1980	In Throughout
	.99 (.29)	.94 (.44)	5.28 (1.42)	.29 (1.18)	6.48 (.30)†	4.50E +09 (10.00)†
				1.29 (.40)	.76 (.13)†	1.03 (1.25)
	3.31 (.43)†	2.37 (.70)	9.90 (2.33)	.09 (1.45)	3.58 (.48)†	2.87 (5.93)
	1.06 (.08)	.96 (.15)	1.44 (.51)			
				1.47 (.73)	1.53 (.15)†	11.76 (1.82)
	1.36 (.19)	1.11 (.30)	2.95 (.81)	10.64 (.95)†	1.26 (.21)	.21 (2.90)
	1.04 (.16)	1.36 (.25)	18.40 (.84)†			
				2.21 (.73)	1.36 (.19)	33.04 (1.81)†
	8.59 (.48)†	2.09 (.39)	1778.02 (22.25)	.94 (1.21)	1.46 (.32)	22,820.66 (36.39)
	1.18 (.17)	1.04 (.27)	1.98 (.74)			
				.24 (.93)	1.78 (.19)	1.98 (1.79)
	.80 (.17)	.48 (.32)†	1.63 (.38)	.79 (.49)	1.09 (.17)	.38 (1.93)
	208 (46)†	116 (46)†	404 (19)†	116 (47)†	183 (47)†	273 (47)†

Another important trend shown in Table 5-1 is that in the area of science achievement, resources often have a significant—and usually similar—effect in more than one of the trajectory equations. However, for the science access and attitude trajectories, there is usually a distinct group of resources that significantly predict the odds of being in the various trajectories.

Science Achievement

The first three columns in Table 5-1 are for models predicting experiences in science achievement. Patterns of significance show that it is a mix of demographic, family, school, and individual variables that are important for science achievement experiences. It is no surprise that race and class are significant predictors of young women's persistence in science achievement. It is also no surprise that it is upper SES women who have an advantage over lower SES women. However, the surprising finding here (but one that was noted earlier) is that young African American women with equal resources are *more* likely than other women to stay in the science achievement pipeline (as opposed to staying out) throughout the six-year period.

Other than social class, none of the other resources in the young women's family of orientation has a significant impact on their chances of staying in the area of science achievement throughout the six-year period. However, young women who form their own families at an earlier age significantly reduce their chances of staying in science achievement. Three individual resources also have a significant causal impact on these chances: young women who score high on the standardized math and science exams and on the 1980 science attitude factor also have significantly higher chances of staying in the science achievement pipeline. Interestingly, the access factors are not related to these chances. Thus, for young women, course taking is not related to staying in the achievement pipeline.

Which young women are more likely to leave the science achievement pipeline after showing early signs of talent? Having a father with a higher status occupation and avoiding early marriage are associated with both an early exit from science achievement and an in-and-out pattern leading to an exit by 1986. In addition, African American women and those from higher SES families are more likely to follow this in-and-out trajectory than they are to stay out.

Interestingly, having friends at school who value education *decreases* the chance of having an early exit but *increases* the chance of the in-and-out pattern (as does being in an academic program). The only individual resources that significantly predict lost talent in science achievement include standardized math and science scores and science access and attitude factor scores. Young women who score higher on these measures are more likely than other young women to have spent some time (as opposed to no time) in the sciences, but they did not stay in.

Science Access

Very few resources significantly predict whether a young woman will maintain access to science throughout the survey period (the same is true for the total sample and for young men). Surprisingly, having a father with a higher status occupation and having a greater internal locus of control significantly *reduce* the chances that a young woman will stay in (as opposed to out) of the access pipeline. Higher math/science achievement factor scores in 1982 increase the chances of staying in the access pipeline. Thus, science achievement affects later access, but not vice versa. The popular notion has always been that it is course taking that brings about high achievement in science. These results question that notion. Here we find that when science trajectories are examined (as opposed to the traditional focus on achievement or course taking at one point in time), taking science courses does not guarantee that young women will have high achievement in science. However, when young women have high achievement, they increase their odds of staying in science courses.

A larger number of resources are significant in the equations predicting exits from science access. Fathers who monitor homework, higher expected age at marriage, an interest in school, and a greater amount of time spent on homework are all resources that increase young women's chances of being in science in 1980 but exiting after 1980. A higher math/science achievement factor score decreases these chances. It is interesting to look at the relation between resources and early exits because here we are predicting something that has an ambiguous value. That is, it is better to have been in the sciences for at least some time than not at all. On the other hand, it is unfortunate when young women show early promise in an area of science that remains unfulfilled.

Table 5-1 shows that being African American, having a mother who monitors homework, attending a private school, having progressive attitudes about women's place in the home, and high math/science achievement factor scores increase a young woman's chances of being in the in-and-out trajectory that ends up out of the science access pipeline. High self-concept, locus of control, and math and science scores *reduce* these chances.

Science Attitudes

The last three columns in Table 5-1 present information on resources that predict experiences for young women in the science attitude pipeline. The first finding of interest here is the fact that the resources that are important predictors are very different in the equation predicting odds of an in-and-out trajectory versus the equation predicting an early exit. It is disproportionately family resources that predict the former and individual resources that predict the latter.

The resources that increase the odds of an in-and-out trajectory ending up out of the area of science attitude (as opposed to staying out) include a mother with more education, a father who monitors homework, and a high score on the 1980 math/science achievement factor. Resources that decrease the odds of being in this trajectory include a father with more education, a mother who monitors homework, friends who place a high value on education, and a high self-concept.

These patterns provide insight into the nature of the causal mechanisms at work when comparing young women who show signs of talent but eventually exit the sciences (in any area) and those who never show signs of talent and stay out. The "lost talent" group shows a mix of resources that do not always work in a positive way for them. In other words, they do not consistently have certain advantages over those who stay out. This is part of the explanation for their exit. When comparing the group of women who stay in the sciences to those who stay out, these anomalies are much less likely to occur. That is, the reason they are able to stay in is that they consistently have resources that act to keep them in.

When predicting early exits from the area of science attitude, it is mothers who monitor homework, a greater amount of dating, interest in school, high educational and occupational expectations, and higher math/science achievement and attitude factor scores in 1980 that increase the odds of being in this trajectory. Resources that decrease the odds include enrollment in a private school, high grades and standardized science scores, high educational aspirations, and a high math/science access factor score in 1980. Remember the comparison groups here. Neither group had much experience with science attitudes. We are looking at the odds of an early exit as compared to never being in this area. Thus the fact that young girls in private schools or those with high grades have a lower chance of being in this area makes more sense in this light, for they are more likely to have never had positive attitudes about science than to have had them and then lowered them.

Very few resources significantly predict the odds of a young woman staying in the science attitude area as opposed to staying out. High occupational expectations and a high score on the math/science access factor score in 1984 increase these odds. Rural residence and a mother who monitors schoolwork decrease these odds.

The findings in Table 5-1 give us some sense of the critical resources that predict young women's experiences in science. However, to understand this process fully, we must consider the possibility that unique causal processes exist for groups of women who vary on two key characteristics—race and class.

Race and Class Variations in Science Resources and Success

RESOURCES.   Are some women better equipped than others for success in science by virtue of larger amounts of critical resources? Table 5-2 provides the information necessary to answer this question. Consider family resources, for example. There are significant differences between race

(Text continued on page 161)

TABLE 5-2 Means (and Standard Deviations) for Females' Family, School, and Individual Resources, by Race and Class (HSB Sophomore Cohort)

	RACE		CLASS	
	African American	*Other*	*Lower SES*	*Upper SES*
Demographic Characteristics				
1980				
Rural Residence				
(1 = Yes; 0 = No)	.21 (.41)*	.33 (.47)*	.37 (.48)*	.27 (.44)*
Race—African American				
(1 = African American;				
0 = Other)			.16 (.37)*	.06 (.24)*
Race—Hispanic				
(1 = Hispanic; 0 = Other)			.16 (.37)*	.07 (.26)*
Family Resources				
1980				
SES Quartile	1.73 (.78)*	2.54 (1.11)*		
Number of Siblings	3.52 (1.87)*	2.88 (1.73)*	.03 (.18)*	.09 (.28)*
Father Living In Household				
(1 = True; 0 = False)	.46 (.50)*	.76 (.43)*	.90 (.30)*	.93 (.26)*
Mother Worked When				
Respondent Was in				
Elementary School				
(1 = True; 0 = False)	.80 (.40)*	.61 (.49)*	.64 (.48)*	.62 (.49)*
Mother's Occupation				
(1 = Technical, managerial,				
professional; 0 = Other)	.26 (.44)	.24 (.43)	.16 (.36)*	.34 (.47)*
Mother's Education				
(1 = At least some college;				
0 = Other)	.24 (.42)	.26 (.44)	.06 (.23)*	.48 (.50)*
Father's Occupation				
(1 = Technical, managerial,				
professional; 0 = Other)	.11 (.31)*	.31 (.46)*	.06 (.23)*	.55 (.50)*
Father's Education				
(1 = At least some college;				
0 = Other)	.32 (.47)	.33 (.47)	.16 (.36)*	.53 (.50)*
Mother Monitors Schoolwork				
(1 = Yes; 0 = No)	.89 (.31)	.89 (.32)	.87 (.34)	.91 (.29)*
Father Monitors Schoolwork				
(1 = Yes; 0 = No)	.64 (.48)*	.77 (.42)*	.68 (.47)	.84 (.37)*
Mother's Educational				
Expectations				

(continued on next page)

TABLE 5-2 *(continued)*

	RACE		*CLASS*	
	African American	*Other*	*Lower SES*	*Upper SES*

Family Resources (continued)

1980 (continued)

(1 = College education or
more; 0 = Other) .69 (.46)* .59 (.50)* .45 (.50) .72 (.45)*

Pocket Calculator in Home
(1 = True; 0 = False) .61 (.49)* .80 (.40)* .67 (.47) .91 (.29)*

1982

Mother Keeps Track of Progress
in School
(1 = True; 0 = False) .90 (.29)* .87 (.33)* .86 (.35)* .90 (.31)*

Father Keeps Track of Progress
in School
(1 = True; 0 = False) .64 (.48)* .76 (.54)* .68 (.47)* .81 (.39)*

Parents Know Where Student Is,
What Student Does
(1 = True; 0 = False) .77 (.42)* .87 (.34)* .85 (.36)* .88 (.33)*

How often Parents Attend
PTA Meetings
(1 = Never; 2 = Once in
while; 3 = Often) 1.41 (.62)* 1.23 (.51)* 1.21 (.49)* 1.28 (.59)

How Often Parents Attend
Parent-Teacher Conference
(1 = Never; 2 = Once in
while; 3 = Often) 1.48 (.65) 1.47 (.64) 1.44 (.62)* 1.50 (.66)*

1994

Ever Married
(1 = Yes; 0 = No) .08 (.27)* .23 (.42)* .26 (.44)* .14 (.35)*

Had Child
(1 = Yes; 0 = No) .26 (.44)* .16 (.36)* .22 (.42)* .09 (.29)*

School Resources

1980

School Type
(1 = Private; 0 = Public) .04 (.18)* .11 (.31)* .06 (.24)* .15 (.36)*

Program
(1 = Academic; 0 = Other) .28 (.45)* .35 (.48)* .22 (.41)* .49 (.50)*

Percent of Teachers Considered
Excellent[P] 25.85 (16.87) 27.95 (18.03) 26.15 (16.78)* 29.58 (18.99)*

Teacher Influence on
Curriculum, Content, and
Teaching Techniques[T]

TABLE 5-2 *(continued)*

	RACE		CLASS	
	African American	*Other*	*Lower SES*	*Upper SES*

School Resources

1980

(Scale from low to high: 3 to 18)	12.86 (2.88)*	14.04 (2.47)*	13.59 (2.66)*	14.27 (2.33)*
Percent of Class Time Teachers Spend on Instruction^T				
$(1 = 0–2; 9 = 31+)$	8.25 (1.96)*	8.63 (1.39)*	8.55 (1.55)	8.66 (1.32)
Percent Female Teachers in Sample^T	.59 (.49)*	.47 (.50)*	.50 (.50)	.46 (.50)
Teachers' Education^T				
$(1 = $ High School; $8 = $ Doctorate)	5.60 (.98)*	5.47 (.90)*	5.52 (.95)	5.46 (.85)
Female Math/Science Teacher in Sample^T				
$(1 = $ Yes; $0 = $ No)	.15 (.36)	.13 (.34)	.16 (.36)*	.10 (.31)*
Number of Years of Math Required for Graduation^P	1.81 (.62)*	1.59 (.72)*	1.60 (.66)	1.62 (.75)
Number of Years of Science Required for Graduation^P	1.60 (.62)*	1.43 (.64)*	1.45 (.60)	1.43 (.67)
Rate School on Teacher Interest in Students				
$(1 = $ Good, excellent; $0 = $ Poor, fair)	.52 (.50)	.55 (.50)	.51 (.50)*	.58 (.49)*
Closest Sophomore Friend at School				
· Gets Good Grades				
$(1 = $ True; $0 = $ False)	.84 (.37)	.84 (.37)	.80 (.40)*	.84 (.37)*
· Is Interested in School				
$(1 = $ True; $0 = $ False)	.69 (.46)*	.78 (.42)*	.64 (.48)*	.68 (.47)*
· Attends Classes Regularly				
$(1 = $ True; $0 = $ False)	.93 (.26)	.90 (.30)	.90 (.30)*	.92 (.27)*
· Plans to Go to College				
$(1 = $ True; $0 = $ False)	.72 (.45)*	.67 (.47)*	.51 (.50)*	.65 (.48)*
Friends' Feelings About Students with Good Grades				
$(1 = $ Thinks well of; $0 = $ Other)	.43 (.50)*	.38 (.49)*	.37 (.48)	.36 (.48)
Program				
$(1 = $ Academic; $0 = $ Other)	.31 (.46)*	.40 (.49)*	.26 (.44)*	.54 (.50)*
Rate School on Teacher Interest in Students				

(continued on next page)

TABLE 5-2 *(continued)*

	RACE		CLASS	
	African American	*Other*	*Lower SES*	*Upper SES*

School Resources (continued)

1980 *(continued)*

(1 = Good, excellent;				
0 = Poor, fair)	.54 (.50)*	.64 (.48)*	.59 (.49)*	.66 (.47)*
Closest Senior Friend at School				
• Gets Good Grades				
(1 = True; 0 = False)	.88 (.32)*	.91 (.29)*	.86 (.34)*	.90 (.30)*
• Is Interested in School				
(1 = True; 0 = False)	.86 (.35)*	.73 (.45)*	.70 (.46)	.71 (.45)
• Attends Classes Regularly				
(1 = True; 0 = False)	.96 (.19)*	.93 (.26)*	.91 (.28)	.92 (.27)
• Plans to Go to College				
(1 = True; 0 = False)	.77 (.42)*	.73 (.44)*	.59 (.49)*	.70 (.46)*

Individual Resources

1980

Self-Concept Scale	−.18 (.70)*	.12 (.73)*	.15 (.76)*	−.00 (.69)*
Locus of Control Scale	−.08 (.66)*	.07 (.63)*	−.07 (.63)*	.22 (.58)*
Work Orientation Scale	.06 (.66)*	−.12 (.70)*	−.11 (.69)*	−.06 (.66)*
Family Orientation Scale	−.18 (.64)*	.05 (.60)*	.00 (.63)*	.06 (.59)*
Sex-Role Attitudes				
• Working Mother Is a				
Good Mother				
(1 = Agree;				
0 = Disagree)	.31 (.46)*	.20 (.40)*	.21 (.41)	.21 (.21)
• Man Should Achieve,				
Woman Keep House				
(1 = Disagree; 0 = Agree)	.20 (.40)	.17 (.38)	.14 (.35)*	.22 (.42)*
• Woman Is Happiest in Home				
(1 = Disagree; 0 = Agree)	.11 (.31)	.12 (.32)	.09 (.28)*	.16 (.37)*
Popular				
(1 = Very; 0 = Somewhat				
or not at all)	.75 (.43)	.78 (.42)	.73 (.44)*	.82 (.38)*
Amount of Dating				
(1 = Almost every day				
or every day; 0 = Other)	.04 (.19)*	.06 (.24)*	.06 (.23)	.05 (.23)
Age Expect to Get Married	24.58 (3.79)*	22.58 (3.13)*	22.51 (3.42)*	23.08 (3.00)*
Age Expect to Have First Child	24.97 (4.04)*	24.60 (3.15)*	24.28 (3.40)*	25.02 (2.99)*
Interested in School				
(1 = True; 0 = False)	.84 (.36)*	.78 (.42)*	.77 (.42)*	.81 (.39)*
High School Grades				
(1 = A's or B's; 0 = B's				
or less)	.21 (.40)*	.34 (.47)*	.32 (.47)*	.44 (.50)*

TABLE 5-2 *(continued)*

	RACE		CLASS	
	African American	*Other*	*Lower SES*	*Upper SES*
Individual Resources *(continued)*				
1980 *(continued)*				
Standardized Math Score	42.42 (7.80)*	49.31 (9.41)*	45.98 (8.90)*	51.77 (9.20)*
Standardized Science Score	41.17 (7.83)*	49.93 (9.20))*	46.86 (9.10)*	51.84 (8.95)*
Time on Homework per Week				
(1 = 3+ hours; 0 = Other)	.50 (.50)*	.59 (.49)*	.53 (.50)*	.66 (.47)*
Educational Expectations				
(1 = College degree or more;				
0 = Other)	.45 (.50)	.41 (.49)	.28 (.45)*	.58 (.49)*
Educational Aspirations				
(1 = Disappointed if don't				
go to College; 0 = Other)	.80 (.40)*	.64 (.48)*	.58 (.49)*	.76 (.43)*
Occupational Expectations				
(1 = Professional job;				
0 = Other)	.38 (.49)	.39 (.49)	.30 (.46)*	.51 (.50)*
1982				
Interested in School				
(1 = True; 0 = False)	.86 (.35)*	.78 (.41)*	.78 (.42)*	.81 (.39)*
High School Grades				
(1 = A's or A's & B's; 0 = B's				
or less)	.25 (.43)*	.40 (.49)*	.32 (.47)*	.44 (.50)*
Time on Homework per Week				
(1 = 5+ hours; 0 = Other)	.31 (.46)*	.37 (.48)*	.31 (.46)*	.42 (.49)*

* T-Test is significant at .05 level.
[T] Item is from Teacher Survey.
[P] Item is from Principal Survey.

and class subgroups on a majority of these resources. In the case of class contrasts, there are significant differences between upper SES and lower SES women on each of the family resources, and these invariably are in the direction of upper SES women having more family resources. (Some but not all of these resources will be higher, by definition, in the upper SES group given the items used to measure SES. For more information on this measure, see the Appendix.) Not only do the upper SES women have parents with more education and higher occupational status, but their parents have higher expectations for their children and are more involved in their academic and social lives. In addition, upper SES women are about half as likely as lower SES women to marry or have a child early.

Although a majority of the race contrasts on family resources show an advantage for non–African American women, this is not the case in all situations. Women who are not African American do come from higher SES families, and have fathers who have higher job status and who are more likely to be living in the home. Their fathers are also more likely to monitor their progress in school, and both their parents tend to know more about the student's whereabouts and activities. These women are also more likely to have a calculator in the home and to have fewer siblings, and are less likely to have a child early. However, African American woman do have the advantage on a number of family resources, and most of these have to do with their mothers. Their mothers were more likely than other mothers to work when the daughter was in elementary school, thus perhaps providing a positive role model. In addition, these mothers have significantly higher educational expectations for their daughters and are more likely than other mothers to keep track of their children's progress in school. Finally, even though young African American women are more likely than other women to have a child at an early age, they are *less* likely to marry at an early age.

Earlier we discovered that gender often worked through individual resources to affect science experiences. Do women in different race and class groups vary in the extent to which they have these important individual resources? Table 5-2 suggests that there are differences and that they are considerable. These data also give additional insight into how young African American women, but not lower SES women, sometimes beat the odds and succeed in the white male domain of science.

Consider class differences in individual resources among young women. Although lower SES women do have a significantly higher self-concept than do upper SES women, they score lower on other personality scales (such as locus of control and work orientation), hold more conservative sex-role attitudes, expect to enter family roles earlier, are less interested in school, get poorer grades and standardized test scores, spend less time on homework, and have lower educational expectations. One of the most striking class differences involves these expectations. Over twice as many young women from upper SES homes (58%) as from lower SES homes (28%) expect to get a college degree or more.

Consider now the information on race differences in individual resources among young women. Here we see that, even more so than in other areas of resources, young African American women sometimes prevail over other women. It is true that non–African American women have a higher self-concept, locus of control, and work orientation. They also spend more time on homework and have higher grades and standardized math and science scores. However, young African American women have a lower orientation toward family and more liberal sex-role attitudes (recall their greater tendency to have working mothers). They date less and expect to marry and have children at later ages (even though, as we observed above, they actually have children earlier). Finally, and perhaps most unexpectedly, they express a greater interest in school than do other young women. Note that a good number of the items on which African American women show deficits in individual resources involve behaviors (e.g., grades, time spent on homework, standardized test scores). When these young women have the advantage, it often involves attitudes. And there are no race differences on some attitudes (e.g., educational expectations).

The final set of resources that is compared across class and race groups in Table 5-2 is school resources. It is not surprising that the litany of deficits associated with being a young girl from a lower SES background continues here. Young women from upper SES backgrounds are over twice as likely as those from lower SES backgrounds to be attending a private school and to be in an academic program. They are also more likely to have teachers who are considered excellent, who are viewed as being interested in the students, and who have influence on curriculum, content, and teaching techniques in the classroom. The upper SES women have an additional advantage at school that goes beyond programs and teachers. They are more likely than other young women to have school friends who get good grades, are interested in school, attend classes regularly, and plan to go to college. Lower SES women do, however, have one advantage over their upper SES counterparts. The sample of math and science teachers from their schools was more likely than the sample from the upper SES women's schools to include a female math or science teacher.

Differences by race in school resources provide some additional insights into our earlier finding that young African American women sometimes do better in science than other women. Table 5-2 shows that non–African American women *are* more likely than African American women to be in private schools (almost three times more likely) and academic programs. Their teachers are more likely to have influence over what happens in the classroom and to spend a greater amount of class time on instruction. But this is where the clear advantage stops. Young African American women are more likely to have female teachers in their school sample, and their teachers in general tend to have more education. In addition, the schools that they attend require more math and science for graduation. Some differences in school peer groups favor non–African American girls and some favor African American girls. In their sophomore year, non–African American girls are more likely to have friends who are interested in school, but African American girls are more likely to have friends who plan to go to college and who think well of students with good grades. In their senior year of high school, non–African American girls are more likely to have friends who get good grades, but the young African American girls are more likely to have friends who are interested in school, attend classes regularly, and plan to go to college.

SCIENCE TRAJECTORIES.   To what extent do women's experiences in science over time vary with their race and social class? Table 5-3 shows the percent of women in race and class subgroups who followed the various science trajectories in achievement, access, and attitudes. A quick look at this table suggests that—once again—class, but not race, is related to science experiences in a simple, straightforward manner. Regardless of the aspect of science, lower SES women are much more likely than upper SES women to stay out of the science pipeline throughout the six-year period. The most extreme contrast is in the area of science achievement, where almost three times as many lower SES (43%) as upper SES (15%) women never enter the science pipeline. Conversely, upper SES women are more likely to be in each of the areas of science

TABLE 5-3   Over-Time Experiences (Trajectories) in the Sciences for Subgroups of Women (HSB Sophomore Cohort)*

TRAJECTORY	*ACHIEVEMENT*			
	Race		*SES*	
	African American	*Other*	*Lower*	*Upper*
Out Throughout	35.2%	29.4%	42.6%	14.7%
In and Out, Out 1986	40.8%	34.5%	30.4%	41.4%
Left After 1980	.4%	2.4%	2.8%	1.5%
Left After 1982	.2%	1.0%	.7%	1.1%
Left After 1984	1.1%	8.9%	4.3%	12.3%
In 1986, but Not Throughout	21.6%	18.8%	17.0%	21.7%
In Throughout	.7%	5.0%	2.1%	7.2%
N	679	4550	2623	2406

* Trajectories for Activities are not presented since there were insufficient measures at some time points.

† Given the small number of attitudes measured in the 1986 survey, attitude trajectories are created for 1980–84. Some categories change, e.g.: "in 1986, but not throughout," should be "in 1984, but not throughout," and should be "in and out, out 1984."

throughout the survey period. Again, the greatest contrasts are in the area of science achievement. Over three times as many upper SES women as lower SES women stay in the science achievement pipeline (7% versus 2%). It is this area that the upper SES women are least likely to stay out of and the most likely to be in. Lower SES women are also least likely to stay out of achievement than other areas, but they are almost equally unlikely to stay *in* any of the three areas.

Although upper SES women are more likely than lower SES women to be in the sciences, the loss of talented young women from the sciences is also greater in this group. Upper SES women are more likely than lower SES women to have entered science and left it—especially in the areas of achievement and access.

Throughout this research, unexpected findings on the situation of young African American women in science have been revealed. The trajectory information in Table 5-3 reveals even more insight into race and science. Earlier, in a descriptive analysis of the science pipeline, we saw that young African American women are overrepresented in the "out throughout" trajectory of the science achievement pipeline but not in the science access and attitude pipelines (Tables 3-2 through 3-4). In our causal analyses, we saw that, when other factors were controlled,

ACCESS				ATTITUDES†			
Race		SES		Race		SES	
African American	Other	Lower	Upper	Arican American	Other	Lower	Upper
41.2%	50.1%	57.9%	39.7%	37.0%	47.0%	56.8%	38.2%
26.4%	20.6%	16.5%	26.1%	3.9%	1.4%	2.0%	1.4%
9.6%	6.7%	8.0%	6.3%	12.4%	12.1%	10.8%	13.2%
2.9%	4.2%	2.8%	5.3%	1.9%	1.9%	1.6%	2.2%
1.6%	4.0%	1.7%	5.8%	1.9%	1.9%	1.6%	2.2%
16.3%	11.2%	11.4%	12.4%	41.0%	33.6%	26.5%	39.7%
2.1%	3.1%	1.8%	4.3%	3.8%	4.1%	2.3%	5.4%
458	3278	1763	1872	366	2998	1400	1910

African American women are more likely than other women to spend time in achievement and access (Table 4-9). Figures in Table 5-3 showing the breakdown of trajectory experiences for African American women and other women confirm the complexities of these earlier findings.

When other resources are not controlled, African American women are more likely than other women to be out of and less likely to be in the science achievement pipeline. Thirty-five percent of African American women but only 29 percent of other women remain out of this area. Less than 1 percent of African American women stay in this area, while over five times as many other women stay in (5%).

There is a different race pattern in access and attitudes. Here African American women are less likely than other women to remain out of these pipelines and as likely (if not slightly more likely) to remain in. There are minimal differences between the two racial groups in the amount of lost talent. However, in all areas of science, African American women are more likely than other women to go in and out of science and to end up out of it altogether.

PREDICTING SUCCESS IN SCIENCE FOR SUBGROUPS OF WOMEN.   The final question to be asked about the different groups of women is whether the causal process leading to success in science varies by subgroup. Table 5-4 presents results that will aid in answering this question. Unfortunately, because the subgroups are small (especially for African American women), logistic regression models could not be used. ANOVA models are more robust and will provide estimates on smaller samples, but they limit the number of resources included as independent variables and tell us nothing about the direction of effects. Nevertheless, ANOVA results in Table 5-4 do provide some useful information.

First consider differences by social class in the models predicting science experiences. Certain resources have similar effects for lower and upper SES women in each of the areas of science. In the science achievement model, this includes resources such as early marriage, friends' value on education, and math and science scores. In the access model, this includes race, early marriage, and attitudes about math and science. Additional variables that have a similar effect in the science attitude model are school program (e.g., academic versus nonacademic) and access to math and science courses. However, each model has a large number of resources that are significant for one SES group but not the other. For example, mother's work status when the young woman was in elementary school affects the science achievement and science attitude experiences of lower but not upper SES women. Having a mother who monitors schoolwork is associated with experiences in the area of science achievement only for upper SES women. Self-concept helps explain the science achievement and science access of upper SES women but not lower SES women. The opposite is true when one is considering science attitudes. Thus these findings suggest that social class interacts with a considerable number of resources in affecting science experiences. Many resources have different effects on success in science depending on the social class of the young woman.

Turning to the ANOVA models for the race subgroups, Table 5-4 shows that, as with social class, the effect of resources on young women's experiences in the sciences often varies with race. Even fewer resources have similar effects for women in the two race subgroups than was the case for women in the class subgroups. And the similarities in process are greatest in the area of science attitudes and smallest in the area of science achievement. Thus we find significant evidence that race and resources interact in their effect on success in science, especially science achievement. Although researchers typically speak in general about how resources affect young women's chances of success in science, our results suggest that these general statements may be misleading when so many of these effects are conditional on the racial identity of the young woman.

The single resource that significantly affects the science achievement trajectory of African American and non–African American women is the value that friends put on education. Marital status and attitudes about math and science significantly affect access trajectories of both groups of young women. Finally, mother's occupation, school program, and access to math and science significantly affect the attitude trajectory that both groups of young women follow.

One of the most intriguing findings presented in Table 5-4 is that when other resources are taken into account, social class (as measured by SES quartile) is significantly related to experiences in each area of science for non–African American women but *not* for African American women. From our earlier analyses we know that when SES has an effect on science experiences, it is invariably a dampening effect. Somehow, young African American women, but not other women, escape the yoke of class. For them, it is other family resources, in addition to school and individual resources, that help predict their success in science. It is the case that although overall SES is not significantly related to the science experiences of young African American women, one element of SES— mother's occupational status—does help predict variations in science attitude trajectories.

Other resources that have a significant impact on the science experiences of non–African American but not African American women in-

TABLE 5-4 ANOVA Coefficients for Models Predicting Science Trajectories for Subgroups of Women (HSB Sophomore Cohort)

INDEPENDENT VARIABLES	ACHIEVEMENT			
	Class		Race	
	Lower SES	Upper SES	African American	Other
Race (1 = African American; 0 = Other)	1.19	.04		
Family				
1980				
SES Quartile			1.36	6.95*
Mother Worked When Respondent Was in Elementary School				
(1 = True; 0 = False)	8.24*	.88	8.12*	2.42
Mother's Occupation				
(1 = Technical, managerial, professional; 0 = Other)	5.11*	1.11	2.77	2.09
Father's Occupation				
(1 = Technical, managerial, professional; 0 = Other)	.59	1.89	.55	6.63*
Mother Monitors Schoolwork				
(1 = Yes; 0 = No)	.17	6.17*	1.10	5.73*
Father Monitors Schoolwork				
(1 = Yes; 0 = No)	.72	.32	5.92*	.49
1984				
Ever Married				
(1 = Yes; 0 = No)	56.00*	29.64*	.57	79.55*
School				
1980				
School Type (1 = Private; 0 = Public)	.06	1.81	.19	1.00
Program (1 = Academic; 0 = Other)	1.54	.90	.44	4.57*
Friends' Educational Behavior Scale†				
(4 = High; 0 = Low)	14.83*	7.45*	3.79*	27.92*
Individual				
1980				
Self-Concept Scale†	.10	3.76*	26.04*	.19
Locus of Control Scale†	.54	.44	3.29	.78
Sex-Role Attitudes†				

ACCESS					ATTITUDES			
Class		Race			Class		Race	
Lower SES	Upper SES	African American	Other		Lower SES	Upper SES	African American	Other
5.06*	8.35*				22.51*	4.16*		
		1.32	6.25*				.46	3.99*
.09	.12	.22	1.11		7.44*	.67	3.30	3.09
.57	.42	.05	1.02		1.35	4.85*	4.15*	4.21*
.00	.15	1.03	.48		.55	5.23*	2.08	4.21*
.75	3.11	.00	.27		.01	.61	2.64	.05
.11	.03	1.40	.01		.20	.26	.00	.06
7.28*	8.12*	5.27*	16.34*		17.95*	4.36*	.59	15.74*
8.75*	.22	.98	4.07*		9.70*	.27	1.80	2.57
3.09	16.15*	.75	19.35*		7.75*	9.37*	15.06*	16.71*
7.26*	.00	2.35	1.16		2.60	.23	.28	.39
1.31	4.56*	.83	6.22*		6.93*	.38	1.71	.63
.64	.15	.08	.26		1.53	8.88*	2.32	8.99*

(continued on next page)

TABLE 5-4   *(continued)*

INDEPENDENT VARIABLES	ACHIEVEMENT			
	Class		*Race*	
	Lower SES	*Upper SES*	*African American*	*Other*
Individual *(continued)*				
1980 *(continued)*				
Working Mother Is a Good Mother				
(1 = Agree; 0 = Disagree)	.02	1.08	1.25	.43
Amount of Dating†				
(1 = Almost every day or every day;				
0 = Other)	3.29	.53	.00	.06
Standardized Math Score†	39.08*	17.33*	.97	58.99*
Standardized Science Score†	22.97*	61.67*	.49	84.89*
Math/Science Achievement Factor Score†				
Math/Science Access Factor Score†	2.86	10.26	2.99	9.70*
Math/Science Attitude Factor Score†	3.18	5.16*	.27	8.65*
F	8.51*	9.04*	3.84*	6.16*

* Significant at ≤ .05.
† Covariate.

clude father's occupational status, mother's monitoring of homework, school program, math and science scores, and math and science access and attitudes in the science achievement model. In the science access model, resources involving school type, school program, self-concept, dating, and achievement in math and science in addition to SES affect the trajectory experiences of non–African American but not African American women. Father's occupation, marital status, and locus of control are the resources that have a significant impact for the former but not for the later group of women in the area of science attitudes.

In this chapter we presented results from a multivariate model that predicted science experiences for young women. We found, first of all, that the important predictors of science experience vary with the area of science being considered. In general the findings show a mix of family, school, and individual resources that predict success in science. Some resources (e.g., sex-role attitudes, locus of control, and self-concept) that were expected to have consistently positive consequences were often not important when other resources were controlled. Other resources such as experiences in other areas of science and scores on standardized

ACCESS				ATTITUDES			
Class		Race		Class		Race	
Lower SES	Upper SES	African American	Other	Lower SES	Upper SES	African American	Other
7.43*	.02	.11	2.63	6.37*	.24	5.45*	.00
.94	2.91	.61	3.75*	2.28	.20	.66	.12
.19	.01	.22	.00	4.54*	2.45	3.71	1.33
.64	3.10	.84	1.29	.54	1.22	1.02	3.11
1.09	13.76*	.00	15.93*	36.17*	45.89*	4.59*	71.47*
				5.71*	.09	.29	.49
42.99*	139.05*	11.22*	152.80*				
4.66*	9.62*	2.33*	10.14*	4.95*	5.07*	3.18*	7.23*

math and science exams had the consistently positive consequences that were expected. A look at the resources and science experiences of groups of women who varied by race and class showed some unexpected findings. Although young women from lower SES families have consistent disadvantages in science resources and experiences, the same is not true for African American women. Sometimes these young women have resource advantages and end up with more positive experiences in science than do other young women.

6

CONCLUSIONS

This research has taken a comprehensive look at the science experiences of young women in the United States. Using several nationally representative, longitudinal data sets, it has focused on multiple aspects of science experience, including achievement, access, attitudes, and activities in both math and science. Science experiences beginning in seventh grade and continuing through the post–high school years have been examined. The emphasis has been on lost talent. The findings support the work of others in showing that young women start out on a par with young men in the science arena but lose ground over time. The goal here was to describe the science experiences of young women and young men at multiple points in time and to follow the young people in order to chart out their science trajectories—their experiences over time in various areas of the sciences. Using this approach it is possible to gauge the extent to which women (especially those who had shown promise) exit from the sciences and when this exiting occurs. It is also possible to understand the reasons for these exits and the unique characteristics of the women who continue on in science.

The explanatory model used here focuses on gender as a causal factor that works independently (e.g., as a result of differential treatment—gender discrimination) as well as indirectly through the different levels of resources available to children on the basis of their gender. In this chapter a brief summary of the major findings of the study and their implications are presented. Throughout the summary, findings are contrasted with results from earlier research on women in science. In some cases these comparisons will provide support for previous research. In other cases the comparisons will question or suggest qualifications on results from other research.

Science Experiences

The first research goal was simply to describe the math and science experiences of young women and men from seventh grade on in the areas of achievement, access, attitudes, and activities.

ACHIEVEMENT. Because few researchers have looked at gender differences in both math and science achievement, it is often concluded that women fall behind men in math and science in the high school years (Oakes, 1990). However, we saw that young women fall behind in science before they fall behind in math. Even in seventh grade, girls score lower than boys on standardized science exams. During this same year there are no significant differences by gender in math scores. By tenth grade, however, girls get lower scores on both standardized math and science exams, and this continues in the final year of high school.

In contrast to conclusions from other researchers (DeBoer, 1984a; Stockard & Wood, 1984), we do not find much support for the notion that girls get better grades in math classes at the same time that they are scoring lower on standardized exams. Indeed, in most years we find few gender differences in math grades. When differences are found, they tend to be small and are as likely to favor males as females. We also find few gender differences in science grades, but when they do occur they are small and favor boys. Thus it is fair to conclude that young women taking math and science courses often get grades that are similar to those of the young men. At the same time, young women score lower on standardized science exams by seventh grade and on math exams by tenth grade. Keep in mind that in the early years of high school most young people—male and female—are taking math and science, and that it is not until tenth grade and beyond that individuals have the opportunity to opt out of these courses. Thus in the early years, it is the same women who are competing almost equally with men in the classroom who are falling behind on standardized exams. In addition, these same women consistently—throughout the high school years studied here—have higher overall grade point averages than the young men. Some researchers have concluded that gender differences in math knowledge are declining (Linn & Hyde, 1989). Our research provides some support for this by showing that the women who graduated from high school in 1984 were more likely than those who graduated in 1982 to be scoring in the top quartile on standardized math exams. In spite of these declines, we do not find that the gender gap has disappeared. In their senior year of high school, young men in our sophomore sample were 28 percent more likely than young women to score in the top quartile on the standardized math exam.

A similar contrast between science achievement and achievement in general is found in the post–high school years, when we find that young women are *more* likely than young men to enter and to graduate from college. However, they are *less* likely to have a job in math or science.

ACCESS.   Our findings on gender differences in access to math and science show a long-term trend in which women take fewer and fewer courses in math and science. In the early years of high school—through tenth grade—there are few gender differences in course taking. When these differences do occur, they are small and almost as likely to favor females as males. However, when examining attendance in specific courses, such as algebra, biology, and computer education, boys are slightly overrepresented even in the eighth grade. By tenth grade, girls are slightly less likely to be taking trigonometry, calculus, chemistry, physics, and computer education. Girls are also less likely to be planning on taking more years of math and science, and these plans turn into a reality by twelfth grade. In their senior year of high school, boys are more likely than girls to have a math or science concentration and to have taken more math (e.g., algebra II and calculus) and science (e.g., physics and chemistry) courses. Like other research, our findings show some of the greatest differences in science courses, especially physics (Oakes, 1990; Linn & Hyde, 1989). However, unlike other research, we do not find the gender differences in math and science course taking in high school to be disappearing (Rallis & Ahern, 1986). Our findings show that the gender differences continue in the post–high school years, when young men are more likely than young women to have taken postsecondary math and science courses and to claim math or science as a field of study.

ATTITUDES.   As with science access, our research found few differences between girls and boys in their attitudes about science in the early high school years. This contrasts with those who conclude that girls' attitudes are more negative even in the early years (Linn & Hyde, 1989; Dossey et al., 1988). Thus, in seventh and eighth grade girls are no more anxious than boys about math or science and are just as likely to believe that math knowledge is necessary for a good job. A majority of girls (far more than boys) disagree with ideas about boys being better in math and science or about math and science being more useful for boys. In fact, girls are more likely than boys to say that science will be useful in their future and to look forward to science classes. However, even in seventh grade, girls are less likely to believe that science knowledge is needed for a good job and to aspire to a job in math or science. Thus we cannot conclude, as some have, that even at a young age girls do not see science as being useful in their future in general (Fox, 1976; Fennema & Sherman, 1977; Oakes, 1990; Mullis & Jenkins, 1988). We can conclude, however, that girls do have more negative attitudes on some specific issues having to do with the relevance of science to future jobs, and aspirations to science jobs. Although girls start out liking math and science as much as boys, their negative attitudes in these areas may be more important for later science achievement (Fox et al., 1979).

In contrast to some research that shows that girls' and boys' attitudes about math and science do not diverge until later (Aiken, 1970; 1976), our research indicates that by tenth grade girls have acquired more negative attitudes. They are less likely than boys to say that math is one of their best subjects or that it will be useful in their future. They are more likely than boys to be tense or scared about math class. Fewer girls than boys expect to study math or science after high school or aspire to an occupation in math or science. However, during this same year they continue to disagree with the notion that math is more useful for boys and are just as likely as boys to find math interesting. As seniors, girls are more likely than boys to expect a four-year degree and a professional job, but they are less likely to expect to concentrate in math or science in postsecondary school. In the post–high school years, boys become more likely than girls to expect a college degree, but girls remain more likely to expect a professional job.

ACTIVITIES. Other researchers have given little attention to gender differences in science activities. Are there differences in the extent to which girls and boys use computers, calculators, and microscopes, or join science and math clubs? The limited research that has looked at this issue finds early gender differences in science activities but does not follow up on the young people to see whether these differences continue (Oakes, 1990; Furr & Davis, 1984; Becker, 1986; Zimmerer & Bennett, 1987). Interestingly, our research shows a different trend in the area of science activities than we saw in science achievement, access, and attitudes. Here, girls start out with a deficit and *gain* some ground over time. In the middle school years, young boys are more likely than young girls to have talked to a scientist or attended a computer club. They are also more likely to have used a computer for a significant amount of time during the week and to have items such as computers and microscopes in their home.

In tenth grade boys still show some advantages: they are more likely to have conducted an experiment, to have items such as computers and calculators in the home, and to have used a computer for a significant amount of time during the week. But girls are spending more time on math and science homework. In the years after high school, girls become *more* likely than boys to have used a pocket calculator and to have used a computer terminal (ever or on a job), even though boys continue to be more likely to have used computers in their education. This trend in use of computers may derive from the fact that jobs in the female sector of the labor market (e.g., clerical and secretarial) increasingly involve the use of computers.

Science Trajectories and Lost Talent

In this research we have promoted the advantages of a trajectory approach in describing young women's (and men's) experiences in the science pipeline. Although a limited number of researchers have used the concept of a science pipeline and have even followed students over time, much of the work uses a single item, such as planned major or interest in science careers, to measure the pipeline (Office of Technology Assessment, 1988; Berryman, 1985). Our research is unique in using multiple measures of science experiences at four points in time to create science trajectories for young women and men (in the HSB sample) in three areas of science—achievement, access, and attitudes (there were too few measures of activities at certain time points to create activity trajectories). An examination of these trajectories suggests that very few students— male or female—stayed in the sciences throughout the six-year period studied. In most cases, the most common trajectory is the "out throughout" pattern, where students were not in the pipeline in any year. (Recall that in order to be "in" the pipeline, the student had to score in the top quartile on a factor that represented multiple aspects of experience in that area of science for that year.) Another common pattern for both boys and girls is a haphazard in-and-out pattern. Other researchers have also found this to be a common pattern (Berryman, 1983; Office of Technology Assessment, 1988). A comparison of the three areas of science suggests that many more students end up in the science attitude pipeline than in the achievement or access pipelines.

In spite of these gender similarities in science experiences, we found considerable divergence in the science experiences of young women and men. In each of the areas of science, males were more likely than females to be in the science throughout the six-year period. These differences were largest in access and attitudes and smallest in achievement. Young women are least likely to maintain access throughout the study period, and young men are least likely to maintain achievement throughout the study period. In fact, if one considers both the women who stay in the science achievement pipeline and those who end up in this pipeline in 1986, it is young women who represent the largest group in the science achievement pipeline. This finding goes against the general notion, promoted in the literature, that some of the greatest gender differences in the sciences are in areas involving achievement.

When looking at the science experiences of young women, we saw that they had their most successful experiences, overall, in the area of attitude. Over one-third of the young women we studied end up in this area (recall that due to a shortage of items in 1986, we only followed young people to 1984 in this trajectory). All women do not experience positive science attitudes, however. Nearly half of the women in the sample are not in the science attitude pipeline in any year. In contrast, women have the least success in the science access pipeline. Nearly half are never in this pipeline, and nearly three-fourths are out of this pipeline permanently following their sophomore year of high school.

We wondered how much overlap there was between the three areas of science. Is the same group of women successful in science achievement, access, and attitudes? Since the available research shows a connection between attitudes, access, and achievement in areas involving math and science, we expected considerable overlap in these areas (Linn & Hyde, 1989; Oakes, 1990). Our findings, however, showed little overlap. No more than one-third of young women who are in one area of science throughout the six-year period are in another area throughout this period. The largest overlap occurs for those who have high access. These young women are the most likely to be involved in the two other areas of science.

The science trajectories also provide a measure of lost talent. They reveal how many young people who show promise in science end up out of the science pipeline. Researchers commonly refer to the fact that young women start out with high achievement and interest in science but lose ground in these areas over time. However, very few researchers have offered an estimate of the amount of lost talent, as we do here. The area in which there is the greatest amount of lost talent is science achievement. Almost half of the young women in the sample who show signs of promise in this area are out of the sciences by the final survey year. This number is slightly less for young men (women are 7% more likely than young men to exit the science achievement pipeline). There is also a considerable amount of lost talent in science access. Slightly more than one-third of young men and women with promise exit this pipeline— gender differences are virtually absent. Finally, loss of talented youth from science is smallest in the science attitude pipeline and here it is young men who are more likely to exit (21% versus 16%).

Gender, Resources, and Success in Science

Our examination of gender differences in resources that have been shown to be important for positive science experiences suggested that there are considerable gender differences and that the group with the advantage varies with the type of resource being considered. Young men are given more resources in the home. For example, they are more likely than young women to have a pocket calculator in their home, to have a father who keeps track of their progress in school, and to have parents who attend PTA meetings and parent-teacher conferences. The largest gender difference in resources occurs in the early marital and childbearing behaviors of the young people. Young women are over twice as likely as young men to have been married or to have had a child by the time they are two years out of high school. Young men also have more personality resources. Their greater orientation to work and lesser orientation to family, along with their higher math and science test scores, give them potential advantages in science. On the other hand, young women have a distinct advantage in having more (general) school resources—chief of which is peer groups with an emphasis on education. The young women also have the advantage of higher self-concepts and higher commitment to and achievement in school, as well as higher educational aspirations and occupational expectations.

To examine how these resources varied with science experiences, we looked at the resources of women who had followed various paths in science. With regard to family resources, many of these appear to be related to time in the sciences. Young women who pursue science are more likely than others to have parents who are more involved in their children's social and academic lives and to have more education and higher status jobs. Both mothers' and fathers' actions are highly related to science success. Some of the most extreme differences in resources involve the young girl's marriage and childbearing experiences. Young women who stay in the science achievement pipeline are ten times less likely to have married and thirty times less likely to have had a child (2 years out of high school) than are those who stay out of science. The school variables that vary most with science experiences were program (e.g., academic or nonacademic) and peer group. Some interesting patterns emerge when examining individual resources. Women who stay in science date less than do other women and have a lower self-concept. They have unexpectedly high family orientation and low work orientation. However, these same girls tend to feel that they have more control over their lives and do not necessarily feel unpopular (except for those who maintain positive science attitudes). Young women who stay in science also have much higher educational achievement and expectations than do other women. Those who succeed in one area of science are much more likely than others to have resources in the other areas. For example, young women who stay in the science achievement pipeline are over four times more likely than those who stay out to have taken advanced math in their sophomore year of high school.

When causal models were used to look at the way in which resources affect science experiences for young women and young men, we discovered that a *consideration of gender is often important for understanding how a resource will affect experiences in science.* This is especially true in the area of experiences regarding science access, where a large majority of the resources that are important for success have an impact that varies by gender. In the case of science achievement, the resources that are important for success are almost as likely to have similar effects as they are to have different effects for young women and young men.

The evidence presented by these models provides strong support for the notion that gender per se is often a critical factor in determining experiences in science. When the amount of family, school, and individual resources that young people have is taken into account, gender still has a significant impact in many of the equations predicting experiences in science achievement, access, and attitudes. In the areas of access and attitudes, the gender effect often involves a disadvantage for young women. They are less likely than young men with equal resources to spend time in these pipelines. However, in the area of science achievement, when resources are equalized it is the young woman who has the advantage of spending more time in the pipeline. Gender is also an important factor in predicting lost talent in science, especially in science achievement. Thus although young women with equal resources are more likely than young men to stay in this area throughout the six-year period examined, there is also a greater exiting of female talent than male talent.

Results from our causal models also highlight the fact that the way in which resources affect science experiences varies by gender. Thus gender can have a direct impact on science experiences, but it can also indirectly affect them through its association with family, school, and individual resources.

Women and Science: Who Survives?

What is the causal process leading to success in science for young women? In other words, what are the effects of resources when inequalities in other resources are controlled? A careful modeling of science trajectories for young women shows some interesting findings. Predictors of success vary widely depending on which area of science is being considered, and very few resources in the model predict continued success in access to science. One of the most unexpected findings in this research is that young African American women with the same resources as other women are more likely to have at least some experiences in science achievement and access. Interestingly, others have also found gender differences to reverse when looking at African American youth (Matthews, 1984). Another surprising finding is that having a father with a higher status occupation and having more feeling of control over one's life reduce the chances of a young woman maintaining access to the sciences.

In general our findings show a mix of demographic, family, school, and individual resources that predict success in science for young women. In contrast to research on Hispanics in general, we find that young Hispanic women do not have different experiences in science than other women (Oakes, 1990). Growing up in a rural community reduces the chances of staying in the science attitude pipeline but has no effect on experiences in the other areas. When authors review the literature on family resources, they often make general conclusions about the import of SES for young girls' science experiences (Ethington & Wolfe, 1988; Oakes, 1990). Our findings suggest the need to place some conditions on these conclusions. We find that family SES is important for predicting experiences in science achievement but much less important for predicting experiences in science access and attitudes. Here parental behaviors—like monitoring homework—make more of a difference (although girls with mothers and fathers who have more education do have more positive experiences as regards science attitudes).

Similarly, broad conclusions about the effect of early marriage and childbearing cannot be made. Our findings show that young girls who get married earlier have less positive experiences in science achievement, but that early childbearing has little effect on positive experiences. In addition, we find that neither early marriage nor early childbearing has much influence on science access and attitudes.

Like other researchers, we find that school factors like school type and especially school peers also influence young women's science experiences (Boswell, 1985; Fox et al., 1979). Other research that has looked at the effects of peer groups in more detail has shown that peer systems that stress romance are a critical factor in steering young women away from math and science. Fear of peer rejection and feelings that men do not want women who hold science jobs are related factors that inhibit women in science (Fox, 1975, 1976; Fox et al., 1979; Holland & Eisenhart, 1991). Finally, our findings are in agreement with other research in showing that some of the most consistent predictors of the route in science that young women will follow are individual characteristics that involve their early science experiences (Ethington & Wolfe, 1988; Ware, Steckler, & Leserman, 1985). However, our look at the separate areas of science experiences suggests that the type of early experience that is important varies with the area of science being examined. For example, we find that early access to science is important for staying in the science attitude pipeline, but not in the achievement and attitude pipelines. Others who have taken a less comprehensive look at science achievement (e.g., those using single indicators of achievement at one point in time) consistently report that course taking (access) is one of the critical predictors of this outcome (Fox et al., 1979; Wise, 1985). We find that early achievement *is* important for future achievement and access. Early attitudes are also important for continued success in achievement. Others have shown a similar relationship between confidence in math and science (but not *general* self-confidence) and achievement (Armstrong, 1980; Armstrong & Price, 1982; Fox et al., 1979). We do not find early science attitudes to be related to continued access, as some have suggested (Fennema & Sherman, 1977; Boli et al., 1985; Armstrong, 1980), but our measures of science attitudes do not include the specific questions about one's own abilities in math and science that researchers often use.

General personality characteristics such as locus of control and self-concept have no effect on experiences in science achievement, as some have suggested (Fennema & Sherman, 1977), and they have only minimal effects in the other two areas. Surprisingly, sex-role attitudes do not appear to be important as causal predictors. Similarly, individual characteristics such as popularity, amount of dating, or time spent on homework have little causal influence. Much has been written about math as a male domain (Fox et al., 1979; Fox et al., 1985; Weitzman, 1979). Like some, we find mixed results in this area (Sherman, 1980). Our findings that girls who date less, are less popular, and have more liberal sex-role attitudes are not more likely to persist in science suggest that these are not the vehicles through which women are taught that math is a male domain, as some have suggested (Fox et al; 1979). We do, however, find that young girls' early attitudes about math and science affect their chances of continued success in the science achievement pipeline. That is, young girls who see math as useful in their future, have positive attitudes about math class, and expect to major in science are those who have the highest chance of continued high achievement in science. Our findings are in agreement with those of others who have suggested that it is not general personality traits such as self-confidence but rather specific attitudes about math that make a difference for women in science (Fox et al., 1979).

When the causal process leading to exits from science is contrasted with the causal process leading to continued success, it becomes clear that young women who exit the science pipeline have a mix of resource effects. Sometimes resources work to provide success, and sometimes they do not. On the other hand, those who stay in the sciences tend to have resources that have consistently positive effects on their science experiences.

As the above discussion suggests, our conclusions about the causal process leading to persistence in the sciences for young women often diverge from those of other researchers. A good part of this divergence stems from the radically different methodological approach we have employed. When we created predictive models similar to those that are popularly used, we also generated results that are different from those that emerged from our multidimensional trajectory approach. In addition, although we found many resources to be *correlates* of science experiences, the number of resources that were statistically significant in *causal* models that controlled for differences in other resources was substantially reduced. Many researchers limit their analyses to bivariate correlations between gender and resources or between resources and science experiences for young women, and cannot make conclusions about the causal process leading to science experiences. Finally, some researchers look at the causal process leading to success in science for samples of young men and women and then make conclusions about factors that would affect young women's success. Our analyses show that gender often interacts with resources to affect science experiences—i.e., resource effects vary by gender. Thus, conclusions about factors affecting young women's success in science must come from samples of women only.

Race, Class, and Success in Science

Throughout this book we have argued that an understanding of women's science experiences cannot be complete without consideration of potential race and class differences in science resources and experiences. Our findings provide strong support for this argument. We found, for example, considerable race and class variation in the kind of science trajectory that young women follow. And although class differences are always in the direction expected, race differences are not. Regardless of the area of science, lower SES women are much more likely than upper SES women to stay out of the sciences, and upper SES women are much more likely to stay in. For example, more than 3 times as many lower SES women as upper SES women never enter the science achievement pipeline. Although upper SES women are more likely to be in the science pipeline, the loss of talented young women is also greatest in this group.

A look at race differences in science experiences showed that African American women are more likely to stay out of and less likely to stay in the area of science achievement. However, when examining access and attitudes, we found that African American women are less likely than other women to stay out and as likely to remain in. Race differences in lost talent are minimal.

Our examination of differences in the science resources of subgroups of women in the HSB sample showed significant race and class differences on a majority of resources. SES differences consistently favor young women from upper SES families. These women have advantages on family resources (e.g., parents with more income, education, and higher expectations), school resources (e.g., interested teachers, peers who put a high priority on education, and a greater chance of being in academic programs and private schools), and individual resources (e.g., greater feelings of control, higher expected ages at marriage and childbearing, more time spent on homework, and higher educational expectations).

Our look at race differences in resources showed that there is *not* a consistent advantage for either African American or non-African American women. It is true that African American women are lower on a good number of family, school, and individual resources. For example, young African American women tend to come from lower SES families with more siblings, and they are less likely to have a pocket calculator in their home. They are less likely than other girls to be in private schools or academic programs. They score lower on self-concept, orientation to work, and standardized math and science exams. However, African American women have advantages over other women on other important resources, many of which involve the influence of their mother as well as their own positive attitudes. African American women in our sample are more likely to have had a working mother in elementary school, who perhaps provided an important role model. Their mothers have higher educational expectations for their daughters and are more likely to keep track of their daughters' progress in school than are other mothers. In addition, even though African American women are more likely than other women to have a child at an early age, they are less likely to marry at an early age. African American women are also more likely than other women to have liberal sex-role attitudes and expectations for later marriage and childbearing. In addition, they express a greater interest in school. These advantages that African American women show on some important resources help explain why these women sometimes have more positive experiences in science than do other women.

Our consideration of the causal impact of these resources in predictive models for the subgroups of women showed that race and class often interact with resources to affect science experiences. These findings lead to the conclusion that one cannot make general statements about predictors of success in science for young women without consideration of their race and class. One of the many intriguing findings emerging from this research is that SES (as measured by a scale of family indicators) is a predictor of experiences in each area of science for non–African American women *but* not for African American women.

Implications of the Study

Results from this research suggest that experiences in science are complex phenomena that occur in multiple areas of both math and science over time. To understand fully what happens, researchers must consider both math and science as well as achievement, access, attitudes, and activities in these two arenas. In addition, they must consider them not at just one point in time but at multiple points. Considerable confusion can result from the limited focus typical of much research. By focusing on math only, researchers fail to see that it is in the arena of science where young women first fall behind their male peers. By focusing on a single aspect of experience, such as achievement or access, they fail to see that young women are not having identical experiences in each of these areas of science. In fact they fall behind in achievement before they fall behind in access or attitudes. In the area of activities they start out well behind their male peers as early as seventh grade, but actually make some gains over time when they end up in white-collar jobs in which they find themselves using calculators and computers.

Perhaps the most important implication of this research is that science experiences are not snapshot events that can be captured at one point in time (or even predicted at one point in time using earlier time points). It is essential that groups of young women (and men) be followed over time in order to capture the dynamics of science experience. Both young women and young men experience considerable "in's" and "out's" in science. A cross-sectional look at the group that was high on science achievement in their sophomore year of high school would contain a very different population if the researcher had chosen the senior year of high school. The more important question is,

"Who stays in science and why?" This, in addition to questions about the exiting of talented youth, can only be answered by research designs that follow young people through the critical years of their schooling and chart their trajectories. In contrast to cross-sectional (or even many traditional longitudinal) analyses, which consistently find negative effects of gender by showing that young women fall behind young men in math and science achievement and access by their senior year of high school, the trajectory approach shows that in the area of science achievement, equally qualified women are actually *more* likely to end up in the sciences.

Another important implication of this research is that gender per se often explains variation in science experiences—even when other resources are controlled. In two areas of science—access and attitudes—it is women who have the disadvantage. Thus equally qualified young women are discouraged from staying in these areas. However, it is equally qualified young *men* who are discouraged in the area of science achievement. Researchers need to spend more time examining the differential treatment of qualified boys and girls in order to understand the mechanisms through which gender discrimination takes place in science. Cultural assumptions about the appropriate roles for males and females become institutionalized into gender belief systems that shape the behaviors of all of the relevant players—parents, teachers, and students. But how can these be measured, when they are so taken for granted that individuals are often unaware of them? Work by the Sadkers (1986) and others that uses observational rather than survey techniques such as those employed here is an essential step in unraveling these gender belief systems. The Sadkers found that although teachers often treated students differently on the basis of gender, they tended to be unaware of this differential treatment.

A recent report by the American Association of University Women (1992) concluded that while gender differences in math achievement are small and declining, those in science achievement are neither small nor declining. Our findings confirm that math differences are declining. Girls in the younger cohort of high school students are more likely than those in the older cohort to score in the upper quartile on standardized math exams in their sophomore year of high school. However, we must be cautious about concluding that gender differences in math achievement have been reduced. Differences on math grades can already be seen in eighth grade, and differences on standardized math scores are present by tenth grade. Both differences tend to increase (with one exception—grades in tenth grade) throughout high school. Furthermore, the differences are statistically significant even when they are their smallest. Until all gender differences in math achievement have disappeared, statements about their small and declining size need to be made with caution, lest we gain a false security about gender equality here.

Never before have researchers looked carefully at the science resources and experiences of girls with different race and class characteristics. Oakes (1990) has argued a need for this kind of analysis, and some preliminary work has been done— but usually on only one or two rather than all three statuses of gender, race, and social class (e.g., Matthews, 1984; National Science Foundation, 1988; Grant & Sleeter, 1986). This research shows that young women's experiences in science vary greatly across race and class groups. For example, we cannot conclude that young African American women fall behind their white counterparts, for they actually have more resources and more positive experiences in some areas of science. Unfortunately, young women from lower SES backgrounds have disadvantages in science that cannot be surmounted.

Our findings on the role of gender in science lend to considerable optimism, since they show that women are not always disadvantaged. Indeed, science is a field that only a minority of both young women *or* young men pursue consistently. All young people need encouragement in this area of education. When we do find gender differences favoring males in some areas, they are small. When looking at certain resources, such as peer groups, overall grades, and college attendance, it is young women who have the advantage. And sometimes it is equally qualified *males* who leave the sciences. However, this optimism must be checked somewhat, since all is not rosy for young women. Young women are more likely than young men to experience declines in all areas of science in the high school years and are less likely to stay in the sciences. Even those who are equally qualified suffer in some areas of science. Part of the explanation for these gender differences can be attributed to the lesser resources that young girls receive in the home and in the school. Families and schools continue to see science as a male domain. In our sample, it is the young men who are more likely to have fathers who are involved in their educational activities. By contrast, it is the family that is seen as a female domain, and this is reflected in our findings. Young women are over twice as likely as young men to have been married or have had a child by the time they are two years out of high school. These family roles make continuation in the sciences difficult if not impossible. And although our findings show that young women have at least as many general educational resources in the school, others who have looked more specifically at the science resources and expectations that teachers, counselors, and school administrators have for their male and female students have found a male bias (Frazier & Sadker, 1973; Klein, 1985; Sadker & Sadker, 1986; AAUW, 1992).

The fact that women's lower standardized math and science scores were found here to be one of the major routes through which gender negatively affects science experiences suggests that, in one way or another, families and schools are more successful at providing critical math and science information to boys than to girls. Educators and evaluators need to continue to pursue standardized exams that allow young women to compete fairly with young men. Many have suggested that standardized math exams are biased to favor males and that a select group of women who are less prepared than their male counterparts end up taking these exams. Those who have evaluated these tests carefully suggest that the largest gender differences often occur on problem-solving items and that female deficits here are related to the tendency of women to opt out of advanced math courses that emphasize problem solving. Other aspects of the test environment can also affect girls' ability to perform. Some have found that when it is a woman administering the test, girls perform better than they do with a male tester. Women's lower confidence in their math and science abilities also contributes to the lower scores (see Linn & Hyde, 1989; see also Eccles & Jacobs, 1986; AAUW, 1992; Pederson, Shinedling, & Johnson, 1968).

Where have the advances for women been made, and where is there still a considerable female disadvantage? More women are continuously in the science achievement pipeline than in the other science pipelines. Unfortunately, it is also in this pipeline where the biggest drain of talented young women takes place. It is in the science access pipeline where we find the fewest women consistently pursuing science. Other research has shown that once women get into science courses, they are taught similar amounts of science and receive grades similar to (or better than) those of their male counterparts (Hanson, Schaub, & Baker, in press; Baker & Jones, 1993; DeBoer, 1984a). The key thus appears to be getting women into the science courses.

What resources do we need to offer to young women to keep them interested in science? Some resources cannot easily be distributed to all women. Primary among these is social class. This resource is highly correlated with continued success in science, but we cannot realistically hope for short-term solutions here. But other resources can be more easily offered to all women. Families need to be involved in their daughters' school and schoolwork, especially in math and science. Since the women who stay in science have parents who know where they are and what they are doing as well as school peer groups that value education, parents need to be actively involved in their daughters' social life as well. In

addition, they need to encourage high educational and occupational expectations, self-confidence in math and science, and progressive ideas
about women's roles outside of the home, and to discourage early marriage and family formation. When parents provide computers, calculators, and microscopes at home, they also increase the chances that their
daughter will enjoy science. At the school level, we find that private
schools, schools that require more math and science courses for graduation and have active, involved teachers, and academic programs within
schools are the environments that are the most likely to encourage interest in science. These are environments that families and schools can
seek to make available for all children. Although this research did not
provide detailed information on the classroom level, others have studied
this resource and made suggestions about classroom environments that
would encourage all students, regardless of gender. Young women tend
to perform better in classrooms that have female role models, and in
which students are all female (or in which females are strongly represented). They also do better in classrooms where feedback is extensive
and constructive, expression of ideas is encouraged from all, the relevance of learning science is clear, learning is cooperative but individual
achievement is also rewarded, students do not mindlessly memorize but
rather apply their learning to solving real problems, and teachers have a
high regard for the ability of males *and* females in science (Linn & Hyde,
1989; Oakes, 1990; Brody & Fox, 1980; Matyas, 1986; Boli et al., 1985).

Young women who pursue science are involved in a delicate balancing act between home and career roles. Very few of the young
women in our sample ended up in science occupations, and those who
did often put off marriage and childbearing to do so. Research has shown
that one of the largest drops in persistence in science careers occurs after graduate school (National Science Board, 1987). What factors are involved here? Some have suggested that the strong emphasis put on early
productivity in science careers (at a time when many women have heavy
family responsibilities), perceived competitiveness in science jobs and
the related perception of science as a male domain, difficulties in finding jobs for women in two-career families, and continued beliefs about
women's lesser abilities in science all combine to make science an occupation that is perceived as (or experienced as) difficult for women
(Linn & Hyde, 1989; AAUW, 1992; Rosser, 1990; Vetter, 1992; Fox, 1995,
in press; Zuckerman, 1991; Devine, 1992; Morgan, 1992).

To overcome these problems, employers need to provide flexible
work environments in which all employees can be productive regardless
of family responsibilities. They need to have family leave policies that allow both men and women to take maternity/paternity leave and other

time off to care for ill family members. Other changes that would improve the work environment for female scientists include special attention to the needs and difficulties of two-career families (e.g., personnel offices that assist the spouse of a potential employee in locating a job) and an emphasis through policies and procedures on the elimination of differential treatment on the basis of gender.

In describing young women's experiences in the sciences, we discovered a tremendous amount of in's and out's. Others who have used alternate measures of science experience have reached similar conclusions (Office of Technology Assessment, 1988). We cannot assume, then, that once young women are in the sciences, they will stay there. Nor can we assume that when they leave they will not be returning. Researchers and educators who use the pipeline analogy need to be mindful of these findings. Even though the path by which students approach science careers is compared to a pipeline, it must be thought of as a very permeable pipeline. Our resources should not be solely aimed at a science elite but rather at all students, since many may attempt to enter the pipeline later (and perhaps be underprepared). Since so many girls *and boys* end up leaving the science pipeline—after showing aptitude and interest—a better analogy might be that of a permeable funnel. Early success and training certainly do not guarantee ultimate success in this science training process. Those who use the science pipeline analogy need to keep in mind factors other than training, namely statuses that reflect positions in the social structure. Not just gender but race and social class statuses often keep qualified young people out of science.

In an age of technology, where well-educated workers are increasingly seen as economic resources, the education system in the United States continues to produce scientists and technicians that are disproportionately white and male. As females and minorities become an increasingly large percentage of work cohorts, educators and employers may finally become interested in the full participation of all young people, regardless of gender or race, in science.

APPENDIX

MEASURES AND ANALYSIS DESIGN

Measures of Resources

Means, standard deviations, and coding information for the items used to measure family, school, and individual resources in the HSB sophomore cohort are presented in Table 3-1. (Recall that predictive models using the resources as independent variables will be applied only to the HSB sophomore data.) Means and standard deviations are provided for the total sample as well as for the male and female samples.

With the exception of a few variables, complete measurement information is provided in Table 3-1. Some explanations are necessary, however. With regard to the SES variable, the National Center for Education Statistics (NCES) created this variable from information on the mother's education, father's education and occupation, family income, and material possessions in the home. It standardized the information and created four quartiles.

Mother's and father's occupation were coded by the NCES using 16 broad U.S. Census categories. Since these categories do not constitute a continuous level of measurement along some status variable, we created a variable that compared professional jobs (1) to all other jobs (0).

A note on the HSB's approach to collecting parental information is necessary. Questions on parental education and occupation refer to the parent(s) in the home. This may be a stepfather (or stepmother) or male (or female) guardian. If the student does not have a particular parent (or stepparent or guardian) in the home, he/she receives a missing value on this variable. Nine percent of the sample did not have a father (or father substitute) in the home, and 1.5 percent did not have a mother (or mother substitite) in the home. Because these numbers are not alarmingly high, the decision was made to include information on parents in the analyses, since parental influence is of major interest in this research.

One of the school-related resources in the model has to do with the attitudes and activities of classmates. The HSB survey included four questions about the respondent's best friend in the sophomore class: whether the friend gets good grades, is interested in school, attends class regularly, and plans to go to college. In this study, the four items were each scored 0 or 1, with 1 reflecting more positive characteristics. In the multivariate analyses, a summated index that ranges from 0 to 4 was created from these items.

Four composite personality variables were included as individual resources. These measure self-concept, work orientation, family orientation and locus of control. As with the SES measure, the NCES combined these items, standardized them, and provided them to the researcher as a composite measure.

The composite measure of self-concept included four items: "I take a positive attitude toward myself"; "I feel I am a person of worth; on a equal plane with others"; "I am able to do things as well as most other people"; and "On the whole I am satisfied with myself." A high score reflects a high self-concept.

Orientation to work was measured as a composite of three items. Respondents were asked to rate how important the following were in their life: "Being successful in my line of work"; "Having lots of money"; and "Being able to find steady work." The family orientation measure was based on three items as well: "Living close to family and relatives"; "Finding the right person to marry and having a happy family life"; and "Getting away from this area of the country". High scores on the work and family orientation variables reflect a strong orientation to work or family, respectively.

With regard to the locus of control measure, an *internal* locus of control refers to the belief that one's actions and efforts, rather than fate or luck, determine one's successes, whereas an *external* locus of control refers to the opposite pattern. The NCES used four items to compute this composite scale: "Every time I try to get ahead, something or somebody stops me"; "Good luck is more important than hard work for success"; "Planning only makes a person unhappy, since plans hardly ever work out anyway"; and "People who accept their condition in life are happier than those who try to change things." Higher scores on this composite variable reflect a more internal locus of control.

Another individual characteristic, occupational aspirations for age 30, was coded by the NCES using the 16 broad categories described in the above discussion of mother's and father's occupations. We created an aspirations variable that compared aspirations for professional jobs (coded 1) to aspirations for all other jobs (coded 0).

It should be noted that science experiences were used as both independent and dependent variables in analyses. That is, experiences in the science pipeline (achievement, access, and attitudes) were being predicted, but they were also resources for achievement. (See the next section for an explanation of why we did not predict activities with the multivariate models.) Models predicting a particular outcome did not, however, contain measures of that outcome as predictor variables. For example, in models predicting science achievement, science achievement was not included as an individual resource. However, science access and attitudes were.

Measures of Experiences in the Sciences

In each of the three data sets, a number of items measured student experiences in areas of science including achievement (e.g., standardized math and science scores), access (e.g., course taking), attitudes (e.g., attitudes about math and science classes and about abilities in these areas), and activities (e.g., participation in science fairs and use of calculators and computers). Means and standard deviations for these items are included in Tables A-1 to A-4 for the LSAY, NELS, HSB sophomore cohort, and HSB senior cohort. Means and standard deviations are provided for the total sample as well as for females and males. Measurement information is provided in parentheses following each item. Variables were coded in a dichotomous fashion so that responses to each item would reflect a position either in or out of the science pipeline. This information was then put into bar charts for each data set and area of science experiences, so that the cohorts' over-time experiences in the science pipeline could more easily be assessed.

Two of the variables used to measure science experiences in the HSB samples require some additional explanation: postsecondary field of study and occupation. In the 1984 and 1986 survey years, the HSB survey included questions about all jobs and postsecondary experiences since high school (asked in 1984) and since the 1984 survey (asked in 1986). The NCES coded occupations using detailed U.S. Census categories. Field of study codes involve conventional academic subdivisions of knowledge and training. We created two variables (for each of the two years) from this information on field of study and occupation. The field of study variable measured whether the respondent had claimed math or science as a field of study in any postsecondary school attended in the period under question. The majors that were categorized as math or science included mathematics, biological sciences, computer and information sciences, engineering, health sciences, and physical science. When we reported descriptive information on the created math/science field of study variable, only those who had attended postsecondary school in the period under question were included (others were coded as missing).

TABLE A-1 Means (and Standard Deviations) for Science Variables by Gender (LSAY)

	Total	*Females*	*Males*
Achievement			
1987			
Top Quartile, Math	.25 (.43)	.26 (.44)	.24 (.43)
Top Quartile, Science	.25 (.43)	.22 (.41)*	.28 (.45)*
1988			
Top Quartile, Math	.25 (.43)	.24 (.43)	.26 (.44)
Top Quartile, Science	.25 (.43)	.22 (.42)*	.28 (.45)*
1989			
Top Quartile, Math	.25 (.43)	.25 (.43)	.25 (.44)
Top Quartile, Science	.25 (.43)	.21 (.41)*	.28 (.45)*
Mostly A's in Math	.27 (.44)	.25 (.43)	.28 (.45)
Mostly A's in Science	.25 (.43)	.24 (.43)	.25 (.44)
1990			
Top Quartile, Math	.25 (.43)	.23 (.42)*	.27 (.44)*
Top Quartile, Science	.25 (.43)	.22 (.41)*	.28 (.45)*
Access			
1987			
Math Class, High Ability	.33 (.47)	.35 (.48)*	.31 (.46)*
Science Class, High Ability	.28 (.45)	.29 (.45)	.27 (.44)
1988			
Math Class, High Ability	.22 (.42)	.22 (.42)	.22 (.42)
Science Class, High Ability	.26 (.44)	.29 (.45)	.24 (.43)
Enrolled, Pre-Algebra	.20 (.40)	.22 (.41)	.19 (.39)
Enrolled, Algebra	.18 (.39)	.17 (.38)	.19 (.39)
1989			
Math Class, High Ability	.24 (.43)	.25 (.43)	.23 (.42)
Science Class, High Ability	.30 (.46)	.27 (.44)*	.33 (.47)*
Enrolled, Honors Math	.39 (.49)	.37 (.48)	.40 (.49)
Enrolled, Honors Science	.27 (.44)	.25 (.44)	.28 (.45)
1990			
Math Class, High Ability	.22 (.41)	.39 (.43)	.36 (.40)
Science Class, High Ability	.38 (.49)	.25 (.49)*	.19 (.48)*
Enrolled, Honors Math	.26 (.44)	.26 (.44)	.25 (.44)
Enrolled, Honors Science	.26 (.44)	.27 (.44)	.26 (.44)
Attitudes			
1987			
Low Anxiety, Math	.14 (.35)	.15 (.36)	.13 (.33)
Low Anxiety, Science	.16 (.37)	.15 (.36)	.17 (.37)
Plan to Attend Four-Year College	.65 (.48)	.68 (.46)*	.61 (.49)*

TABLE A-1 *(continued)*

	Total	Females	Males
Attitudes *(continued)*			
1987 *(continued)*			
Aspire to Math/Science Occupation	.10 (.31)	.06 (.24)*	.15 (.35)*
Disagree: Math Is More Useful for Boys	.63 (.48)	.76 (.43)*	.51 (.50)*
Disagree: Science Is More Useful for Boys	.59 (.49)	.71 (.46)*	.49 (.50)*
Need Math for Good Job	.75 (.43)	.75 (.44)	.75 (.43)
Need Science for Good Job	.40 (.49)	.34 (.48)*	.46 (.50)*
Disagree: Boys Are Better at Math	.61 (.49)	.76 (.43)*	.48 (.50)*
Disagree: Boys Are Better at Science	.58 (.49)	.69 (.46)*	.48 (.50)*
1988			
Low Anxiety, Math	.15 (.35)	.15 (.36)	.14 (.35)
Low Anxiety, Science	.17 (.38)	.18 (.38)	.16 (.37)
Plan to Attend Four-Year College	.61 (.49)	.64 (.48)*	.58 (.49)*
Aspire to Math/Science Occupation	.06 (.23)	.03 (.16)*	.09 (.28)*
Disagree: Math Is More Useful for Boys	.66 (.47)	.79 (.41)*	.54 (.50)*
Disagree: Science Is More Useful for Boys	.62 (.49)	.75 (.43)*	.51 (.50)*
Need Math for Good Job	.75 (.44)	.74 (.44)	.75 (.44)
Need Science for Good Job	.43 (.50)	.36 (.48)*	.49 (.50)*
Disagree: Boys Are Better at Math	.61 (.49)	.78 (.41)*	.46 (.50)*
Disagree: Boys Are Better at Science	.61 (.49)	.74 (.44)*	.49 (.50)*
Disagree: Mathematicians/Scientists Are Nerds	.75 (.44)	.81 (.40)*	.69 (.46)*
1989			
Low Anxiety, Math	.10 (.30)	.12 (.32)*	.07 (.26)*
Low Anxiety, Science	.13 (.33)	.15 (.36)*	.11 (.31)*
Plan to Attend Four-Year College	.67 (.47)	.69 (.46)*	.65 (.48)*
Aspire to Math/Science Occupation	.06 (.23)	.03 (.17)*	.09 (.28)*
Disagree: Math Is More Useful for Boys	.65 (.48)	.77 (.42)*	.54 (.50)*
Disagree: Science Is More Useful for Boys	.63 (.48)	.74 (.44)*	.52 (.50)*
Need Math for Good Job	.69 (.46)	.70 (.46)	.69 (.46)
Need Science for Good Job	.44 (.50)	.40 (.49)*	.49 (.50)*
Disagree: Boys Are Better at Math	.64 (.48)	.77 (.42)*	.51 (.50)*
Disagree: Boys Are Better at Science	.60 (.49)	.72 (.45)*	.48 (.50)*
1990			
Low Anxiety, Math	.10 (.30)	.10 (.30)	.09 (.29)
Low Anxiety, Science	.12 (.32)	.12 (.33)	.11 (.31)
Plan to Attend Four-Year College	.63 (.48)	.67 (.47)*	.60 (.49)*
Aspire to Math/Science Occupation	.06 (.24)	.03 (.17)*	.10 (.30)*
Disagree: Math Is More Useful for Boys	.71 (.46)	.82 (.38)*	.59 (.49)*
Disagree: Science Is More Useful for Boys	.67 (.47)	.79 (.41)*	.55 (.50)*
Need Math for Good Job	.68 (.47)	.66 (.48)*	.70 (.46)*
Need Science for Good Job	.43 (.50)	.40 (.49)*	.46 (.50)*
Disagree: Boys Are Better at Math	.68 (.47)	.81 (.39)*	.54 (.50)*
Disagree: Boys Are Better at Science	.67 (.47)	.79 (.41)*	.54 (.50)*

(continued on next page)

TABLE A-1 *(continued)*

	Total	Females	Males
Activities			
1987			
Ever Talked to a Scientist	.21 (.41)	.16 (.36)*	.27 (.44)*
Ever Entered a Science Fair	.39 (.49)	.38 (.48)	.40 (.49)
This Year Used a Computer for 10+ Hours	.27 (.44)	.19 (.39)*	.33 (.47)*
Computer in Home	.44 (.50)	.39 (.49)*	.48 (.50)*
Microscope in Home	.29 (.45)	.22 (.41)*	.36 (.48)*
1988			
This Year Used a Computer for 10+ Hours	.25 (.43)	.17 (.37)*	.32 (.47)*
1989			
This Year Used a Computer for 10+ Hours	.22 (.42)	.16 (.37)*	.28 (.45)*
1990			
This Year Used a Computer for 10+ Hours	.19 (.39)	.14 (.34)*	.24 (.43)*

* Significant at ≤0.05.

When we included this variable in the multivariate analysis, we included those who did not attend postsecondary school with those who did not major in math or science in category 0, since we did not want to limit our causal analysis to those who had attended postsecondary school. As with the field of study variables, the variables measuring occupations were combined into a new variable (in the 1984 and 1986 survey years), which measured whether any of the occupations that the respondent had had since high school (asked in 1984 survey) or since 1984 (asked in the 1986 survey) were in math or science. Occupations defined as math and science occupations include engineers, mathematical specialists (e.g., actuaries, mathematicians, statisticians), life and physical scientists (e.g., chemists, biologists, physicists), college and university math and science teachers, and engineering and science technicians. Like the field of study variable, when the occupation variable was used in multivariate analyses, all respondents who answered the question were given a valid code (0 if no occupation or no occupation in math or science; 1 if an occupation in math or science), not just those who had had occupations since high school.

In the causal analysis of experiences in the science pipeline, students' dynamic, over-time patterns were measured using trajectories. Recall that only the HSB sophomore cohort was used in this analysis. Given the large number of indicators of pipeline experiences for each area of experience in the sciences and each year of measurement, principal components factor analysis with varimax (orthogonal) rotation was used as a data reduction technique. Items included in this factor analysis are the HSB sophomore measures of achievement, access, and attitudes shown in Table A-3. Given the small number of activities indicators for most years and the desire not to use single indicators of science experience in the causal analysis, no trajectories were created nor causal analysis performed for the activities area of pipeline experiences. For each year and area of experience combination (e.g., access to the science pipeline in 1980), the most cogent factor (in some cases factors) was used to represent experiences. Eigen values for the factors are presented in Table A-3. The Kaiser criterion was used to determine which factors to include (eigen value greater than or equal to 1). If there was more than one factor, the average of the factor scores was computed for each individual. Once quartile cutoffs for the factors were determined, seven trajectories were then created for each area of science experience. These trajectories represent typical patterns of experiences and can be used to assess the issue of lost talent in science. The first trajectory is the "in pipeline" trajectory. Students who were in the top quartile on the factor score for each survey year (1980, 1982, 1984, and 1986) were placed in this trajectory. A second trajectory included those who ended up in the top quartile in 1986 but were not in it each of the previous years. Three other trajectories were created to include young people who left the pipeline later (after 1984) or earlier (after 1982 or after 1980). A sixth trajectory was created to include students who had experienced a variety of ins and outs but who did not end up in the science pipeline and did not fit into the above patterns of experiences. Finally, a trajectory was created to represent the experiences of those who were not in the top quartile of the science measures for any year. It should be noted that measurement of science attitudes vis-à-vis the trajectories diverges somewhat from the achievement and access measures. Because there were very few measures of attitudes in 1986, this year was not used, and experiences in this area are measured with 6, not 7, trajectories. In addition, the only attitudes available in 1984 are general education attitudes not specific to science. These qualifications should be kept in mind when examining the trajectory results.

These trajectories represent a unique way of measuring over-time patterns of experiences in the sciences. They are especially helpful in understanding the nature and extent of talent loss in science among young women. When used as the outcome in the lost talent model, they will contribute to an understanding of how gender directly and indirectly (through resources) affects the exiting of talented women as reflected in the "early exit" and "later exit" trajectories.

TABLE A-2 Means (and Standard Deviations) for Science Variables by Gender (NELS Eighth-Grade Cohort)*

	Total	*Females*	*Males*
Achievement			
1988			
GPA: 3.0 or More	.52 (.50)	.57 (.49)†	.48 (.50)†
A's and B's in Math	.12 (.32)	.11 (.13)†	.13 (.11)†
A's and B's in Science	.13 (.33)	.12 (.14)†	.15 (.11)†
Top Quartile, Math	.24 (.44)	.24 (.44)†	.25 (.45)†
Top Quartile, Science	.25 (.44)	.22 (.42)†	.28 (.46)†
High-Ability Math	.32 (.47)	.31 (.46)†	.33 (.48)†
High-Ability Science	.25 (.43)	.22 (.41)†	.27 (.44)†
1990			
A's and B's in Math	.17 (.38)	.17 (.38)†	.16 (.37)†
A's and B's in Science	.16 (.37)	.17 (.37)	.16 (.36)
Work Hard in Math	.56 (.50)	.64 (.48)†	.49 (.50)†
Work Hard in Science	.51 (.50)	.57 (.50)†	.46 (.50)†
Professional Job at 30	.40 (.49)	.46 (.50)†	.35 (.47)†
Access			
1988			
Advanced Math Taken	.41 (.49)	.40 (.49)†	.42 (.50)†
Advanced Science Taken	.28 (.45)	.26 (.44)†	.29 (.46)†
Attended Algebra	.37 (.49)	.37 (.49)†	.38 (.49)†
Attended Math	.69 (.47)	.69 (.47)	.69 (.47)
Attended Science	.59 (.49)	.59 (.49)	.60 (.49)
Attended Biology	.19 (.40)	.17 (.38)†	.21 (.41)†
Attended Computer Education	.35 (.48)	.33 (.48)†	.37 (.49)†
1990			
Algebra II Taken	.27 (.46)	.27 (.45)	.27 (.46)
Trigonometry Taken	.07 (.29)	.07 (.28)†	.08 (.30)†
Precalculus Taken	.02 (.17)	.02 (.14)†	.03 (.19)†
Calculus Taken	.02 (.14)	.01 (.12)†	.02 (.16)†
Chemistry Taken	.17 (.39)	.17 (.38)†	.18 (.40)†
Physics Taken	.05 (.23)	.04 (.21)†	.06 (.25)†
Computer Education Taken	.28 (.45)	.26 (.44)†	.30 (.45)†
Attitudes			
1988			
Expect College Degree	.65 (.47)	.68 (.46)†	.62 (.48)†
Science/Engineering Job at 30	.08 (.28)	.05 (.21)†	.12 (.33)†
Ask Questions in Math	.75 (.43)	.74 (.44)†	.76 (.42)†
Look Forward to Math	.46 (.50)	.47 (.50)†	.45 (.50)†
Math Useful in Future	.16 (.37)	.16 (.37)†	.17 (.37)†
Ask Questions in Science	.80 (.40)	.81 (.39)†	.80 (.40)†

TABLE A-2   *(continued)*

	Total	Females	Males
Attitudes *(continued)*			
1988 *(continued)*			
Look Forward to Science	.42 (.49)	.45 (.50)†	.39 (.49)†
Science Useful in Future	.35 (.48)	.38 (.48)†	.33 (.47)†
Attitudes			
1990			
Plan College after High School	.69 (.47)	.73 (.46)†	.65 (.48)†
Math Courses' Emphasis on Further Study in Math	.39 (.48)	.41 (.48)†	.37 (.47)†
Science Courses' Emphasis on Further Study in Science	.22 (.40)	.23 (.41)	.22 (.40)
Math One of Best Subjects	.42 (.50)	.39 (.49)†	.46 (.50)†
Activities			
1988			
Computer at Home	.40 (.49)	.36 (.48)†	.45 (.50)†
Calculator at Home	.95 (.22)	.95 (.22)	.95 (.22)
Math Homework, 4+ Hours	.08 (.28)	.09 (.29)†	.07 (.28)†
Science Homework, 4+ Hours	.03 (.18)	.03 (.18)	.03 (.18)
Attended Science Fairs	.28 (.45)	.28 (.45)†	.28 (.46)†
Attended Science Club	.05 (.22)	.04 (.19)†	.06 (.24)†
Attended Math Club	.06 (.23)	.05 (.22)†	.06 (.25)†
Attended Computer Club	.08 (.27)	.06 (.24)†	.09 (.30)†
1990			
Computer at Home	.39 (.49)	.35 (.48)†	.43 (.50)†
Computer Used in Math	.16 (.37)	.14 (.35)†	.17 (.38)†
Math Homework, 4+ Hours	.12 (.33)	.14 (.35)†	.10 (.31)†
Science Homework, 4+ Hours	.09 (.30)	.10 (.31)†	.08 (.28)†
Conduct Own Science Experiment	.20 (.39)	.17 (.37)†	.24 (.41)†

* N (1988) = 25,599; N (1990) = 20,706.

† Significant at ≤ .05.

Analyses

To answer the first research question about gender differences in experiences in the sciences, the percent of young women and men who had positive science experiences was examined. This was done for the three data sets representing three different periods in the science pipeline and for the multiple indicators of each of the four areas of science experience in each of the survey years as presented above. *T*-tests were performed to make conclusions about whether gender differences are statistically significant at the .05 level. As noted in the measurement section, this information was presented in both table and bar-chart form.

A second way of describing experiences is to examine the number of young women and men who were in each of the four science trajectories. The complexities of the multiple dimensions of experience were integrated into this descriptive analysis. Experiences within one area of science were examined for those who scored high in other areas of science. The results from this analysis tell us, for example, how many of those who stayed in the science achievement pipeline throughout the survey years also stayed in the science access pipeline, and whether these numbers vary for young women and men.

The second research question addresses the issue of the ways in which gender might affect science experiences both directly and through resources. To answer this question, multivariate analyses of variables represented in our model of gender and lost talent in science are performed with Analysis of Variance (ANOVA) and logistic regression analyses. First, the continuum of trajectory experiences is used as a dependent variable in ANOVA models that look for the ability of independent variables to detect variation in trajectory experiences. Second, given the implicitly categorical nature of the outcome variable (trajectories), logistic regression models provide an excellent technique for looking at the impact of model variables on the odds of being in a particular trajectory. Comparisons are made contrasting the odds of being in each of the trajectories with the odds of being in the "out of pipeline throughout" trajectory. Although it might have been preferable to use the "in the pipeline throughout" group as the comparison group, the N here was so small that it was disqualified as a good comparison group. Logistic regression coefficients represent the effect of a unit change in the independent variable on the log of the odds of being in category 1 of the dependent variable (category 0 = "out throughout" trajectory; 1 = another trajectory). The antilogs of these coefficients provide a more intuitive understanding of the effects. These transformed coefficients can be interpreted as the effect on the odds of being in category 1. For example, if the logistic coefficient for an independent variable had an antilog of 2.0, that would mean that with each unit increase in that variable, the odds of being in category 1 of the dependent variable would increase by a factor of 2 (i.e., the odds would double). The model *chi*-square that tests the fit of the model against a null model is also provided. It is the logistic regression equivalent of the *F*-test in OLS regression.

Logistic analyses begin with an examination of the direct effect of gender on the odds of being in a given trajectory as opposed to being in the "out throughout" trajectory. This is done in areas of science experience involving achievement, access, and attitudes. To assess this direct effect, a full model that includes gender and all resource variables (family, school, and

TABLE A-3 Means (and Standard Deviations) for Science Variables by Gender (HSB Sophomore Cohort)*

	Total	Females	Males
Achievement			
1980			
A's and B's in Math	.41 (.49)	.54 (.50)†	.39 (.49)†
Top Quartile, Math	.28 (.45)	.26 (.44)†	.30 (.46)†
Top Quartile, Science	.28 (.45)	.22 (.42)†	.33 (.47)†
Eigen Value	1.852		
1982‡			
Top Quartile, Math	.21 (.41)	.18 (.39)†	.25 (.43)†
Top Quartile, Science	.26 (.44)	.20 (.40)†	.32 (.47)†
A's and B's in High School	.17 (.37)	.21 (.41)†	.12 (.32)†
Eigen Value	2.357		
1984			
Attended Postsecondary School	.56 (.50)	.60 (.49)†	.52 (.50)†
Had Math/Science Job Since High School	.01 (.10)	.00 (.07)†	.02 (.13)†
Eigen Value	1.053		
1986			
Had College Degree	.07 (.57)	.07 (.76)	.06 (.24)
Had Math/Science Job Since 1984	.03 (.17)	.01 (.11)†	.05 (.21)†
Eigen Value	1.085		
Access			
1980			
High School Math, Had 1⁺ Years	.84 (.37)	.84 (.37)	.84 (.37)
High School Science, Had 1⁺ Years	.78 (.42)	.78 (.42)	.77 (.42)
High School Math, Plan 2⁺ Years	.48 (.50)	.46 (.50)†	.49 (.50)†
High School Science, Plan 2⁺ Years	.35 (.48)	.34 (.47)†	.37 (.48)†
Advanced Math Taken	.24 (.43)	.24 (.43)	.25 (.43)
Eigen Value			
Factor 1	1.962		
Factor 2	1.089		
1982			
Math Concentration	.09 (.29)	.09 (.28)†	.10 (.30)†
Science Concentration	.10 (.30)	.07 (.26)†	.13 (.33)†
High School Math, Had 3⁺ Years	.35 (.48)	.31 (.46)†	.39 (.49)†
High School Science, Had 3⁺ Years	.22 (.41)	.19 (.39)†	.25 (.43)†
High School Algebra II Taken	.50 (.50)	.49 (.50)†	.51 (.50)†
High School Calculus Taken	.09 (.29)	.08 (.26)†	.12 (.32)†
High School Physics Taken	.21 (.41)	.16 (.37)†	.26 (.43)†
High School Chemistry Taken	.38 (.49)	.36 (.48)†	.40 (.49)†
High School Honors Math Taken	.22 (.41)	.20 (.40)†	.24 (.42)†

(continued on next page)

TABLE A-3   *(continued)*

	Total	*Females*	*Males*
Access (continued)			
1982 (continued)			
Eigen Value			
Factor 1	4.136		
Factor 2	1.048		
1984			
Field of Study, Math/Science	.25 (.43)	.22 (.41)†	.29 (.45)†
Postsecondary Math, Had 2[+] Courses	.47 (.50)	.41 (.49)†	.55 (.50)†
Postsecondary Science, Had 2[+] Courses	.40 (.49)	.38 (.48)†	.43 (.50)†
Had Math/Science Job Since High School	.01 (.10)	.00 (.07)†	.02 (.13)†
Eigen Value	2.048		
1986			
Field of Study, Math/Science	.24 (.43)	.21 (.40)†	.28 (.45)†
Had Math/Science Job Since 1984	.03 (.17)	.01 (.11)†	.05 (.21)†
Eigen Value	1.200		
Attitudes			
1980			
Math Useful in Future	.59 (.49)	.57 (.50)†	.61 (.49)†
Math Interesting	.32 (.47)	.33 (.47)†	.32 (.47)†
Math Class, at Ease	.69 (.46)	.67 (.47)†	.71 (.45)†
Math Class, Not Tense	.69 (.46)	.67 (.47)†	.71 (.45)†
Math Class, Not Scared	.68 (.47)	.63 (.48)†	.73 (.44)†
Math Class, Don't Dread	.69 (.46)	.68 (.47)†	.71 (.45)†
Expect 4[+]-Year Degree	.39 (.49)	.40 (.49)†	.38 (.49)†
Professional Job at 30	.34 (.47)	.39 (.49)†	.30 (.46)†
Expected Field of Study, Math/Science	.24 (.42)	.17 (.37)†	.31 (.46)†
Eigen Value			
Factor 1	2.395		
Factor 2	1.231		
Factor 3	1.011		
1982			
Expect 4[+]-Year Degree	.44 (.50)	.45 (.50)†	.43 (.50)†
Professional Job at 30	.33 (.47)	.36 (.48)†	.31 (.46)†
Expected Field of Study, Math/Science	.27 (45)	.21 (.41)†	.35 (.48)†
Eigen Value	1.608		
1984			
Expect 4[+]-Year Degree	.38 (.48)	.37 (.48)	.39 (.49)
Professional Job at 30	.27 (.44)	.29 (.46)†	.25 (.43)†
Eigen Value	1.416		
1986			
Expect 4[+]-Year Degree	.55 (.50)	.54 (.50)	.56 (.50)

TABLE A-3 *(continued)*

	Total	Females	Males
Activities			
1980			
Calculator at Home	.80 (.40)	.78 (.41)†	.82 (.39)†
1982			
Calculator at Home	.88 (.33)	.88 (.33)	.88 (.33)
Computer at Home	.08 (.27)	.06 (.24)†	.10 (.30)†
1984			
Calculator Used	.90 (.30)	.92 (.27)†	.87 (.33)†
Calculator Used in High School	.82 (.38)	.84 (.37)†	.80 (.40)†
Computer Used	.47 (.50)	.48 (.50)†	.45 (.50)†
Computer Used in High School	.16 (.36)	.15 (.36)	.16 (.37)
Computer Used in Education	.33 (.47)	.32 (.47)†	.34 (.48)†
Computer Used in Job	.17 (.37)	.22 (.41)†	.12 (.32)†
Micro-computer Used	.24 (.43)	.20 (.40)†	.29 (.45)†
Micro-computer Used in Education	.12 (.33)	.09 (.28)†	.15 (.36)†
Micro-computer Used in Job	.03 (.18)	.04 (.19)	.03 (.18)

* All variables are coded 1 = True; 0 = False.

† Significant at ≤0.05.

‡ Two other variables measuring the log of gains in math and science scores were also included in the trajectories but are not shown here.

individual) is examined. Reduced-form models are used to assess the indirect effect of gender through the family, school, and individual resource variables. Here a series of equations entering model variables in the order they appear in Figure 1-1 is used. This analysis begins with an examination of models with only gender in the equation (Tables 4-6 through 4-8, column 1)—showing the total effect of gender. Next models that add family and demographic (column 2) and then school resource variables (column 3) and then individual resources (column 4) are examined. Comparisons of the gender coefficient and the model *chi*-square in the various models contribute to an understanding of the indirect process through which gender might affect science experiences. For example, if the total effect of gender (in the model where gender is the only predictor) is reduced when family resources are entered, then it can be concluded that some of the effect of gender is felt indirectly through these variables. If the gender effect is reduced additionally with the inclusion of the individual variables, then the results suggest that some of the indirect effect is through these variables as well. Other possible scenarios involve a total effect of gender that is not reduced with the resource variables, suggesting a purely direct gender effect, or a total effect of gender that is significant and substantial but that becomes small and nonsignificant with the addition of resources variables, suggesting an effect that is largely indirect.

TABLE A-4   Means (and Standard Deviations) for Science Variables by Gender (HSB Senior Cohort)

	Total	*Females*	*Males*
Achievement			
1980			
A's and B's in Math	.45 (.50)	.46 (.50)*	.42 (.49)*
Top Quartile, Math	.35 (.48)	.29 (.46)*	.41 (.49)*
A's and B's in High School	.34 (.47)	.39 (.29)*	.28 (.45)*
1982			
Had Math/Science Job Since High School	.01 (.12)	.01 (.09)*	.02 (.14)*
Attended College Since High School	.38 (.49)	.39 (.49)	.37 (.48)
A's and B's in in Postsecondary School	.26 (.44)	.27 (.45)*	.24 (.43)*
1984			
Attended College Since 1982	.38 (.49)	.37 (.48)	.39 (.49)
A's and B's in Postsecondary School	.29 (.45)	.32 (.47)*	.25 (.43)*
Had Math/Science Job Since 1982	.03 (.18)	.02 (.13)*	.05 (.22)*
1986			
Attended College Since 1984	.30 (.46)	.29 (.48)*	.31 (.46)*
Considered Medicine	.06 (.24)	.07 (.26)*	.05 (.21)*
Had Math/Science Job Since 1984	.05 (.23)	.03 (.17)*	.08 (.27)*
Access			
1980			
High School Math, Had 3+ Years	.34 (.47)	.29 (.45)*	.39 (.49)*
High School Science, Had 3+ Years	.24 (.42)	.20 (.40)*	.27 (.44)*
Algebra II Taken	.52 (.50)	.49 (.50)*	.54 (.50)*
Calculus Taken	.09 (.29)	.08 (.26)*	.11 (.32)*
Physics Taken	.22 (.42)	.16 (.37)*	.29 (.45)*
Chemistry Taken	.40 (.49)	.38 (.49)*	.43 (.50)*
Advanced Math Taken	.24 (.42)	.22 (.41)*	.26 (.44)*
1982			
Postsecondary Math, Had 1+ Years	.44 (.50)	.38 (.48)*	.52 (.50)*
Postsecondary Science, Had 1+ Years	.44 (.50)	.41 (.49)*	.47 (.50)*
Field of Study, Math/Science	.04 (.19)	.06 (.23)*	.01 (.12)*
Had Math/Science Job Since High School	.01 (.12)	.01 (.09)*	.02 (.14)*
1984			
Postsecondary Math, Had 2+ Courses	.63 (.48)	.56 (.50)*	.69 (.46)*
Postsecondary Science, Had 2+ Courses	.60 (.49)	.58 (.49)*	.62 (.49)*
Postsecondary Computer, Had 1+ Courses	.56 (.50)	.50 (.50)*	.63 (.48)*
Field of Study, Math/Science	.27 (.44)	.23 (.42)*	.31 (.46)*
Had Math/Science Job Since 1984	.03 (.18)	.02 (.13)*	.05 (.22)*
1986			
Field of Study, Math/Science	.25 (.43)	.22 (.41)*	.28 (.45)*
Had Math/Science Job Since 1986	.05 (.23)	.03 (.17)*	.08 (.27)*

(continued on next page)

TABLE A-4   *(continued)*

	Total	*Females*	*Males*
Attitudes			
1980			
Math Useful in Future	.62 (.49)	.58 (.49)*	.65 (.48)*
Math Interesting	.43 (.50)	.43 (.50)	.43 (.50)*
Expect 4+-Year Degree	.47 (.50)	.45 (.50)*	.48 (.50)*
Expected Field of Study, Math/Science	.24 (.42)	.17 (.37)*	.31 (.46)*
Professional Job at 30	.40 (.49)	.42 (.49)*	.38 (.48)*
1982			
Expect 4+-Year Degree	.51 (.50)	.49 (.50)*	.52 (.50)*
Professional Job at 30	.35 (.48)	.36 (.48)*	.34 (.47)
1984			
Expect 4+-Year Degree	.44 (.50)	.42 (.49)*	.47 (.50)*
Professional Job at 30	.30 (.46)	.31 (.46)*	.28 (.45)*
1986			
Expect 4+-Year Degree	.41 (.49)	.41 (.49)	.40 (.49)
Activities			
1980			
Calculator in Home	.86 (.35)	.85 (.36)*	.87 (.34)*
1984			
Calculator Used	.92 (.27)	.94 (.24)*	.90 (.30)*
Calculator Used in Education	.57 (.50)	.56 (.50)*	.58 (.49)
Calculator Used in Job	.44 (.50)	.43 (.50)	.44 (.50)
Computer Used	.57 (.50)	.59 (.49)*	.55 (.50)*
Computer Used in Education	.38 (.48)	.34 (.48)*	.41 (.49)*
Computer Used in Job	.28 (.45)	.36 (.48)*	.20 (.40)*
Micro-computer Used	.27 (.44)	.22 (.41)*	.32 (.47)*
Micro-computer Used in Education	.12 (.32)	.09 (.23)*	.15 (.36)*
Micro-computer Used in Job	.06 (.24)	.05 (.22)*	.07 (.25)*

* Significant at ≤0.05.

The final way in which gender can affect science experiences is by interacting with the resource variables. To understand this influence, interaction terms between gender and resources variables are created and tested for significance in the ANOVA models. In addition, a more careful look at the nature of the interactions is achieved by performing logistic analyses separately for young women and men. If, for example, the effect of science achievement on access to science is much larger for boys than for girls (controlling on all other characteristics), then it can be concluded that gender interacts with achievement by inhibiting the positive effects of girls' but not boys' achievements.

Previous research has shown that the effects of gender on experiences in the science pipeline often vary with two other important social statuses—social class and race. We acknowledge this potential diversity by examining the science experiences and the factors affecting them among groups of young women from various race and class groups.

The causal models also provide insight into the interplay between the various aspects of science experiences. By including measures of other science experiences in each model, an examination of the influence of success in one area of science on success in another area is possible. Of special interest is the way in which these cross-influences vary for girls and boys.

A note on some of the difficulties in estimating a causal model with so many independent variables is in order. In our descriptive analyses we provide information on over 60 family, school, and individual resources that are potentially important for success in the science pipeline. Certain variables, such as the school variables from the principal and teacher surveys, could not be included in the models because of large amounts of missing data. More importantly, ANOVA models only allow 20 independent variables, and logistic regression models have very little success in estimating coefficients when the number of independent variables is large. Consequently, the ANOVA models are limited to 20 independent variables, as are some of the logistic regression models. Some of the logistic regression models also include a larger number of independent variables. Generally, it is sample size that determines whether a solution can be found for a large number of independent variables in a logistic regression analysis. This variation in models could not be avoided. Decisions on which variables to include come from theory and preliminary descriptive analyses.

The NCES provides weights to control for sample attrition and non-response in the HSB survey. All analyses were based on weighted data. When tests of significance were performed, the sum of the weights was adjusted to equal the size of the sample. This is a necessary adjustment, since the HSB weights adjust the sample size to the national population of high school youths and contribute to extremely small standard errors and a large likelihood of finding significance.

In sum, the descriptive and causal analyses described above, together with the multiple longitudinal data sets, provide results that will contribute to our understanding of the nature of lost science talent among young women and the causes of this talent drain. Answers to questions about how many women leave the sciences and when they leave are provided. Answers to questions about the ways in which gender affects experiences in science, both directly and indirectly through important resources, are also provided.

REFERENCES

Alexander, K. L. & Eckland, B. K. (1974). Sex differences in the educational attainment process. *American Sociological Review, 29,* 668–682.

American Association of University Women (AAUW). (1992). *How schools shortchange girls.* Washington, DC: American Association of University Women Educational Foundation.

Alper, J. (1993). The pipeline is leaking women all along the way. *Science 260:* 409–411.

Armstrong, J. M. (1985). A national assessment of participation and achievement of women in mathematics. In S. F. Chipman, L. R. Brush, & D. M. Wilson (Eds.), *Women and mathematics: Balancing the equation* (pp. 59–94). Hillsdale, NJ: Lawrence Erlbaum Associates.

Armstrong, J. M. and Price, R. (1982). Correlates and predictors of Women's Mathematics participation. *Journal of Research in Mathematics Education. 13:* 99–109.

Association for Women in Science (AWIS). (1993). *A Hand up: Women mentoring women in science.* Washington, DC: Author.

Astin, H. (1974). Sex differences in mathematical and science precocity. In J. C. Stanley, D. P. Keating, & L. H. Fox (Eds.), *Mathematical talent: Discovery, description, and development* (pp. 70–86). Baltimore: Johns Hopkins University Press.

Atkinson, P., & Delamont, S. (1990). Professions and powerlessness: Female marginality in the learned professions. *The Sociological Review, 38,* 90–110.

Auster, C. J., & Auster, D. (1981). Factors influencing women's choice of nontraditional careers: The role of family, peer, and counselors. *The Vocational Guidance Quarterly, xx:* 253–263.

Baker, D. P. and Jones, D. P. (1993). Creating gender equality: Cross-national gender stratification and mathematical performance. *Sociology of Education 66:* 91–103.

Barber, L. A. (1995). U.S. women in science and engineering, 1969–1990: Progress toward equity? *Journal of Higher Education, 66,* 213–234.

Beck, E. M., Horan, P. M., & Tolbert, C. (1978). Stratification in a dual economy. *American Sociological Review, 43,* 704–720.

Becker, H. J. (1986). *Computer Survey newsletter.* Baltimore, MD: Johns Hopkins University Center for Social Organization of Schools.

Becker, J. R. (1981). Differential treatment of females and males in mathematics classes. *Journal of Research in Mathematics Education, 12,* 40–53.

Berryman, S. E. (1983). *Who will do science?* New York: Rockefeller Foundation.

Berryman, S. E. (1985). The adjustments of youth and educational institutions to technology generated changes in skill requirements. Research Report Series, RR–85–08. Washington, DC: National Commission for Employment Policy.

Blau, P. M. and Duncan, O. D. (1967). *The American occupational structure.* New York: Wiley.

Boli, J., Ramirez, F., & Meyer, J. (1985). Exploring the origins and expansion of mass education. *Comparative Education Review, 29,* 145–170.

Boswell, S. L. (1985). The influence of sex-role stereotyping on women's attitudes and achievement in mathematics. In S. F. Chipman, L. R. Brush, & D. M. Wilson (Eds.), *Women and mathematics: Balancing the equation* (pp. 175–197). Hillsdale, NJ: Lawrence Erlbaum Associates.

Bourdieu, P. (1973). Cultural reproduction and social reproduction. In E. Brown (Ed.), *Knowledge, education, and cultural change* (pp. 71–112). London: Tavistock.

Brock (1986, November 30). Altering the work force. *Washington Post.*

Brody, L., & Fox, L. H. (1980). An accelerative intervention program for mathematically gifted girls. In L. H. Fox & K. Tobin (Eds.), *Women and the mathematical mystique* (pp. 164–178). Baltimore: Johns Hopkins University Press.

Brophy, J., & Good, T. (1974). *Teacher-student relationships.* New York: Holt, Rinehart & Winston.

Brown, R. W. (1990). *Proceedings of the National Conference on Women in Mathematics and the Sciences* (S. Z. Keith & P. Keith, Eds.). St. Cloud, MN: St. Cloud State University.

Brush, L. R. (1980). *Encouraging girls in mathematics: The problem and the solution.* Cambridge, MA: ABT Books.

Brush, S. G. (1991). Women in science and engineering. *American Scientist, 79,* 404–419.

Casserly, P. L. (1980). Factors affecting female participation in advanced placement programs in mathematics, chemistry, and physics. In L. H. Fox & D. Tobin (Eds.), *Women and the mathematical mystique* (pp. 138–163). Baltimore: Johns Hopkins University Press.

Casserly, P. L., & Rock, R. (1985). Factors related to young women's persistence in mathematics. In S. F. Chipman, L. R. Brush, & D. M. Wilson (Eds.), *Women and mathematics: Balancing the equation* (pp. 225–247). Hillsdale, NJ: Lawrence Erlbaum Associates.

Catsambis, S. (1994). The path to math: Gender and racial-ethnic differences in mathematics participation from middle school to high school. *Sociology of Education, 67,* 199–215.

Chafetz, J. S. (1984). *Sex and advantage: A comparative, macro-structural theory of sex-stratification.* Totowa, NJ: Rowman and Allanheld.

Charles, M. (1992). Cross-national variation in occupational sex segregation. *American Sociological Review, 57,* 483–502.

Chodorow, N. (1978). *The reproduction of motherhood: Psychoanalysis and the sociology of gender.* Berkeley: University of California Press.

Cole, J. (1987). *Fair science: Women in the scientific community.* NY: Columbia University Press.

Cole, J. and Zuckerman, H. (1984). The productivity puzzle: Persistence and change in patterns of publication among men and women scientists. In P. Maehr and M. W. Steinkamp (Eds.), *Women in Science.* Greenwich, CT: JAI Press.

Commission on Professionals in Science and Technology. (1986). *Professional women and minorities.* Washington, DC: Author.

Condry, S. M. and Dyer, S. (1976). Fear of success: Attribution of cause to. *Journal of Social Issues 32,* 63–83.

Crowley, J. E., & Shapiro, D. (1982). Aspirations and expectations of youth in the U.S. *Youth and Society, 13,* 391–422.

Culottta, E. (1993). Women struggle to crack the code of corporate culture. *Science, 260,* 398–404.

DeBoer, G. (1984a). A study of gender effects in the science and mathematics course-taking behavior of a group of students who graduated from college in the late 1970's. *Journal of Research in Science Teaching, 21,* 95–103.

DeBoer, G. (1984b). Factors related to the decision of men and women to continue taking science courses in college. *Journal of Research in Science Teaching* 21:325–329.

Devine, F. (1992). Gender segregation in the engineering and science professions: A case of continuity and change. *Work, Employment, and Science, 6* (4), 557–575.

Dossey, J. A., Mullis, I. V. S., Lindquist, M. M., & Chambers, D. L. (1988). *The Mathematics Report Card: Are we measuring up?* Princeton, NJ: Educational Testing Service.

Eccles, J. S., Adler, T., Futterman, R., Gott, S. B., Kaczala, C. M., Meece, J. L., & Midgley, C. (1985). Self-perceptions, task perceptions, socializing influences, and the decision to enroll in mathematics. In S. F. Chipman, L. R. Brush, & D. M. Wilson (Eds.), *Women and mathematics: Balancing the equation* (pp. 95–121). Hillsdale, NJ: Lawrence Erlbaum Associates.

Eccles, J. S. & Jacobs, J. E. (1986). Social forces shape math attitudes and performances. *Signs: Journal of Women in Culture and Society, 11,* 367–380.

Entwisle, D., & Baker, D. (1983). Gender and young children's expectations for performance in arithmetic. *Developmental Psychology, 19,* 200–209.

Ernest, J. (1976). *Mathematics and sex.* Santa Barbara: University of California Press.

Ethington, C. A., & Wolfe, L. M. (1986). A structural model of mathematics achievement for men and women. *American Educational Research Journal, 23,* 65–75.

Ethington, C. A., & Wolfe, L. M. (1988). Women's selection of quantitative undergraduate fields of study: Direct and indirect influences. *American Educational Research Journal, 25* (2), 157–175.

Fagot, B. I., Leinbach, M. D., & Kronsberg, S. (1985). Differential reactions to assertive and communicative acts of toddler boys and girls. *Child Development, 56,* 1499–1505.

Farmer, H. S. (1976). What inhibits achievement and career motivation in women? *The Counseling Psychologist, 6,* 12–15.

Fennema, E. (1980). Sex-related differences in mathematics achievement. In L. H. Fox (Eds.), *Women and the mathematical Mystique* (pp. 76–93). Baltimore: Johns Hopkins University Press.

Fennema, E., & Peterson, P. (1985). Autonomous learning behavior. In L. C. Wilkinson & C. B. Marrett (Eds.), *Gender influences in classroom interaction* (pp. 17–35). Orlando, FL: Academic Press.

Fennema, E., & Sherman, J. A. (1977). Sex-related differences in mathematics achievement, spatial visualization, and affective factors. *American Educational Research Journal, 14,* 51–71.

Finkbeiner, A. K. (1987). Demographics or market forces. *Mosaic, 18,* 10–17.

Fleming, J. (1982). Fear of success in black male and female graduate students: A pilot study. *Psychology of Women Quarterly, 6,* 327–341.

Fox, L. H. (1975). *Career interests and mathematical acceleration for girls.* Paper presented at the annual meeting of the American Psychological Association, Chicago.

Fox, L. H. (1976). Women and the career relevance of mathematics and science. *Social Science and Mathematics, 26,* 347–353.

Fox, L. H., & Tobin, D., Eds. (1980). *Women and the mathematical mystique.* Baltimore: Johns Hopkins University Press.

Fox, L. H., Brody, L., & Tobin, D. (1985). The impact of early intervention programs upon course-taking and attitudes in high school. In S. F. Chipman, F. R. Brush, & D. M. Wilson (Eds.), *Women and mathematics: Balancing the equation* (pp. 249–274). Hillsdale, NJ: Lawrence Erlbaum Associates.

Fox, L. H., Tobin, D., & Brody, L. (1979). Sex role socialization and achievement in mathematics. In *Sex related differences in cognitive functioning* (pp. 303–332). New York: Academic Press.

Fox, M. F. (1995). Women and scientific careers. In S. Jasanoff, G. Markle, J. C. Petersen, & T. Pinch (Eds.), *Handbook of science and technology studies.* (pp. 205–223). Thousand Oaks, CA: Sage.

Fox, M. F. (in press). Women, academia, and careers in science and engineering. In C. S. Davis, A. Ginorio, C. Hollenshead, B. Lazarus, & P. Rayman (Eds.), *The equity equation: Women in science, engineering, and mathematics.* San Francisco: Jossey-Bass.

Frazier, N., & Sadker, M. (1973). *Sexism in school and society.* New York: Harper.

Furr, J. D., & Davis, T. M. (1984). Equity issues and microcomputers: Are educators meeting the challenge? *Journal of Educational Equity and Leadership, 4,* 93–97.

Gaskell, J. (1985). Course enrollment in the high school: the perspectives of working class females. *Sociology of Education, 58,* 48–59.

George, L. K. (1993). Sociological perspectives on life transitions. In *Annual Review of Sociology* (pp. 353–373). Palo Alto, CA: Annual Reviews Inc.

Giddens, A. (1973). *The class structure of the advanced societies*. London: Hutchinson.

Giele, J. Z. (1988) Gender and sex roles. In N. Smelser (Ed.), *Handbook of sociology* (pp. 291–323). Newbury Park, CA: Sage.

Grant, C. A., & Sleeter, C. E. (1986). Race, class, and gender in educational research: An argument for integrative analysis. *Review of Educational Research, 56* (2), 195–211.

Gravenkemper, S. A., & Paludi, M. A. (1983). Fear of success revisted: Introducing an ambiguous cue. *Sex Roles, 9,* 897–900.

Haggstrom, G. W., Kanouse, D. E., & Morrison, P. A. (1986). Accounting for the educational shortfall of mothers. *Journal of Marriage and the Family, 48,* 175–186.

Hallinan, M. T., & Sorenson, A. B. (1985). Ability grouping and student friendships. *Educational Research Journal, 22,* 485–499.

Hallinan, M. T., & Sorenson, A. B. (1987). Ability grouping and sex differences in mathematics achievement. *Sociology of Education, 60,* 63–72.

Han, W. S. (1969). Two conflicting themes: Common values versus class differential values. *American Sociological Review, 34,* 679–690.

Hanson, S. L. (1994). Lost talent: Unrealized educational aspirations and expectations among U.S. youth. *Sociology of Education, 67,* 159–183.

Hanson, S. L. & Ginsburg, A. L. (1988). Gaining ground: Values and high school success. *American Educational Research Journal, 25,* 334–365.

Hanson, S. L., Schaub, M., & Baker, D. P. (in press). Gender stratification of scientific occupations: A comparative analysis of the science pipeline in seven countries. *Gender & Society.*

Hess, B., & Ferree, M. (1987). *Analyzing gender: A Handbook of social science research*. Newbury Park, CA: Sage.

Hilton, T. L., & Berglund, G. W. (1974). Sex differences in mathematical achievement: A longitudinal study. *Journal of Educational Research, 67,* 231–237.

Holland, T. C., & Eisenhart, M. A. (1991). *Educated in romance: Women, achievement, and college culture*. Chicago: University of Chicago Press.

Hollenshead, C., Wenzel, Lazarus, B., & Nair. (in press). Influences on women graduate students in engineering and science: Rethinking a gendered institution. In C. S. Davis, A Ginorio, C. Hollenshead, B. Lazarus, & P. Rayman (Eds.), *The equity equation: Women in science, engineering, and mathematics.* San Francisco: Jossey-Bass.

Hopper, E. (1973). Educational systems and selected consequences of patterns in mobility and non-mobility in industrial societies. In R. Brown (Ed.), *Knowledge, education, and cultural change* (pp. 17–69). London: Tavistock.

Horan, P. M. (1978). Is status attainment research atheoretical? *American Sociological Review, 43,* 534–541.

Horner, M. (1972). Toward an understanding of achievement-related conflicts in women. *Journal of Social Issues, 28,* 157–175.

Hueftle, J. J., Rakow, S. J., and Welch, W. W. (1983). *Images of science*. Minneapolis: University of Minnesota, Science Assessment and Research Project.

International Association for the Evaluation of Educational Achievement. (1988). *Science access in seventeen countries: A preliminary report.* New York: Pergamon Press.

Jacobs, J. A. (1995). Gender and academic specialties: Trends among recipients of college degrees in the 1980s. *Sociology of Education, 68,* 81–98.

Kerckhoff, A. C. (1976). The status attachment process: Socialization or allocation? *Social Forces, 55,* 368–381.

Kerckhoff, A. C. (1984). The current state of social mobility research. *Sociological Quarterly, 25,* 139–53.

Kerckhoff, A. C., & Campbell, R. T. (1977). Black-white differences in the educational attainment process. *Sociology of Education, 50,* 65–77.

Klein, S. S. (Ed.). (1985). *Handbook for achieving sex equity through education.* Baltimore: Johns Hopkins University Press.

Lake, A. (1975, January). Are we born into sex-roles or programmed into them? *Women's Day,* pp. 24–25.

Lee, V. E. (1987). *Identifying potential scientists and engineers: An analysis of high school–college transition* (Report). Washington, D.C.: Office of Technological Assessment Contractor.

Leontief, W. and Duchin, F. (1986). *The future impact of automation on workers.* New York: Oxford University Press.

Linn, M., & Hyde, J. (1989). Gender, mathematics, and science. *Educational Researcher, 18,* 17–19, 22–27.

Long, S. (1990). The origins of sex differences in science. *Social Forces, 68,* 1297–1315.

Long, S., Allison, P., & McGinnis, R. (1993). Rank advancement in academic careers: Sex differences and the effects of productivity. *American Sociological Review, 58,* 703–722.

Lyall, S. (1987, April 26). A women's college looks to men, skeptically, for survival. *New York Times,* E8.

Maccoby, E., & Jacklin, C. (1974). *The psychology of sex differences.* Stanford, CA: Stanford University Press.

Marini, M. M. (1984). Women's educational attainment and the timing of entry into parenthood. *American Sociological Review, 49,* 491–511.

Marini, M. M., & Greenberger, E. (1978). Sex differences in occupational aspirations and expectations. *Sociology of Work and Occupations, 5,* 147–178.

Marsh, H. W. (1989). Sex differences in the development of verbal mathematics constructs: The high school and beyond study. *American Educational Research Journal, 26,* 191–225.

Mattews, W. (1984). Influences on the learning and participation of minorities in mathematics. *Journal for Research in Mathematics Education, 15,* 84–95.

Matyas, M. L. (1986). *Persistence in science-oriented majors: Factors related to attraction among male and female students.* Paper presented at the annual meeting of the American Educational Research Association, San Francisco.

McDonald, K., & Parke, R. D. (1986). Parent-child physical play: The effects of sex and age on children and parents. *Sex Roles, 15,* 367–378.

McKnight, C., Crosswhite, F., Dossey, J., Kifer, W., Swafford, J., Travers, K., & Conney, T. (1985). *The underachieving curriculm: Assessing U.S. school mathematics from an international perspective*. Champaign, IL: Stipes.

Meece, J. L., Wigfield, A., & Eccles, J. S. (1990). Predictors of math anxiety and its influences on young adolescents' course enrollment intentions and performance in mathematics. *Journal of Educational Psychology, 82,* 60–70.

Mickelson, R. A. (1989). Why does Jane read and write so well? The anomaly of women's achievement. *Sociology of Education, 62,* 47–63.

Milton, G. A. (1958). *Five studies of the relation between sex role identification and achievement in problem solving*. Unpublished manuscript. Yale University, Department of Industrial Administration and Department of Psychology, New Haven.

Morgan, C. S. (1992). College students' perceptions of barriers to women in science and engineering. *Youth and Society, 24* (2), 228–236.

Morse, L., & Handley, H. (1985). Listening to adolescents: Differences in science classroom interaction. In L. Wilkinson & C. Marrett (Eds.), *Gender influences in classroom interaction* (pp. 37–56). Orlando, FL: Academic Press.

Mullis, I. V. S., & Jenkins, L. B. (1988). *The Science Report Card: Elements of risk and recovery*. Princeton, NJ: Educational Testing Service.

National Center for Education Statistics. (1993). *High school and beyond 1980: Sophomore and senior cohort third follow-up (1986)* (2nd release). Chicago: National Opinion Research Center (producer). Ann Arbor, MI: Inter-University Consortium for Political and Social Research (distributor).

National Center for Education Statistics (1992). *National educational longitudinal study of 1988. First follow-up: Data file user's manual*. Chicago: National Opinion Research Center (producer).

National Center for Education Statistics. (1994). *NAEP 1992 trends in academic progress*. Washington, DC: U.S. Department of Education.

National Commission on Excellence in Education. (1983). *A nation at risk*. Washington, D.C.: U.S. Department of Education.

National Science Board. (1987). *Science and engineering indicators—1987* (NSB No. 87–1). Washington, DC.: Author.

National Science Board. (1993). *Science and engineering indicators—1993*. Washington, DC: U.S. Government Printing Office.

National Science Foundation (1988). *Women and minorities in science and engineering* (NSF No. 888–301). Washington, D.C.: Author.

National Science Foundation. (1993). *Indicators of science and mathematics education*. Washington, DC: Author.

National Science Foundation. (1994). *Women, minorities, and persons with disabilities in science and engineering* (NSF No. 94–333HL). Washington, DC: Author.

Oakes, J. (1985). *Keeping track: How schools structure inequality*. New Haven: Yale University Press.

Oakes, J. (1990). *Lost talent: The underparticipation of women, minorities, and disabled persons in science*. Santa Monica: Rand.

Office of Technology Assessment. (1988). *Elementary and secondary education for science and engineering*. Washington, DC: U.S. Congress.

Parsons, T., & Bales, R. F. (1959) *Family socialization and interaction process*. Glencoe, IL: Free Press.

Pederson, D. M., Shinedling, M. M., & Johnson, D. L. (1968). Effects of sex of examiner and subject on children's quantitative test performance. *Journal of Personality and Social Psychology, 10*, 251–254.

Perot, H. R. (1988, November 20). Wake up America! We're wasting our future. *Washington Post*.

Portes, A., & Wilson, K. L. (1976). Black-white differences in educational attainment. *American Sociological Review, 41*, 414–431.

Public Opinion Laboratory (1992). *LSAY Codebook: Student, parent, and teacher data for cohort two for longitudinal years one through four (1987–1991)*. De Kalb: Northern Illinois University.

Rallis, S. F., & Ahern, S. A. (1986). *Math and science education in high school: A question of sex equity?* Paper presented at the annual meeting of the American Educational Research Association, San Francisco.

Rayman, P., & Brett, B. (1993). *Pathways for women in the sciences: The Wellesley Report Part I*. Wellesley, MA: Wellesley College, Center for Research on Women.

Rayman, P., & Brett, B. (1995). Women science majors: What makes a difference in persistence after graduation? *The Journal of Higher Education, 66*, 388–414.

Rheingold, H. L., & Cook, K. V. (1975). The content of boys' and girls' rooms as an index of parents' behavior. *Child Development, 46*, 459–463.

Rice, J. K., & Hemmings, A. (1988). Women's colleges and women achievers: An update. *Signs, 13*, 546–559.

Rosen, B., & Aneshensel, C. (1978). Sex differences in the educational-occupational expectation process. *Social Forces, 57*, 164–186.

Rosenfeld, R. (1980). Race and sex differences in career dynamics. *American Sociological Review, 45*, 583–609.

Rosser, S. V. (1987). Feminist scholarship in the sciences: Where are we now and when can we expect a theoretical breakthrough? *Hypatia, 2*, 5–17.

Rosser, S. V. (1990). *Female Friendly Science*. New York: Penguin Press.

Rosser, S. V. (1992). *Biology and feminism: A dynamic interaction*. New York: Twayne Publishers.

Rossi, A. S. (1964). Barriers to the career choice of engineering, medicine, or science among American women. In J. A. Mattfield, and C. G. Nan Aken (Eds.), *Women and the scientific professions*. Cambridge, MA: MIT Press.

Rossiter, M. S. (1982). *Women scientists in America: Struggles and strategies to 1940*. Baltimore: Johns Hopkins University Press.

Sadker, M., & D. Sadker (1986). Sexism in the classroom from grade school to graduate school. *Phi Delta Kappan, 68*, 512.

Sagan, C. (1989, September 10). Why we need to understand science. *Washington Post*.

Schiebinger, L. (1987). The history and philosophy of women in science: A review essay. *Signs, 12,* 305–332.

Schwager, S. (1987). Educating women in America. *Signs, 12,* 333– 372.

Sells, L. W. (1978). Mathematics—a critical filter. *The Science Teacher, 45* (2), 28–29.

Sells, L. W. (1980). The mathematics filter and the education of women and minorities. In L. H. Fox & D. Tobin (Eds.), *Women and the mathematical mystique* (pp. 65–75). Baltimore: Johns Hopkins University Press.

Sells, L. W. (1982). Leverage for equal opportunity through mastery of mathematics. In S. M. Humphreys (Ed.), *Women and minorities in science: Strategies for increasing participation* (pp. 7–26). Washington, DC: American Association for the Advancement of Science.

Sewell, W. H., Haller, A. O., & Ohlendorf, G. W. (1970). The educational and early occupational status attainment process: Replication and revision. *American Sociological Review, 35,* 1014–1027.

Sewell, W. H., Haller, A. O., & Portes, A. (1969). The educational and early occupational attainment process. *American Sociological Review, 34,* 82–92.

Sewell, W. H., Hauser, R. M., & Wolf, W. C. (1980). Sex, schooling, and early occupational status. *American Journal of Sociology, 86,* 551–583.

Shenhau, Y. S., & Haberfeld, Y. (1988). Scientists in organizations: Discrimination processes in an internal labor market. *The Sociological Quarterly, 29,* 457–462.

Sherman, J. A. (1980). Mathematics, spatial visualization, and related factors: Changes in girls and boys, grades 8–11. *Journal of Educational Psychology, 72,* 476–482.

Sherman, J. A. (1983). Girls talk about mathematics and their future. *Psychology of Woman Quarterly, 7,* 338–342.

Sherman, J. A. & Fennema, E. (1978). Mathematics by high school girls and boys: Related variables. *American Educational Research Journal, 14,* 159–168.

Siegel, P. M. (1965). On the cost of being a Negro. *Sociological Inquiry, 35,* 41–57.

Smith, T. E. (1992). Gender differences in science achievement of adolescents: Effects of age and parental separation. *Social Forces, 71,* 469–484.

Stockard, J. (1985). Education and gender equality: A critical view. In A. C. Kerckhoff, Ed., *Research in sociology of education and socialization,* vol. 5 (pp. 299–326). Greenwich, CT: JAI Press.

Stockard, J. and Wood, J. W. (1984). The myth of female underachievement: A reexamination of sex differences in academic underachievement. *American Education Research Journal, 21:* 825–838.

Teltsch, K. (1991, October 2). Science and math get most support. *New York Times,* B8:4.

Tidball, M. E. (1980). Women's colleges and women achievers revisited. *Signs, 5,* 504–517.

Tift, S. (1989, September 11). A crisis looms in science. *Time* pp. 68–70.

Treiman, D. J., & Terrell, K. (1975). The process of status attainment in the United States and Great Britain. *American Journal of Sociology, 81,* 563–583.

Treiman, D. J., & Hartmen, H. (1981). *Women, wages, and work: Equal pay for equal value.* Washington, DC: National Academy Press.

Turner, R. (1960). Sponsored and contest mobility and the school system. *American Sociological Review, 25,* 855–867.

U.S. Department of Education. (1988). *Nation at risk.* Washington, DC: U.S. Government Printing Office.

Vetter, B. M. (1987). Women's progress. *Mosaic, 18,* 2–9.

Vetter, B. M. (1992). Ferment: yes; progress: maybe; change: slow. *Mosaic, 23* (3), 34–41.

Vockell, E. L., & Lebonc, S. (1981). Sex-role stereotyping by high school females in science. *Journal of Research in Science Teaching, 39,* 563–574.

Ware, N. C., & Lee, V. E. (1985). *Predictors of science major choice in a national sample of male and female college students.* Unpublished manuscript. Radcliffe College, Cambridge, MA.

Ware, N. C., & Lee, V. E. (1988). Sex differences in choice of college science majors. *American Educational Research Journal, 25,* 593–614.

Ware, N. C., Steckler, N. A., & Leserman, J. (1985). Undergraduate women: Who chooses a science major? *Journal of Higher Education, 56,* 73–84.

Weitzman, L. (1979). *Sex role socialization: A focus on women.* Palo Alto, CA: Mayfield.

Weitzman, N., Binns, B., & Friend, R. (1985). Traditional and nontraditional mothers' communication with their daughters and sons. *Child Development, 56,* 894–896.

Wetzel, J. (1988). *American youth: A statistical snapshot.* Washington, DC: William T. Grant Foundation Commission on Work, Family, and Citizenship.

Wilson, K. L., & Boldizar, J. P. (1990). Gender segregation in higher education: Effects of aspirations, mathematics, achievement, and income. *Sociology of Education, 63,* 62–74.

Wise, L. L. (1985). Project Talent: Mathematics course participation in the 1960's and its career consequences. In S. F. Chipman, L. R. Brush, & D. M. Wilson (Eds.), *Women and mathematics: Balancing the equation* (pp. 25–58). Hillsdale, NJ: Lawrence Erlbaum Associates.

Wright, E. O., & Perrone, L. (1977). Marxist class categories and income inequality. *American Sociological Review, 42,* 32–35.

Zimmerer, L. K., & Bennett, S. M. (1987). *Gender differences on the California statewide assessment of attitudes and achievement in science.* Paper presented at the annual meeting of the American Educational Research Association, Washington, DC.

Zuckerman, H. (1991). The careers of men and women scientists. In H. Zuckerman, J. Cole, & J. Bruer (Eds.), *The outer circle: Women in the scientific community* (pp 27–56). New York: W. W. Norton.

INDEX